BLACK SQUAD

THE INSIDE STORY OF
MANCHESTER CITY'S YOUNG HOOLIGANS

AS FEATURED ON BBC3's
FOOTBALL FIGHT CLUB

CARL MORAN

EMPIRE
PUBLICATIONS

First published in 2015

EMPIRE PUBLICATIONS
1 Newton Street, Manchester M1 1HW
© Carl Moran 2015
ISBN: 9781909360372
Printed in Great Britain

Cover photography - Richard Milnes

CHAPTERS

INTRODUCTION   5

1. THE ENGLISH DISEASE   7

2. BOLTON   13

3. WEST HAM   50

4. EVERY SAINT HAS A PAST, EVERY SINNER HAS A FUTURE   77

5. STOCKPORT COUNTY   83

6. EVERTON   101

7. UNITED   131

8. STOKE   180

9. HERE, THERE AND EVERYWHERE   205

10. LIVERPOOL   251

11. BIRMINGHAM ZULU'S   268

12. THERE IS A LIGHT AND IT NEVER GOES OUT   283

Dedicated to all the real City lads, past and present

A NOTE ON HOOLIGANISM

Since the word "hooligan" became associated in the media with football fans, there have always been police whose job is to eradicate and stamp out trouble at football. In the late 1980's there were various operations set up to do just that. Operation Omega saw Greater Manchester police (GMP) set up an undercover operation to infiltrate Man City's hooligan element. Many were arrested and well over a dozen received custodial sentences directly as a result of Operation Omega's work. Manchester City, like many other clubs, have always had a strong hooligan element. From the Kool Kats, Mayne Line crew, Guvnors and Young Guvnors, to name a few. However 2006-07, saw the emergence of a new set of younger lads at Man City who would go on to be known as the Blazing Squad.

INTRODUCTION

WHEN STUDYING PSYCHOLOGY at university, the first part of the course is, believe it or not, to try and work out the mind of a football hooligan; to see what drives them – mad or what. The media, as well as a large portion of the public in general, have always been fascinated with the football casual and hooligan firms. I mean you've only got to look at the amount of films there are based on the subject in the last 10 years alone. This book tells the story of my own involvement as a football lad in Manchester City's youth firm, Blazing Squad. Now I know exactly what you're thinking... what kind of a gay name is that? Isn't that a boy band? The name itself actually started off as a bit of a piss take by our older lads when we were first starting out back in 2006/07. At first there were only around 14 of us, and we were dead young, hence the name Blazing Squad. The name stuck and we love it. Obviously everyone takes the piss, but the way I see it is, what's worse being called Blazing Squad, or having to go around telling everyone you've just been battered by a group of lads that go by the name Blazing Squad. Unlike most other football hooligan books, I'm not telling stories from fights from three decades ago, this book contains incidents from 2006 right up to the 2015 season. Also, unlike a large percentage of football hooligan books, this one isn't full of shit. I'm not trying to make out City are the best mob in the world or that we have never been done. Hopefully, my honesty shows through. This book tells how the dynamic of football violence has changed over the years. From the 1980s, which is regarded as the golden era of the casual, right through to present day and how the "English disease" has spread worldwide. Oh and as for the psychologists, they should go out and buy some clobber and get down to the match and have a proper fucking scrap, now that I would pay to see. That's the only way they will understand what being a lad is all about.

THE ENGLISH DISEASE

FOOTBALL HOOLIGANISM has long been known as the English disease. The term was first coined by the media around 30 years ago. When in fact the term was originally used in reference to the Hooligan gang in Lambeth, London in 1894. The term grew to refer to violence in football through the late 60s and 1970s when mass brawls were commonplace between rival fans.

The casual movement reached its peak in the 1980s culminating in what seemed to be all out warfare at the end of the 1984/85 season and the Heysel disaster involving Liverpool fans in which 39 Juventus fans died. After several high profile incidents, Prime Minister Margaret Thatcher declared "war" on the football thugs, who were seen to be ruining the beautiful game. The government's response to Heysel was to introduce ID cards. These cards were to be given to all football fans wishing to gain admission to the games. The Luton Town chairman at the time, David Evans, just so happened to be a Tory MP, so at Kenilworth Road they put a prototype scheme in place that effectively banned away fans from the games. In 1989 the football spectators act, made the I.D cards compulsory. This was however later abandoned a few months later following the death of 96 Liverpool fans at Hillsborough. I'm sure everybody has their own opinions on that.

Football and violence go hand in hand, and have done so since the game first began. In 1314 Edward II banned football altogether because he thought the violent disorder around football matches may lead to social unrest. The game was banned in Manchester back in 1608 for the same reason and by the middle of the 19th century in Derby, the Riot Act was required to be read to people, trouble broke out and police on horseback were brought in to control a violent crowd. Even things like pitch invasions aren't a new thing at all. In the 1880s pitch invasions were fairly common and were seen as part and parcel of the game. In 1885 fighting broke out in a match between Preston North End and Aston Villa which led to not only many of the players getting involved but several being knocked unconscious. I wouldn't mind seeing that happen to a few players today. The following year and Preston were at it again, clashing with rival fans outside a train station. Many regard this as the first ever incident of football violence in the modern era outside of the football ground itself. Twenty years on and Preston were bang at it again against Blackburn Rovers. This would lead to dozens of Preston fans being tried for hooliganism. There was even a 70 year old women charged with being drunk and disorderly, I didn't even think people lived to being 70 back then but there you go.

Millwall had its ground closed repeatedly in 1920, 1935 and 1950, after numerous fights broke out in the ground with rival supporters. In more recent times City fans would be banned from attending away matches at the New Den due to violence off the pitch. In the 2013 F.A Cup semis against Wigan they all started fighting in the ground, not with their opponents Wigan but against one another. In the 1960s there was an average of 25 reported incidents of hooligan violence at football each year, with Liverpool and Everton fans being involved in more than their fair share. The 70s and 80s saw the birth of casual culture, and football hooliganism wrought havoc up and down the country, as well as abroad. In the 1980s, when casual culture was at its peak, lads were travelling to away games on football specials. The fares were cheap; I wish they still were today. By the 1990s the section 60 had been introduced, this now meant that police could stop, search and record all football fans. A decade later and every football lad's worst nightmare was introduced, the Section 27. The Section 27 is basically a direction to leave order and, when you are issued one, if you don't leave, then you're arrested. So imagine you've travelled hours to an away game, only to be given that. British Transport police (BTP) have been accused (rightly so) of abusing the Section 27. In 2008 GMP were forced to give an apology and compensation was awarded to Stoke fans who were wrongly sent back, naughty GMP.

Casual culture is, for some people, a way of life. For many lads it wasn't just about the fighting, there was more to it than that. As well as the fighting, there is also the music and the iconic casual clothing. For many the three go hand in hand. Now I'm not trying to say every single football lad has the same taste in music, but the indie genre and similar genres, would be most associated with the football casual. Bands such as The Smiths, Stone Roses, Oasis, The Jam, The Clash, The Charlatans, Joy Division, Arctic Monkeys are the music of the casual. Now for the clothes or as it's known, "the clobber". Most firms in the 70s were skinhead boot boys, shaved heads, bomber jackets and Doc Martens. But the days were numbered for the skinhead gangs at the match. The boot boys were, believe it or not, frequently having their steel toecap Docs taken off them, by the police. The skinheads were seen as trouble makers and were extremely easy to spot. A new look was needed to help lads slip under the radar. The demise of the skinhead look at football seemed to coincide with the rise of the casual. The establishment wasn't expecting anybody wearing smart designer gear to be involved in violence at games, at least not at first anyway. So the football casual was born and football would never be the same again.

As well as the casual look taking over the skinhead look at the match, the rise of the casual scene also saw the decline of the famous "Mods". Liverpool is widely considered to be the birthplace of the casual look. Not that the clothes were made there, but in true scouse fashion they were the first to go out to Europe and rob them. In 1977, '78 and 81 Liverpool's team won the European Cup. During that period the "grafters" saw it as a perfect opportunity to travel across Europe and rob the place blind. Many of those shops just weren't expecting it, and certainly couldn't do anything to stop it. Back in those days many of those shops would have both trainers out on display, the left and right foot, so it really was an easy rob. The trainers and clothing robbed on these trips were brought back to Liverpool, not only to be worn, but to be sold for big profit. The casual scene started to spread across the country. In Manchester they weren't known as the casuals at first, but as the Perry boys, mainly because of their love for Fred Perry. The term casual was at first just a term used down south, but it later spread to be used all over. The casuals' attitude as regards to clothes, was to dress to impress. They would take great pride in their appearance and spend shit loads of money on the clothes, to go to the match in. Some things never change. Not just your average thugs, casuals always dressed smart, with a touch of class about them.

Much of the 80s fashion was tennis gear worn by stars like Boris Becker and Bjorn Bjorg. Films such as The Business, and the remake of The Firm, sparked a huge revival in brands such as Fila, Ellesse and Sergio Tacchini. The trainers worn back then were brands such as Nike, Diadora, New Balance but without a shadow of a doubt the main make back then, as is now, was Adidas. The early Adidas trainers were ones such as Forrest Hills, Trimm Trabs, Tobaccos, Gazzelles, Samba, Sl72, Sl80, the list goes on and on. The trainers back then, just as I suppose now, became very collectable – Adidas have re-released these same trainers decades on provoking bidding wars on ebay and queues round the block outside certain stores. The early clothes brands that were a hit with the casuals were makes like Fila, Ellesse, Adidas, Pringle, Lyle n Scott, Fred Perry, Lacoste, to name but a few. In the late 80s and early 90s the rave scene really took off, many lads took to dancing rather than fighting. There was big money to be made at these raves from the sale of ecstasy. By the 1990s the hooligan wardrobe had changed and now featured brands such as Paul n Shark, Henri Lloyd, Rockport, Ben Sherman, Burberry, Paul Smith, Prada and last but not least Stone Island. Back in 2006/07 when I was first starting out the big make for me was Henri Lloyd, which was a personal favourite of mine. Also brands like Armani and Ralph Lauren. A couple of years on came the quilted Barbour jackets, which pretty much everybody in every firm had at some point, in various colours. Until it got ruined by business men in suits in town, when they all started wearing them. In fact it happened quite a lot, the makes or styles football lads wore were getting copped by the general public. They do say imitation is the best form of flattery. Things like the Stone Island cap and Aquascutum scarf, would become standard issue for the modern day football lad. Another brand that has become synonymous with casuals over the years is CP Company, with their goggle jackets. Things like 80s Casual t-shirts have become very popular with lads as well. In the last couple of years one make which happens to be my favourite has become very popular, Ma Strum, especially their jackets.

Anyway that's enough about the clothes and the scene, so now about the best bit, the good old fashioned violence.

BOLTON

A LOT OF PEOPLE might look at this chapter and think Bolton? Really? But on their day they can more than hold their own against the so-called bigger boys, as I've found out, on more than one occasion. I remember telling a West Ham lad about the rivalry between us and Bolton, and him pissing himself laughing saying he didn't think teams like Bolton had firms. A little bit naïve maybe, or just an example of the north/south divide. In the last few seasons it's quietened down an awful lot between us and Bolton. Well to be honest there's been nothing at all. The banning orders on both sides and Bolton being relegated to the championship certainly hasn't helped. But I think it also has something to do with the fact that they don't want it with us. Not many firms put themselves on offer time and time again, like we do. Now Bolton's "hardcore members", if you will, are good lads, very game indeed. But as many people will know, if you take a handful of the main lads out of a fairly smallish firm, it just will not be the same. I became quite friendly with a couple of their lads, which a lot of people might find odd. How could you want to kick the shit out of each other one minute and be mates the next? I would often be at Bolton's top kid's house, getting tattoos done. In fact over the years I became good mates with many lads in the different firms up and down the country and even abroad. While it would be fair to say that Bolton had a fair amount of game lads, they also had an awful lot of what I would call tagalongs, and just general shit bags making up their numbers.

There have been several fights with our youth and Bolton's lads over the last few years. I can't help thinking there should have been many more though. But with excuses like "sorry didn't realise we were playing this weekend" and my personal favourite "can't meet you this time loads of the lads are in Sweden skiing". Although Bolton's younger youth were a similar age to us lot, none of them seem to go anymore. I don't think they did much to enhance Bolton's reputation. I heard of them going to Birmingham and when Birmingham came to the pub they were in, Bolton back-doored it and ran off. They have messed us about on numerous occasions as well, claiming to be at our place, but not showing up. One time in 2010 we went to Astley Bridge in Bolton and sat in their main pub, The 3 Pigeons. Waited for around an hour, got bored, then got off back to Manchester. Now we didn't do a cunt's trick and just turn up and ring them, we made it clear a week beforehand that 20 of us would be coming down, and they still wouldn't show. "Back in the day" when City was still at the old ground Maine Road, there was a pub in town called The Athenaeum, that the lads would use frequently. Now this was well before the police started throwing out banning orders left, right and centre, to any cunt wearing Adidas trainers. So it would be fair to say City's firm would have been greater in numbers than what it is today, certainly on a match day. The Athenaeum was well known to be City's boozer, so much so that in years to come GMP would have it closed down for that very reason. However from what I've been told, despite it being well known to be a pub that City would be in a lot, not many firms were keen to come to it and have a pop. But apparently Bolton did. Now obviously this is well before I went to the match and well before Blazing Squad was formed in '07. The story goes that Bolton turned up to the pub in fairly big numbers to give it City. City's lads have all piled out of the pub and to put it bluntly, smashed Bolton all over the show. It's rumoured that Bolton's lads were asking GMP to escort them back to the train station, so they could go home… before the game had even started.

I first started getting involved in the football scene in 2006, but it was more just the odd game here and there. Blazing Squad were formed in 2007 and not long after there would be a do with Bolton, which would kick off the whole rivalry. This rivalry would continue for several years. It would end up being a bit of a mis-match as well. The first incident took place in Darwin near the train station in a pub called the Railway Arms. Now City played Bolton that day but a meet with Bolton was the last thing on any body's mind, as Millwall were away at Oldham. Oldham isn't too far from town, just a short train journey. City made the short journey to Oldham in very small numbers, we were 10 very young lads – kids eager to make a name for ourselves, be it fighting Millwall, or Oldham or fucking anyone. However the excitement and anticipation was short lived. Didn't see any 'wall lads, or any Oldham lads either, in fact all the City lads saw were pakis and dibble. The police weren't too impressed with the 10 young lad's reason for being in Oldham that day, "just for a day out on the beer". That line didn't wash with the officers, suppose it wouldn't when the majority of the lads were clearly not old enough to go in the pubs. If I remember right, a couple would be back in school on the Monday. I suppose if we were coming through today, we would have been classed as under 5's, rather than youth. The police sent City on their way back to Manchester. But all was not lost, as Bolton were on the phone, explaining that they had had a wasted trip to Blackburn to have a meet with them, but for one reason or another it didn't materialise. So that was that, the ten City jumped on the next train down there, destination Darwin.

Darwin is a small town near Blackburn in the Lancashire countryside, or in other words, in the middle of fucking nowhere. After arriving, City found a pub right by the train station and plotted up there. The lads had a few beers and a few games of pool. Maybe because of the young age the lads were slightly naïve in going down there with just 10 lads and openly telling Bolton where they were and that. Two lads in their mid to late 20s, came into the pub. Now the pub itself was sort of a horse shoe shape, with the bar in the middle. The two lads were spotted outside walking towards the pub. No sooner had they stepped foot through the door, when they were asked "are use Bolton yeah?" to which the two men just kind of shrugged it off and laughed and said "no we hate Bolton, we're Wigan fans". This was met with some scepticism but what are you going to do, just twat a couple of men on the off chance that they're Bolton? And besides surely if it was Bolton, there was hardly going to be just two of them that walked in right? The lads stay was rather brief, adding fuel to the fire that they could well have been Bolton after all. Maybe a couple of lads sent in to scout the pub, possibly not taking City on their word, that there were only 10 of them in there. Now while there was only 10 young kids in there, make no mistake these lads weren't poor defenceless teenagers at all, far from it. In fact many there that day would go on to have battle after battle for City. Several lads present that day would help cement Blazing Squad's name, as one of the best in the business. The pub doors opened once more, in step the 2 lads from before, only this time they had a good 25 of their pals with them, if not more. None of them were kids, they were all blokes. Now there was no pause, or jumping up and down, which often occurs beforehand. Bolton just piled in the pub, and straight into the two City lads at the door. One of which was little Wizz, who would be sent to prison for a fight with Bolton years later. There was only so long that the City lads could try and hold them off, before sheer numbers prevailed. It was going off in the pub big time, and while some City lads were taking a kicking, it wasn't all completely one sided, with a couple of Bolton lads being knocked to the floor. It wasn't just fists, there were pint glasses and bottles flying all over the place, hitting lads on both sides. One lad recalls being kicked and knocked all over the show by some big 30 odd year old Bolton lads, and reaching for a couple of pool balls on the table, and throwing them as hard as he could. He said if he threw it another 10 times he couldn't have got a better shot. The pool ball smashed right into the Bolton lad's face. He crumbled to the floor at once. Having been hit in my face with bricks, bottles, pool balls, iron bars and all sorts, I can sympathise with the kid.

The fighting continued. Bolton's lads were getting the better of things but with many of their lads being old enough to have children, the same age as the City kids, plus with their numbers, it was no great shock. City was now backed into a corner of the pub and getting beaten badly, but nevertheless continuing to fight back against the huge Bolton firm, huge in both size and numbers in comparison. The pub was a right mess by this stage. Blood covered the walls and floor of the pub, there was broken glass everywhere. God only knows what the bar staff and locals were thinking. One of the 10 was pissing blood pretty bad from his head. The corner City were backed into had a big window there, now at this point they realised they needed to get out. There was no way they could make it past all the Bolton lads and out of the door, so that just left one other option, the window. Pool balls were thrown at the window smashing it instantly. One of the lads kicked the rest of it through. The 10 lads had done all they could do, and by no means had they embarrassed themselves at all. The lads clambered through the window while trying to fight Bolton back at the same time. A lad cut his hand and thumb quite bad, and nearly lost it, climbing through the broken window, to get outside. Another got half way to safety, and was then dragged back in through the window by Bolton. Punches, kicks and bottles rained down on the City lad, from all angles. City realised what had happened and raced back to the window, to try and get him out. It was like a tug of war with this lad, until they fought Bolton back, and managed to pull him outside. The 10 City started to make their way up the road and away from the boozer. No sooner had they done that the police turned up, which let's face it was inevitable. A couple of the City lads had to go to hospital, the rest were arrested and thrown in the vans. The pub was a complete mess, I mean proper smashed to fucking bits. So badly in fact it had to be closed for days after while it was sorted out.

The police van en route to the station was a time for the lads to reflect on what had just taken place. "We only had 10, and we will do it again" rang out. Not to say the lads thought they had by any means won the battle, but they did all they could. We went out of their way to put ourselves on offer and had it with the Bolton lads, whose numbers were considerably greater. Afterwards the Bolton lads said fair play to City and they had no idea the lads present were so young, and so few in number, which is utter fucking bollocks, as they had sent two lads in beforehand. I know if the shoe was on the other foot, and I was talking to another firm and knew they was so young, and so few in number, I wouldn't have done what they did. But that's just me, maybe I'm too soft. Bit of bullying from Bolton you have to say. For Blazing Squad this would be the start of what would become an ongoing battle with Bolton for years to come. This day also went some way to show what our younger lot, and Man City in general, was about. Going out of our way for the fight, regardless of age or numbers.... "we only had 10 and we will do it again".

Over a year went by, until the next time that we would meet Bolton. It was May 2009 the final game of the season. With both sides being mid table it was pretty much a nothing game as far as the football goes but our firm didn't see it that way, we wanted revenge for Darwin. It was nearing the end of May and it was a nice hot day, the sun was certainly shining down on Manchester and we were out in top numbers. If I said we were all out in such huge numbers because of Darwin, I would probably be lying. While it's true that was certainly on many people's minds, I think the fact it was the final game of the season had a lot to do with it. Plus it was sunny as fuck outside. If ever people needed an excuse to be out on the piss, then City at home final game of the season, on a mad hot day, was certainly it. Blazing Squad as well as I suppose City's firm in general is relatively small compared to some of the larger firms around. Quality over quantity any day though and we would prove that to be the case time and time again. That being said we had rather good numbers that day for once. Not sure exactly how many City young and old were out together that day, because we was never all in same place, at same time, must have been getting on for the 200 mark though. Well over 50 of that was made up of youth lads, which to this day is still by far the best youth turn out for us lot.

The game was a 4pm kick off, but we were all out on Oldham Street nice and early for it. We met up around half 10 in the morning, in a pub called The City, on Oldham Street. We were numbering around 20, all youth, which was a fairly standard week in week out number for us lot. Now

I knew that Bolton were coming down because I had spent the last few days, well in fact weeks, talking to them about it. I tried saying to them why not meet us away from the ground and away from the town centre. Somewhere dead out of it like Stockport, or even just outside of town like Cheetham Hill or Moss Side where the old ground was, but they were having none of it. This pissed a lot of lads off, including myself. The way we saw it was, if they wanted it with us, surely they would meet us out of the way, where there was little or no police. Anyway there was not a lot we could do about it now, as they refused to do it. They said they were travelling down by train to Victoria Station but were rather vague on the time. Now looking back the smart thing to do would have been to get the 20 lads, and move off Oldham Street, as it was known to Greater Manchester Polic (GMP) as a City area. We should have moved off somewhere out of the way and waited for Bolton. But we were all still fairly young and still learning what's what. I was 19 but I was one of the oldest there, that gives you an idea of how young we all were. Unlike a lot of the London mobs that have youth lads in their late 20s and early 30s, which always made us piss ourselves. Anyway, word got round that there were well over 100 City down near the ground, so with Bolton still not telling us the time they would be arriving, we made our way down there.

Our ground is only a mile or so from town, so we used to just walk it down. But we rarely walked down the main road, to get down there; we used a different route, down the canal. You can get from near Piccadilly station in town to right near the ground, just by following the canal. Only problem is it took a little longer than the road way through Ancoats. But no doubt about it, it was a cracking way of getting about withoutGMP, and maybe more importantly our Football Intelligence Officers (FIO) spotting us. So off we went down there, all the time meeting more and more younger lads on the way. Was a good 30 of us youth now, we came off the canal, and made our way down near the ground. Just in time for Tactica Aid Unit (TAU) vans to pull out along side us, and all jump out. Closely followed by the Vauxhall Zafira, which were the undercover cars for our FIOs. To us lot they may as well have had big fuck off sirens, with a flashing light saying GMP down the side, they stood out a mile off. Well that was great, we had made all that effort going the canal way to avoid police, only to bump into them the moment we step on the road. Was this it? Was our day over before it had even begun?

No sooner had GMP pulled up and surrounded us, the police helicopter appeared above us in the sky. I said to the officer looking up to the sky "is that for us?" He laughed and said, "you know it is Carl". So there we were, 30 or so youth, with around 20 police surrounding us, mostly Tactical Aid Unit, along with 3 or 4 football intelligence officers. Oh, and not to forget the helicopter hovering above. We were all lined up against the wall and Section 60s was given. A Section 60 is basically the police taking down all your details, name, address, date of birth and then recording you, so they have your name and face on film for that day. We used to joke about saying they're nonces and that's why they want to record young kids all the time. Think it's just more to get your clothes on film, so if there's any fighting that day and someone is wearing identical clothes as you, you're fucked. I'll never forget one of the police there coming up to me saying "Mr Moran, aren't you a bit too old for all this crap now?" I remember thinking what's he on about, I'm still a teenager, a fucking kid. He was going on like I'm some middle age man or something. Anyway, after around 15 or so minutes, the police let us go on our way. They seemed happy enough now they knew what area we were in and let us on our way towards the ground. We headed for the Townley, which is a pub on the estate across the main road from the ground. It's a fairly big pub with a beer garden at the back. With it being such a boiling hot day the place was rammed, about 150-160 people were outside the pub, I would say around 90-100 of that was lads. Those who were drinking went and got a beer and that, I was my usual boring self on the orange J2O's. Throughout the day I was on the phone to Bolton asking what the story was, they were now saying they had not long been in town and were in a pub called the Lord Nelson. The pub is no longer there, it's been torn down, and is now just a car park. We knew exactly what pub they were on about as well, it wasn't far from Oldham Street, where we were an hour before. Bolton were seriously starting to get on my nerves though, big time. One minute they were saying they were going to come down to near where we are and meet us. The next minute it was all "we're the away team come and get us" sort of thing. It was bad enough having to listen to their daft farmer accents all day, without them messing us about on top of that. If they were refusing to move and meet us there was only one thing for it, to go back the way we had just come from, to meet them. Only there was one problem... GMP. We now knew why the police had let us all go so easily, they must have had a fairly good idea of where we were heading, the Townley. They must have thought they were in for a fairly easy day with so many of the lads in one place together down near the ground. There was no way we could have moved from that pub, with the amount of FIOs and police dotted about the place. There were cars and cars of them parked outside the pub. No way we could have left the pub and headed back to town without them stopping us. It just wasn't going to happen.

The only thing that I could think of was to leave the pub in twos and threes, a couple of minutes apart, and hope they don't clock on, and arrange a place down the road to meet up. But contrary to popular belief the police aren't stupid, they would realise what we were doing. Bolton were sat on the outskirts of town 25 handed, and we didn't know how the fuck we were going to get to them. Had them lot on the phone laughing their heads off taking the piss saying "we're in your town what are use going to do about it?" The heat wasn't helping at all. It's safe to say that my hair and skin complexion wasn't made for the sun. It was now around 12 o'clock and still 4 hours before kickoff, I was already burnt to fuck, bright red like a tomato. Most of the lads were in shorts, but I had got jeans on and was proper regretting it. Word got round that there was some older Bolton lads knocking about, near another pub by the ground, the Manchester. We couldn't believe our luck, the pub emptied, with everyone going towards the Manchester, looking for these Bolton lads. This was just the thing we needed, for all our younger lot to slip off unnoticed towards town, which was the opposite direction. We couldn't have written it better if we tried, the police started to follow all the older lads going towards The Manchester. We waited until the police were far enough away, then we made our move back towards town. Our older lads had helped us out big time without even realising it.

Me and the other main youth faces set off towards town, and the other lads did the same in small groups; 10, 20, 30, 40 our numbers just kept growing. We must have ended up with getting on for 60 lads, all youth as well, no older lads, making our way back to town to give it these Bolton kids. Told Bolton we were on our way and would be 15 minutes tops. We were marching up towards town, everyone was bang up for it. This was going to be a message sent out to Bolton, and all the other firms, that if you come to Manchester, this is what you get. We were now roughly half way back to town, all the time ringing Bolton telling them to walk down and meet us but once again they were having none of it. They said "we know where we are, so we know where to find them". We were now nearing the shops near Toys R Us on Ancoats, now just a few minutes walk from the Lord Nelson.

We were walking across this field and wasteland, which I am guessing was old terraces or old factories that had since been torn down. Now normally we only fight with fists. We look down on a lot of the other mobs that use blades and other weapons every time they fight. We thought that was a shit bag way to go about things, however a few days previous a couple of these Bolton kids were mouthing off, saying there bringing blades and that. I wasn't sure whether they were, or it was just mouthing off but that, added to what went on in Darwin a year or so earlier, and the attitude was fuck it, these mongs deserve everything they're going to get today. I didn't grab anything, it's not my style but many other of the lads grabbed bricks and bars and what not, which were lying around in the rubble of this wasteland, which is now all fancy apartments and new homes. We didn't have 60 lads anymore that's for certain, but that always happens losing numbers as you go on, just the way it goes, there were still around 45-50 of us though. We must have been no more than 500 metres away from them, when we heard a sound none of us wanted to hear but one we all instantly recognised. It was our friend the police helicopter back circling over our heads, great, just what we fucking needed. We knew that within minutes now police cars and vans would be all over us. We continued on to where we were going, the Lord Nelson, knowing we had a few minutes at best, before GMP would be swarming all over us. I told Bolton to get out of the pub and walk down because we're here now. No sooner had I got off the phone, and had chance to put it back in my pocket, the screech of tyres could be heard nearby. I looked round and it was a couple of TAU vans coming our way. They all dived out the vans and we scattered all over in different directions. That was it, 50 lads all split up and running in different directions, it was going to be some job getting us all back together again, with police chasing us. It ended up with just me and another young lad running through the back streets and that. We managed to get away, but within 5 minutes a good 15-20 lads had been caught trying to get away. With the rest running back towards the ground or down various side streets, back into town. While all this was going on, Bolton still hadn't set foot out of the pub. We met up with a couple more lads and headed for the pub the Lord Nelson. We rang Bolton, explained what had happened, said there was only 4 of us coming to meet them now. We got to the pub and went inside, there was around 20-25 of them inside, all youth. They seemed a bit on edge, and uneasy with us being there, which I thought was bit mad, seen as there was 25 or so of them, and only 4 of us. Maybe they were expecting loads more to burst through the door or something, god knows. The chat was fairly short and brief, and we were on our way. Pretty much said what had happened, said give us half an hour max, for us to get it back together and we're on. At least we now knew they were being honest with their numbers as well, about what they had.

So we went on our way, and went to some posh bar near Piccadilly station called Golf Bar. The canal path brought you out nearby as well so it was a perfect place to regroup, and get it together and then go smash these cunts. We managed to get about 12, 13 lads together at Golf Bar. Numbers which was obviously nothing compared to what they were an hour ago, but what can you do. The numbers didn't even bother me at all; I knew our 13 would go through their 25, like a hot knife through butter. Besides, we were known for having fairly shit numbers but just being game as fuck.

Bolton were now feeling a lot braver, knowing we had lost the majority of our lads, on our way to meet them. Bolton now agreed to leave the pub and meet us on the canal. At the same time, GMP were still driving around the area looking for us. Gladly the helicopter had pissed off somewhere and was nowhere to be seen. We made our way to the top of the canal and onto a bridge, just across the road from Golf Bar. We saw a police van at the top of the street coming down, and we did the worst thing we could have possibly done... panicked and ran. If we hadn't have done that, they might have not even noticed us. But there's nothing like 13 lads running off to attract attention to themselves and obviously now due to us being idiots and running, the police were now back after us. They dived out the van and out on foot after us. Now this really did used to make our day, because there was just fucking no chance they were catching us, we knew it, and they knew it. Yet they would still persist in running after us, if I was them I would just fuck it off and stay in the van and save myself the embarrassment. Then after a few short seconds, when they realised they aren't catching you, you hear the chubby, middle aged, out of breath copper shout "oi stop police, fucking stop there now". Nah you're alright mate. Why they shout daft things like that, I really have no idea, I mean who in their right mind is going to stop just because they shout stop?

Bolton were also on the canal now, oh yeah I even managed to have a chat with them on the phone whilst running away, that's how slow the police were. But no sooner had we finished laughing at the police, more appeared out of nowhere, and made their way down towards us. So the police were heading for us and these ones didn't look as fat, they looked angry, probably pissed off with us giving them the run around every other week. Unless we jumped in the canal, there was nowhere for us to go, we were cornered from both sides by the police and thrown against the wall. More GMP arrived and all began pushing us around mouthing off to us. "We're the biggest firm in Manchester, we're the hardest firm in Manchester, fight us". That would become a well known catchphrase from them over the coming years. To our amusement the rather chubby out of breath policeman, arrived a couple minutes later, looking even more out of breath than before. We were told in no uncertain terms that they had had enough of us and to fuck off home now or be arrested and banned. Well where were Bolton while all this was going on you may ask? Well Bolton had gone the wrong way on the canal and were heading in the opposite direction, fucking idiots. There's no doubt about it Bolton had been well and truly saved, on more than one occasion by GMP that day. There was only one winner that day and that was the police aka "the hardest firm in Manchester". As for Bolton, another few months would pass before we would next bump into each other. This fight would take place in Radcliffe, my side of town, well away from the police. But there's only one word to some up that entire day for me and that was fucking SUNBURN.

Several months had gone by since the anti-climax which was Bolton at home, last game of the 2009 season. Throughout this period, weekly, if not daily contact was maintained with the Bolton lot. Some of which was good natured, just having a laugh, taking the piss, general "banter" I think they call it.

Sometimes though things would get a little out of hand, and go too far. The constant digs back and forth just added to the rivalry. I remember taking a fair bit of stick off some of the lads at the match for being maybe a little bit too friendly with some of the Bolton kids. By that stage, there was some of them that I would class as actual mates. I've always thought the best way to organise stuff with other firms, is to be alright with each other and that, you get nowhere acting cocky and being a nob head. By being friendly you become friends and gain each other's trust and respect, then once you trust each other, it's far easier to organise stuff. A lot of my good mates are main lads in other firms, dotted about all over the place. The lads at City knew all this, and knew it was better for organising stuff, still didn't stop them taking the piss though. Mates or not, when it comes to facing each other, I would want to smash them all over the gaff, as much as the next person, if not more.

December 12th 2009 was the date of the Bolton away fixture. The match itself was to have plenty of goals and end 3–3. Now believe it or not, sometimes the result of the match itself could have a say in the violence which takes place afterwards. For example, you've just lost a game to your rivals by a last minute goal, so you're going to leave the ground fucking fuming aren't you, and maybe make that extra effort to get to them. That being said, this doesn't apply to arranged meets, often arranged days, if not weeks in advance, the score of the match would have no bearing on these. While I do consider myself to be a proper City fan, the ins and outs of the game, even the final score that day, didn't interest me one bit. I couldn't have cared less. This day was a chance to set the record straight and get revenge for Darwin, a couple of seasons before. It had been building up for quite some time now and for most of the lads on both sides there was no love lost. Since the fixture list came out, this had been the one that straight away stood out to us all, it was going to go off big time. Sometimes things just don't go to plan at all, whether that be police getting in the way, or the other firm messing us about etc.

Sometimes you just get a feeling inside and you know it's going to go off, and today it was going to be fucking mental. So to say I was disappointed when around 10 lads didn't show up on the morning would be a huge understatement. So Blazing Squad, which let's face it, had fairly average numbers at best, was now missing 10 or so lads for our big meet, fucking great. Now I can appreciate that Bolton as a firm might not be very well known, especially to people down south. I can see that not many firms would get giddy, looking at the up and coming fixture being Bolton away, but for us, there was a real rivalry there. This really meant something to us lot, and I know it did to them also, I suppose it was a pride thing more than anything. We arranged to meet up in Bury, this was ever so slightly closer to Bolton than Manchester, but at the same time still far enough away from GMP. This meeting up in Bury would only add to the rumour that us and Bury were going together as one, to fight Bolton, which just wasn't true at all. There were a few of us who were mates with a few of them and that was about it. Bolton and other mobs made out it was some big love-in between us and Bury, and we went together week in week out, 25 a piece together as one big firm and it wasn't the case. That being said, I'm not going to deny there hasn't been the odd time, when one or two Bury lads have come out with us, and vice versa, but never in huge numbers like Bolton and other firms may lead you to believe.

So there we were, hours away from this big meet, which we had all been looking forward to since the fixture list came out months before hand and we had lads not showing up for it. Last minute drop outs are the worst, not just in football firms, I mean also in life in general. You know the type, I mean they will swear blind they're going to do something (sometimes even knowing beforehand that they're not) just to give you no notice and let you down on the day. Some coming out with shit excuses about why they can't come, others just turning their phones off, either way it's not what we needed on a day like this. Leading up to the game, several lads were saying they can't be arsed coming because Bolton wouldn't meet us and will fuck us about, like they have before. So I tried my hardest to drum it into everyone's head that Bolton are going to show and it is going to go off. Bolton had made it very clear that whatever we do, don't go into Bolton town centre or near their ground because police will be all over it, and it'd be over before it's started. I agreed with them and we agreed on a spot in Tongue Moor, on an industrial estate, not far from their town centre but far enough, if you know what I mean. I wasn't daft, I had heard this was a big Bolton area and in fact a lot of their older lot are from around that area but we weren't bothered, we just wanted to take the piss and smashing them in their own area would see to that. So me and the City lads agreed to meet up in Bury in the morning, get taxis down to Tongue Moor, smash fuck out of them, then get off back to town, job done. Well that was the plan anyway but things rarely go to plan, and this day would be no exception. We were supposed to meet in Bury at half 10, yet it was more like 11 or even getting on for half past, before most lads turned up. We didn't all turn up as one firm, most turned up in dribs and drabs. We decided against going in Spoons or Yates and went in an Irish bar O'Neill's (now Malloy's). It was now nearing 12, and there were only around 15 of us, we had around 10 no shows and were still waiting on three lads to turn up.

Meanwhile in Bolton town centre we were hearing there was a nice 80 plus City older lads plotted up there. At this point there was a kind of strange relationship between us and our older lot. Some of them are the best lads you could meet, as regards to being game and just being top blokes, that being said there are a few shit bags and dickheads as well, same as every firm though, I should imagine. For a few seasons now we had been fighting youth firms and slapping them about all over so there weren't many youths left that would meet us without their older lads with them. This didn't impress us one bit, we thought it was a huge sign of weakness, hiding behind older lads and that. Especially when chances are they would have had far greater numbers than us in the first place. In the early years I suppose we took pride in being just the younger lot and fighting sometimes under 5s, youths and older firms all together as one. As years went by we became closer to our older lot and had more fights mixed together, after all regardless of age, we are all City.

Back to Bolton, they were in contact with me all day, oh yeah and I do mean all day, I couldn't even eat my Weetabix in peace earlier on. They had seen/heard about the City mob which had in essence took over the town centre and was growing in numbers all the time. I explained that was our older lot, not us and that we were in Bury. "Why are youse in Bury? Why are you there? That's not Bolton" to which I replied, "you made a massive point to us to avoid your town centre and ground, so that's what we have done". We were now just waiting for a couple more lads who would take our numbers to around 18 and then we were off. It would have been very easy for us to go sit with the older lads in Bolton, as a mob of 100 or so lads, taking over their town centre, but that's not what we we're about. We wanted revenge; we wanted to smash them all over. There was no doubt in my mind that today this was going to happen. There was still one thing playing on my mind though, I had a big fucking wad of cash on me and I wasn't about to let the police search me, and try take it off me. I was stuck with about a grand or so, in my pocket. Not the biggest amount of money, by any stretch of the imagination, but still an unemployed teenager walking around with that on him, how would I explain that if I was stopped and searched? Also what if the fight went tits up, and somehow Bolton got hold of my not so hard earned cash, well I wasn't fucking having that. So I belled my cousin who lived nearby and got him to come and collect it all from me, at least now that was one less thing for me to worry about. While I was gone for what must have been all of two minutes, a couple of our lads started fighting with each other – typical City nobody else there to fight, so fight each other. Not what we wanted at all. It was soon split-up, the day went from bad to worse though, when police turned up, a mixture of TAU and a couple FIOs. I still don't know this FIOs name, but I was grateful he was present, as the police woman who was talking to me was fucking mad. She got it in her head I was lying, and giving her false details, and was about to arrest me, until he stepped in to confirm my name. She begrudgingly let me go, god knows what her problem was but she hated me that is for sure.

I told Bolton what the score was, with the police being here, and as soon as they fucked off, we would get taxis down. Problem was, these police just weren't for moving at all, and Bolton were getting very inpatient. Seemed they wanted this fight to happen as much as we did after all, can't fault them there. Now either they didn't take my word that police were with us, or they just wanted a pop regardless because Bolton made their way to Bury. 25 or so Bolton turned up and went in a pub, at the top end of the Street . The Sir Robert Peel I think it was, the irony of football firms about to fight, sat in the pub named after the man who invented the police force, was not lost on me. While we were only a couple hundred metres apart it may as well have been a couple hundred miles, with all the police with us. If the police didn't know what we was doing out before the arrival of Bolton's lot, they did now. Well it was bound to happen wasn't it, the police issued us with Section 27 direction to leave orders, and escorted us to the tram station. The tram is sort of underneath the bus station so the police escorted us down to it. Now we were expecting them to accompany us all the way back to town but to our amazement they didn't. They just left us to it, we couldn't believe our luck. We jumped off the Met at the first stop we could, which was Radcliffe. Quite handy for Bolton, as that's the same way they were heading to get back to Bolton, after we were escorted away. So we had made the short tram journey to Radcliffe, still a bit puzzled to why the police let us get off on our own, but fuck it we weren't complaining. We made our way down the steps and onto the car park, it was all very quiet and deserted, the calm before the storm maybe.

Radcliffe isn't too far from the area I am from Whitefield, so I knew it fairly well. If am being honest, most of it is a shit hole. We got off the car park and headed across the road, by a high school Coney Green, or Riverside, or whatever its name is these days. Beside the school is a road called Banana Path. This banana place was perfect to have it with Bolton. It was just set off back from the main road, with the school on one side and sort of woodland on the other. With it being winter, it was nice and dark as well. We were expecting Bolton any second, yet they were now saying give them 15 minutes, which only meant one thing, they're waiting for more lads. So rather than have 20 lads stood there in the ginnel, in the dark like a bunch of wallies, we went to a nearby pub the Royal Oak and waited there. There was a few benches outside on the front, so we all just sat on there and waited. Couple of the lads went in getting drinks, but I didn't bother, I hadn't had a beer all day. We bumped into three lads who a couple of us knew, well we knew two of them, the third I could only describe as a Harry Potter lookalike. Harry Potter with shopping bags on each arm. I rang Bolton and said to them where to go, they said they were already there, so that was that, we jumped up and were on our way. Half marching, half slow jogging from the pub down this banana thing. I was careful not to go too fast though, as the path was next to a river, and it was a mixture of moss and it was a little bit icy everywhere, so it was fucking slippy. Was around 4 maybe 5 o'clock now, and it was pitch black, the path just lit up by street lamps, half of which didn't seem to work properly, just flickering on and off.

Now I'm the first to admit my eyes aren't great at the best of times, never mind in the dark, so I can honestly say I heard Bolton well before I saw them. The chant came up from us "Yoof Yoof Yoof" and when ever that chant goes up all my hairs go up on the back of my neck, still does even to this day. The marching and slow jogs got faster and soon turned into full on sprints. This was it; this is what we had been waiting for. My heart was proper pounding, whether that was the adrenaline because we was about to fight or just because I was a fat cunt and was running, maybe a bit of both. They finally came into sight around 40, 50 metres away. They weren't running towards us, most bouncing up and down, arms out gesturing, "come on then" sort of thing, looked around 20–25 in number. Cries went out "come on Bolton, fucking come on then". We were now steaming towards them. I remember having my eyes focussed on this one lad, he stood out from the rest as being a lot bigger, and having a lightly coloured jacket. I could finally make them all out, as they were stood nearby to one of the few working street lights, they mustn't have wanted to stand in the dark. Few of the lads had brought bottles and pint glasses from the pub and launched them at Bolton, who at this point it had to be said, weren't looking too sure of themselves. As soon as the glass smashed all over the floor that was it, they were off, running back the way they had come from, with us chasing them. Some were full on sprinting away and a few others were half running and turning round shouting Bolton and stuff like that. Never understood that me. Oh and one cunt had a big grin on his face, what he found so funny about running off like a little girl, I don't know. Could hear lads behind me saying "where are they going, is that it?" talk about anticlimax, wasn't a single punch thrown and they were running away, what's all that about? We continued to chase them for what felt like a couple of minutes but in truth was probably more like 20 seconds or so.

Unbeknown to me and the lads, a couple more taxis pulled up and more lads got out. I'm guessing these Bolton kids that just turned up most have been their main lads or something because now Bolton were no longer running from us, they was bouncing back towards us. Mint, just what we wanted, maybe this wasn't going to be that easy after all, but it's a fight we came for, not a game of tig. "Come on ya Manc cunts" they shouted, in that awful accent of theirs, right you fat inbred cunt you're getting it now, I thought. We squared up to each other and one punched me, but was unsure of himself, and stepped right back. So I've gone to hit him but I've leant forward to much to reach him, because he had moved back. It ended up being a half punch, half push, moved him right back though. Before he has had chance to think – crack! I gave him a big right hander, caught him bang on his chin. His legs went from under him and he fell right back into his pals behind him. No doubt he was going straight on his arse, if they weren't stood behind him. The way he fell back into them reminded me of primary school in PE, when we had to trust the person behind us and fall back and they would catch us. His mates who had caught him now sort of threw him back into me, which I thought wasn't very kind of them. I've gone to whack him again and he has turned away and kneeled down. Clearly didn't want to know anymore. Went down like a boxer in the ring, taking the count for a body shot. For a brief moment I thought fuck him boot him in his head, teach him for being mard but that's not me, I'm not a bully. So I left him and moved on to his mates. I went into a daydream I suppose is the best way to describe it, it always happens to me. I end up just watching everything else that's going on around me, like as if I'm not there and I'm watching it at home on the telly. Always happens to me, just drift off into my own little world.

Then I suddenly snapped out of it, to a wall of noise, shouting from both sides. "These don't wanna fucking know" was shouted from one of our lot, so we ran at them, and they started to back off. But give them their dues they didn't run. We kept the pressure on them, not giving them an inch, or any time to think. Our frontline line of around seven or so lads just full on ran into the middle of them, sticking right to them, we started to separate them. Once a firm separates you can just pick them off and they crumble in no time. No doubt about it we were getting the better of things. I smacked some kid and he walked to the side with a weird pained look on his face, I just threw him to the side. Before I knew it three lads swarmed round the lad, punching and booting him from all angles, felt a little harsh on him if am being honest, far too soft at times me. Some of their lads had had enough and a few started to get off. A shout came out from one of them, I remember laughing to myself, because it sounded like some 60 year old farmer "Stand Bolton! Stand!" to which I would say a good half did. It was now a standoff, a nice little breather I suppose. It felt like we had been battling for half an hour, in reality was probably more like a minute. Then out of nowhere, one of their lads only youngish looking just ran at us, on his own. I mean he just fucking piled right into us all, on his own throwing digs. What a guy, fair play to the kid. Mad little bastard, I can honestly say I've never done that before, nor would I. A lot of the lads ran at Bolton, again backing them off a bit. The mad kid who ran into us was pulled down to the floor and was getting the shit kicked out of him. Well I can't have that, I had a strange admiration for him, for what he had just done, he doesn't deserve to be booted in on the deck. So I gripped him by his head, picked him up and said fuck off and launched him back to his mates. Well I say mates, not one of them made a proper effort to rescue him or owt. The lad was only on the floor for maybe 10 seconds but with punches and kicks raining down off a few lads, that's long enough.

With that we full on ran at Bolton, they turned and ran, proper ran this time, I thought this was it they're done. We had done what we came to do, and we started to slow down. My mate at the side of me had a big grin on his face and started laughing, he must have been thinking the same, we have just done them. We still carried on jogging down after them though. We were now nearing the end of Banana Path, and getting back near the main road, towards the tram stop where we head came from. In the distance we could see metal bars, like barriers, you know the ones to stop crossers, and other motorbikes going past. We didn't know it yet, but them bars would prove the difference between who won and lost this fight. Bolton were on one side of the bars and we were on the other, but it's like none of us wanted to go through first. You could only fit a couple lads through at a time you see. We should have just ran at it, and got through and jumped over as many as we could, as quickly as we could and they would have gone. But regretfully we didn't, we hesitated. What is it they say… more is lost through indecision than wrong decision? Bolton gained confidence from this, well this and the fact yet another car pulled up and 4 more lads jumped out. Bolton all started to pile back over and through the bars towards us and like dickheads we just let them. Their top lad later said them gates saved them and if we had just carried on running at them, they were gone. Bolton now numbered in the thirties, probably around 35 of them. We had about 20. While there was no doubt that there were numerous lads missing that day, it really shouldn't have mattered, as we still had a decent set of lads out. So there are really no excuses, as you're always going to have lads missing and that.

They say football is a game of two halves, and this fight was no different, the tide had well and truly turned, in Bolton's favour. What the fuck is going on here then, I was thinking, we had these on the run, we had them done, they didn't wanna know. Now we found ourselves having Bolton steam into us and lads were starting to get backed off. I thought as long as our frontline doesn't budge and go anywhere, we can do this all day long. Now I've got to be honest and say I didn't see any of this but bricks started flying about, one hit Craig clean on in the face. I remember seeing him out of the corner of my eye, blood pissing everywhere, and being sort of helped to the side, by another one of our lads. Unbeknown to me near the front as soon as the bricks started flying about, some of the lads behind me started to get off. This would be

Harry Potters queue to leave. He was seen legging it with his pals and his shopping bags. Years later I would actually bump into "Harry" in a pub, for a mate's 21st funnily enough just down the road from this banana place. He explained he had just come back from town shopping for clothes, hence the bags, and that he only got off when other people did. Had a good laugh at him being known as Harry Potter, and he said he's been called far worse.

Anyway back to the action, I still thought that everyone had stayed, even though we were now heavily outnumbered, we could have got it back together, and had them on their toes once more. In truth there were now only around 12 of us at the most. They steamed into us again, and again, and again. If am being honest we were getting backed off big time. With every wave of Bolton attack we would seem to lose a couple more lads. It got to the stage where there was around five maybe six of us left. There was now far too many of them to try and fight off. They weren't only just in front of us, they were now swarming round us from all angles. I was on the far left side, and we had a line of five maybe six max going across. Me, Bez, Wizz, Raz, Tom, that's all I remember seeing anyway. I was scrapping with three or four of them at the side there, but not wanting to fully commit and go into them, in case I got pulled into them all. I was more just fighting them off me, to be honest. Didn't want to end up like their kid earlier on the floor, getting booted in, somehow I didn't see them lot helping me up from it. Funnily enough I think that lad was one of the four I was fighting with now, so that's his way of showing fucking gratitude. I remember looking across to my mates and they weren't having much luck either, we were all getting a slap. This wasn't any good, not the way I envisaged it unfolding whatsoever.

Bang,! Bang! I felt punches all over my head and neck

from everywhere, they were now all around us, well they were all around me that's for sure. I was trying to back off away from them all and cover my face from the punches at the same time, got this one dig on my ear and god it killed. My ears was ringing badly now, and I just lost it, I thought fuck it, if I'm going to get leathered badly here, I'm not just going to stand there covering my face, making it easy for them. So I started proper giving it them back, caught a couple of them. They all backed off away from me, well for a few brief seconds at least anyway. I digged some fat kid and he just turned round and ran off, which would have been funny as fuck, if moments after I had about 8 of them smashing fuck out of me. I remember seeing my hat go flying off my head and on the floor, not a chance was I going to attempt to retrieve it, fuck that. It was no good, we were just getting battered.

We managed to get together as a group again. I looked across at the few lads left alongside me, and their faces pretty much summed up how I was feeling. I would have actually loved the police to turn up at this point, that's was how bad it had got. Bolton ran at us one last time, and I'm not even arsed I'll admit it, I turned to the lads and said "come on I've had enough of this let's run". So that's what we did, we ran, I'm not going to make out we were backing off and still fighting with them, because we weren't, we fucking legged it with them behind us. Most of them half-heartedly chased us, I think in truth they were glad to see the back of us. Around half a minute had gone by if that, we had ran back the same way we had come down from, that pub the Royal Oak, when we realised we were missing Tom. We instantly ran back round chanting City, City, City, they must have thought there was loads of us, because they all ran off. Some on foot, some jumped into cars and got off. We later found out a few

Bolton kids were even hiding in the bushes from us. Tom had somehow been left behind, he had taken a bit of a slap, but nothing too serious, could have been a lot worse. As we got back onto the main road heading for the Met, we saw about 8 of them and ran at them and they got off. With that a GMP van pulled up, and I was grabbed and arrested. Must have been the shortest arrest ever though, it's like they couldn't be arsed nicking me, that was fine by me. They threw me in the van, then let me out about a couple minutes later and that was that. Good old Bolton propaganda would later claim that we wanted Bolton to come to Radcliffe, because we had all the Bury lads there with us, which was complete bullshit. Was some mint fight though that's for sure. So that was Radcliffe and it didn't put an end to the City-Bolton thing, it only made it worse!

After Radcliffe it would be fair to say things got a little out of hand, people going to local pubs on non-match days, looking for people. It even went as far as lads finding out addresses, and going to kid's houses. It got a bit fucking daft. The less said about all that the better. Anyway now back to the football. City and Bolton would play each other the first game of the 2011/12 season. We met up in Dry Bar on Oldham Street, which by now was synonymous for being a pub that we would use. In fact over the years Dry has seen more than its fair share of football violence. So we met up there, a handful of older lot, a few lads my age and then loads of new kids, that were starting to come through. We were debating whether to even bother travelling to Bolton, as they really hadn't filled me with confidence that they would even meet us if we did. It was a nice sunny day, sat chilling on the front of Dry Bar with a few Kopperbergs watching the girls go by, which I suppose was another reason why lads weren't in a great hurry to head off to Bolton. In fact most lads (at least half) hadn't bothered coming, just around 20 of us young lot made the relatively short train journey from Victoria to Bolton. Many of the new lads wouldn't be seen again and didn't make it as City lads. Not that you have to pass a test or owt gay like that. Many lads watch all the films and think it's cool to be a football lad, so they think they will have some of that. Then they realise that it's not for them, for whatever reason.

I jumped off the train at Bolton with about seven other lads, the rest had tickets and carried on to Horwich to the ground. We had a little walk round Bolton town centre and couldn't really see much lad wise, so we just went in Yates and had a few beers. We were in there no longer than 20 minutes, when I received a text off Bolton saying "we know where you are Carl, in Yates 20 of youse aren't there". Well I suppose they were half right we were in Yates's but I think they needed to go back to school and learn to count because it was only 7 not 20. This straight away had us all paranoid looking round the pub, which was fairly packed, thinking Bolton were here. I said there's no way we're moving from here now, they know we are here, I don't care how many of them turn up. We waited and waited for them to come piling through the door but it just never happened. Maybe it was a good job seen as there were only a handful of us in there. We gave it another half hour or so and decided nothing was going to happen, so headed back to town to watch the game.

The match itself ended 3–2 to City and just our luck going back to town and not by their ground, as it went off after the game. The fighting itself took place outside Bolton's pubs by the ground. A group of the young City lads saw a large group of Bolton's older mob heading for this pub, so they followed them and attacked them. Fighting broke out and not long after, police have steamed in. By all accounts it wasn't the greatest fight ever but at least the young lads had a go, and attacked a far larger group of Bolton lads. We were kicking ourselves we'd missed it, oh well, that's the way the cookie crumbles sometimes. There was one more big scrap between us lot and Bolton and like several other City fights, it made its way onto YouTube and is a fairly well-known row. There's been a fair few Blazing Squad lads that have been inside but this would see the first lad sent to prison as a result of football violence.

The fighting that took place in Yates's in Bury town centre. That day resulted in several lads doing time in prison, and many bans being given out. The funny thing is City and Bolton weren't even playing that day and a meet hadn't been arranged beforehand either. I'm not sure who Bolton played that day, in fact I've not a clue who they played, or indeed what they were doing in Bury that day. Bury were at home to Stockport County, from what I heard there's no love lost between them two at all. Now I might not be able to recall who Bolton played that day but I 100 percent remember we had Birmingham at home. This I remember because I had spent the week or so leading up to the fixture trying to sort something with one of my pals from their lot. On the morning of the game I was sick, proper fucking ill, being sick and sweating, shaking the lot. I really didn't want to miss the day, so I dragged myself up and started to get dressed, to head out to town. The plan was to get to town, smash them and get a taxi straight back to bed and die in bed for the next few days, safe in the knowledge that is was job done. Although my mum had other ideas, she said I was far too ill to go out fighting, and tell them I would fight them another time instead, "tell them your mum said your too ill to play out". Well I was hardly going to say that, but either way she was right, I was in no fit state to leave the house, never mind anything else. Later I found out that I had food poisoning, self-inflicted so nobody to blame but myself.

I made everybody aware that I was too ill to come out today, Birmingham didn't seem overly bothered by it; neither did my lot to be honest. Now I rate The Zulus as a proper top firm, as do most people I know. But that being said the year previous, well same calendar year, but previous season at least, they hadn't impressed us lot at our place, not one bit. Granted I'm sure a lot of their main lads were missing but even so it got a little embarrassing for them that day. To quote the words of Cliff Lea who at the time was City's main copper "many Birmingham risk were lead away for their own protection". I think that sums it up rather nicely don't you. There wasn't a great battle that day, GMP had seen to that. Although Birmingham's lads were only too happy to be escorted off them, I must say. It wasn't just their kids either, there were a good 25 or so of their older lot combined with around 40 kids. We had around 50 near the ground, when we first come off the estate to attack them. Police solely focused the efforts on to backing us off and not containing their escort. Not that the "Zulu warriors" did a great deal to try and get to us that day. They were pretty poor that day but like I said I know for a fact they're a mint set of lads overall. Several years later we would go on to have one of, if not the best fights I've ever had, in Deep South Birmingham, with the Zulu youth.

Anyway, because of what happened the season before, many lads couldn't be arsed with Birmingham and would rather go meet someone else. Also that day there was a City charity do on and there were supposed to be well over 100 older lads in attendance. Now the youth lads stayed in town for a while, seeing if they bumped into any Zulus, or indeed any other mobs passing through. They then decided to go to Bury, to give it County I'm guessing. By the time they get the tram down there it was during the game, so near enough everyone was in the ground. There was a handful of Bury lads in a pub called the Traff, situated bang in the middle I would say of their town centre. News had got round of a Bolton firm in Bury town centre. Now this was music to the City lad's ears, Bolton were out and only up the road, fucking perfect. The Bury lads present in the pub wanted to wait until after the game, until they were all there, until they made their move for Bolton. The City lads weren't too keen on fucking about, so they just set off there and then and made their way to find Bolton. So around 15 City left the pub, with a couple of Bury lads also. The walk was a relatively short one, past the town hall, across the road and there you are. Bolton were supposed to be in one of the pubs on the front. So three lads went on ahead looking through windows and popping their heads in pubs to see if Bolton were about. The idea being to just send three of them in, to tell Bolton that City are here, and to come outside. The lads approached Yates's Wine Lodge, with the rest of the bunch not too far behind. Unbeknown to City lads at the time, as well as being 12 or so Bolton kids inside, there was also an older Bury lad in there. He looked out the window and seen the 20 or so lads approaching Yates's and presumed it was Bury's firm. On seeing this he literally dives on this Bolton lad, who was standing a few feet away, and starts raining punches on him. City were still oblivious to this one-man attack on Bolton. He was expecting the Bury lads knowing he was in there, to come steaming in but nobody knew he was there. So the three City lads open the doors to have a look inside Yates's, at this point still unsure if Bolton are even in there. Now the Yates's in Bury is pretty much a standard size boozer, but has 2 sets of double doors to go through before your inside. You've got the bar straight in front of you, stairs to the toilets in the corner on the left hand side. It's roughly a rectangular shape bar but the entry where the doors are comes in a bit because it has two sets of double doors you have to go through. It's that what makes nobody notice the brave/mad Bury lad on his own, because he was in a corner. Without coming right inside Yates's and turning back on yourself, you couldn't see. So while being twenty foot away at most, nobody knew he was even there.

The City lads burst through the second set of double doors and for a couple seconds are looking around scouting for lads I suppose. Little Wizz is the first lad in and for some reason pulls his hood down in front of his face. Fuck knows why he did that, maybe just a natural reaction from coming in from outside or something. However this would prove to be his undoing later on. Now Bolton had noticed them, Wizz cracks one of the Bolton lot and it goes off big time in the doorway. A handful of Bolton lads run into the City lads in the doorway. Punches are exchanged, in the small area in between the two sets of double doors. Madness continued, as the rival lads go at it toe to toe. About five from each side traded punches for around half a minute. At the same time, these daft double doors keep swinging back and forth, getting in everybody's way. Bolton were backed off out of the area in between the doors and there was now a standoff for a couple seconds. City lads were shouting "come outside Bolton, come outside and have it". City lads even take a couple of steps back, as they're saying it as in gesturing to Bolton to follow them out. Bolton refused to come outside though, I mean it's one thing holding a door but another being out in the open fighting. Also I must say there wasn't as many Bolton as there was City there. Whilst they might have not fancied their chances outside, they never fully backed away from the doorway. City lads ran back into Bolton and the fighting continued. This time both sides being slightly cautious and maybe not wanting to fully run into the other, more just holding their ground and refusing to back down. Those daft doors swinging both ways certainly weren't helping. Punches and kicks were traded between the two sets of lads, with the odd daft things like bar stools thrown about. I've got to say I've never been one for the whole chair throwing business, not my thing, just makes you look gay as fuck. Also what damage is throwing a chair at somebody's legs going to do, really? I say legs, because that's where the majority of them seem to hit people. Having this fight in the narrow entrance suited Bolton because City's superior numbers counted for nothing. Which certainly was the case as half the lads never got close enough to do owt, there just wasn't enough room.

The fighting broke off, with the opposing lads on each side of their respective doors, not wanting to back away. By now the police were on their way, a van was spotted at the top of the street and this was City's queue to leave. City have backed away from Yates's and walked off up the street, a Bolton lad ran out a chucked a pint glass, catching someone clean in the face. He then ran back inside, it's a shame none of them would come outside earlier on, before City were getting off. Now you remember the Bury lad, the one that was in there own his own right, well he was on top of the Bolton kid, going to town on him. Another Bolton lad sees what's going on, comes running over, upper cuts the Bury lad, and sends him flying into some tables and chairs, then on his arse. He quickly jumps back to his feet to find the lad who he was hitting, is running off. He grabs guess what.. a chair, and throws it at him, but for a change its actually a decent throw, launching it into his side. The Bolton lad half heartedly throws it back. The Bury lad runs into him once again, bombarding him with blows, until a couple more Bolton lads run over and join in. They're now at the far end of Yates's, by the bar. There are innocent bystanders leaving their seats, rushing to the other end of the gaff. The Bury lad has now been pulled to the floor and a few of them are hitting and booting him. All this is going on at the same time as the fighting in the door way is happening and just after. While the lad was on the floor in a foetal position with his hands covering the side and back of his head. Now the next part really pisses me off for a couple of reasons. As the Bury lad lays curled up on the floor, some fat bastard, who has absolutely nothing to do with it, walks over and starts booting him. It's not about booting people on the floor who've clearly had enough and are curled up in a ball. To top it off he wasn't Bolton at all, the silly fat shit bag turns out to be an ex-Burnley lad who had got talking to the Bolton lads briefly at the bar a few minutes earlier. Shortly after police would arrive on the scene and arrests would be made. Months after little Wizz would receive an 18 month sentence for his part that day.

So that was Bolton. The rivalry for us is still there, it hasn't gone away, although they don't seem to want to know anymore. Looking back I think we were always too eager if anything to meet them, any place any time, to put right things from Darwin. Any firm that gets done and then doesn't go out of their way to avenge that, well questions need to be asked about them. At the same time though we're big enough to admit when we got done and say fair play you did us. Besides you learn more about your lads, and indeed yourself, from times like that, rather than just slapping firms about. Everybody gets done sometimes, apart from United obviously, they've never been done ever apparently. With Bolton, I think firms really do underestimate them, especially southern mobs. That being said, it's true at times Bolton have proper fucked us about, ran off, refused to meet us on several occasions. Me and their main lad Kirk had a laugh filming together, in some pub in Bolton, for Football Fight Club. On that day he assured me they were more than happy to meet us, however they still haven't done so. On their day, with their proper lads, they're very good. Capable of turning any firm over, I don't care who you are, we can certainly vouch for that one.

WEST HAM

MY FIRST EVER TASTE of football violence and what it was all about was West Ham at home in the cup back in 2006. It was a midweek night match, in the middle of March. The game itself ended 2-1 to West Ham, knocking City out. I was only 16 at the time and had gone to the game with my mate Piggy. At this point back in 2006 I'm not going to lie and say I was a "lad" and part of the City firm because I wasn't. I was just a 16 year-old scally, bouncing about in his Paul & Shark tracksuit. Even though we were only 16 I was fearless, by that age I had already had a stupid amount of fights. I do mean shit loads. There was nothing I loved more than fighting - fighting and Coronation Street... At this point I didn't know a great deal about football firms or owt but I knew enough to know that West Ham carried a big reputation as a top mob. So I thought this was a good night and hoped it kicked off with this lot. I'm not entirely sure what I was expecting to happen; maybe some 100 a side big fuck off fight. I think I was a little naïve about police presence at the games, the amount of them and all the FIOs. So after the match we headed over to the crossroads pub (now known as The Manchester) which is on the estate, just across the road from our ground. I'm sure before the game the pub was split into two halves, one side for home and one side for away fans but I've never seen that happen any other time. But I'm sure it happened that day anyway and I remember thinking well that's just going to kick off isn't it. There are no away fans pubs near our ground, just all City. I thought maybe after the game West Ham would return back to the boozer and maybe this is where it would all kick off. But obviously police would be escorting them to their coaches or back to the train station in town. The longer West Ham were about, the more there was a chance of violence flaring up.

After the match Me and Piggy tried getting back in the pub but they were saying they're not letting anymore in, it was already too full. We weren't too arsed, as there were loads of people outside. Now I can't really say if they were all lads or what, because back then I wasn't a lad myself. There was a good 120 of us outside the pub and it was increasing by the minute, god knows how many lads were inside the pub as well. News spread that GMP were keeping West Ham in the ground, for at least 10 minutes, then escorting them. Well I reckoned a good 10 minutes at least had passed since the final whistle, so we should be expecting them anytime now. Sure enough West Ham were put in a big escort and escorted from the ground to the coaches. Which was bang in our direction. There were police around near us but it wasn't anything special, could only see about 10 maybe 12, they wasn't going to do much if it went off. More and more lads now started to pile out of the pub and we made our way towards the main road. I was tagging along and going with the flow, seeing if owt happened. There were fucking loads of us by this point, talking around 150 easy, all eagerly waiting for this West Ham ICF escort to come.

We didn't have too long to wait "they're here, West Ham are fucking here now" some big bald cunt stood by me shouted, eyes lighting up and with excitement in his voice. I could now see them, not sure how many of them, if I had to guess I would say 200 maybe 250 of them, with more than enough police around them, as I am sure you can imagine.

Police on foot, horses and a few vans, not to mention the helicopter flying about. The 150 or so City split up into smaller groups, all going in slightly different ways, but all with the same purpose, to get to the main road and attack that escort. The way I saw it was we're from Manchester, they're from east London, and if they thought they can come up here, with all those lads and take the piss, they've got another thing coming. I saw people climbing over this green fence to get to the main road, so I did the same. Put both hands over the fence and gripped it tight, so I could pull myself over. The police weren't too keen on this idea and showed their disapproval, by smacking everyone with coshes. I got my knuckles wacked, not nice at all, especially when it's cold. GMP were being extremely heavy handed, I am guessing to try and stop any fighting before it even started. They weren't shy using their coshes on us, that's for sure. Some fat GMP cunt with a goatee just shouting "move the fuck back, move the fuck back now". He was like some kind of robot, just repeating himself constantly. Even after we had moved back, he still persisted in saying it and waving his baton about. Now by this point I had lost my mate somewhere, god knows where he had gone. It was madness, lads being chased all over the show by police, even seen police being chased off by lads, which made my day.

The West Ham escort had now stopped dead in its tracks. Police must have thought best to hold the escort there, while the rest of them dealt with City and pushed us back. I thought they would have rushed West Ham off as quickly as possible, obviously not. West Ham were now only about 50–60 metres away and could see the commotion and began to push the police escort and began to edge closer towards us. More police were arriving all the time but even so they were very heavily outnumbered. Whereas before the police held a nice line, they were now scattered about all over in different groups near us. A group of around 20 plus police had part surrounded a group of 60 or so City, against the outside of a pub called Mary D's. With that more police steamed over to help contain the group. A group of 50 or so ran round the corner shouting "fucking come on West Ham" and ran at their escort. The group seemed to multiply in number with every few seconds, and now they must have been a good 70, 80 strong, me included. We charged directly into the police lines, which was all that separated us and West Ham. The police were definitely taken back at first by this and were probably in two minds whether to push us all back, or stay and stop West Ham getting free. We were now trading insults and there was a lot of finger pointing going on. A few pint glasses and bottles were being chucked about as well. But there was just about enough police in between us to keep us apart on. There would be a handful of City who managed to get through and attack West Ham. They was quickly pulled out by police and pushed back. Cries of 'ICF, ICF, ICF' went up which infuriated us lot. We felt we were doing everything we could to get to them but they maybe could have been doing more.

This continued for another half a minute or so, with only a handful being able to get close enough to throw punches. Then everyone around me started running back, I thought what the fuck is going on here, why is everyone running?. Then I felt a huge thud in my back and turned round to see a giant horse at the back of me. So that's why everyone had started running, because mounted police were coming into us. The officer on the horse said in some depressing Birmingham accent to me, "run or the horse is going to run into me again". More like he was going to get the horse to run into me again. Me being the cocky kid that I was replied "nah I'm not fucking running nowhere". With that the horse half rammed into me and started to trample on my legs, I thought I don't fancy getting trampled on by this huge horse, so I started walking off. Well I tried to walk off, but the policeman on the horse, didn't want to let me go. "Get down off your horse you fucking prick" I shouted at him, no sooner had I said that I was pulled to the floor from behind by three or so GMP, they sat on me with their knees pressed down on my neck, as they do, so I wasn't going anywhere. One of them was only the cunt with the goatee from a few minutes previous, the one who was whacking everybody with his cosh. The depressed Brummie on the horse proceeded to tell some tale to his fellow officers of how I was punching the horse. I started laughing and said I didn't at all, got a swift elbow in the face for my troubles. I was then dragged to my feet and thrown against the wall at the side of the pub. At this point there were around 8 of them round me, throwing me around. "is there something amusing, kid?" one of them goes to me. I paused for a second and replied "is this the highlight of your careers, loads of you pushing a 16 year-old boy about". They weren't too impressed with that, and I thought I was in for a right kicking off them. Two more police came round the corner, their bosses I'm guessing from the way they were talking to them. "What's happening here with this chap then? He coming in or what?", "no fuck it Section 27 and on his way". Now of course I didn't have a clue what Section 27 was, but to be honest I didn't care, I just knew it meant I wasn't getting arrested. So I got my first Sec 27 that night, albeit under a different name, Pat Mooney, well I wasn't going to give them my real name was I? So I went off on my way, finally found Piggy, and got off back to Whitefield. Feeling very smug inside thinking because I gave them a fake name, I had somehow got one over on GMP.

So the horses did the job, that 100 police with batons out couldn't do, and dispersed the mob of City. While it may not have been a full on fight with West Ham, it was still my first taste of football violence. Little did I know at that point that it would later take a vice like grip over me, and become my life, for the best part of a decade. As for those police horses, that may have been my first encounter with them, but wouldn't be my last. Over the years, the horses would take a dislike to me, the riders anyway. That March evening back in 2006, would be the first and last time I saw a West Ham firm at our place, good job we don't mind travelling isn't it. Next stop east London.

The first game of the 2007/08 season was West Ham away. With it being August, it was another hot day, and there would be lots of City going down to the East End, fans and firm alike. This would be my first trip to the capital. In fact at this point, I could probably count on my hands, the amount of times I've left Manchester. Not really sure what I was expecting London to be like, just like Eastenders I suppose. I soon discovered there aren't too many Londoner's left in London, in fact there weren't a great amount of people who seemed to be able to even speak English, and I thought parts of Manchester were bad. Anyway myself and Piggy booked the trip well in advance, the day the fixtures came out – £60 return Piccadilly to Euston. We had arranged to meet up with loads more lads down there. I had seen West Ham's firm close up for myself just over a year previous, but this time we wanted to bump into them without police in the middle. West Ham carries a very big reputation name wise, to the general public. They were supposed to be right up there as one of the best "back in the day". In recent times films such as Cass, Rise Of The Foot Soldier, Green Street and The Firm, have only enhanced West Ham's reputation even more, in the eyes of the media and general public. So we made our way from Euston across to east London. An hour or so before kickoff the place was just rammed with West Ham everywhere. With little pockets of City dotted about, not in a big group as per. We found a pub not too far from the ground and went in, only 5 or so of us at this point. Was massive this place, like a big supporters club or something, was a good 500 people in there, all West Ham. We got a beer and went to back of the pub in the corner and just kept ourselves to ourselves. We were getting some right funny looks so we had a couple and got off. Bumped into some more lads and headed to another pub. On our way we saw this lad pissing with blood; it was only one of our mates. He had been glassed by a few West Ham in a pub round the corner. Only it turns out that was the pub we'd been in earlier, we must have just missed him. We jogged back to the pub but the doorman wasn't letting any more in and police were everywhere ushering people towards the ground. So we just went in the game.

The game itself ended 2-0 to City. We were all kept in the ground for a few minutes after the game, we being the away fans of course. We weren't all put in an escort to my surprise, we were left to do our own thing. It had been a long day and if am being honest I just wanted to get off back home, I was fucked. We heard a lot of noise in the distance, shouting and stuff. Me not being the tallest of people I couldn't really see what was going on. Jogged down to see but by the time we got there the police were all over it. It seemed a larger group of West Ham had attacked a few City lads walking down, and it had gone off. Little pockets of fighting were breaking out, a few yards away from us a City fan got glassed and bottled right outside this pub. We got on the famous Green Street, just reminded me of Cheetham Hill Road really. We heard later of more fights going on, on the train on the way home there were more City fans with cut faces, from being glassed and bottled. That was my first away day to London, and while pretty uneventful, the next trip to West Ham would be one of Blazing Squad's most famous rows, a favourite of mine even to this day.

Not just this away day but the whole weekend is right up there for me. The weekend of the 28th February and 1st March 2009. West Ham away being the 1st of March but the night before that I had an unlicensed boxing match. So for weeks leading up to this weekend I could think of nothing else. Won the boxing match, went to town after to get pissed, not wanting to go too wild as I was up in a few hours, for the away day down there. It was Tom's birthday, his 21st, so I knew on the way down it would be a big party. So with that in mind I left town about half 2 so I could get a couple of hours sleep, then got ready and back to town to meet the lads. Safe in the knowledge that tomorrow was going to be a fucking mental day. We all met up in town pretty early about 6:30am it was, near the taxi rank at the back of Piccadilly station. We had booked a 16 seater but 18 of us had turned up. Now whether the driver didn't realise we had an extra couple of passengers, or just didn't care, I'm not fully sure, either way we were off. The trip down is obviously far slower by car than by train and the fact we were in a mini bus would mean it would take even longer. Everyone was in good spirits, drinking, drugs, singing and dancing, it was a party on the way down. A small number travelling with us had tickets to the game but the vast majority of us, me included, had no intention of seeing the game and couldn't care less. I just wanted to fight West Ham. Wanted to give them a proper kicking, not a little scuffle outside the ground where police are all over, a proper meet out of the way, with no old bill, no cameras, just us and them. Then we would see if West Ham really did warrant the reputation which they had acquired over the years. See we were all dead young, 90 percent of us were still teenagers and we wanted the big reputation. And going all the way to east London and meeting their lads, smashing them all over, well you couldn't really ask for a better opportunity than that. As teenage hooligans I suppose we craved the big reputation and we wanted City to be known as one of the best in the business.

On the way down the lads who had been present at the boxing last night were bigging me up and telling the lads about my fight. They were maybe exaggerating my exploits a little but I wasn't going to stop them. Music was blasting out all the way down. The usual Manchester classics like the Smiths, Oasis, Stone Roses etc were on the go. But there were two songs witch stuck in my head from that day, MGMT 'Kids' and Joy Division 'Love Will Tear Us Apart'. We blasted them out all the way down. To the Joy Division classic we changed the words to "City taking over your town, again". Even now over 6 years on, I still sing 'City taking over your town again', whenever I hear that song. Now you've all seen the film Football Factory right, well the part in that where they are at the services, and just robbing everything, that scene could have been based on City youth. We joke around and say the prices at service stations are so high, due to all the football lads passing through and robbing it blind. Sounds a little daft and farfetched I know but if you were there and seen the amount of shit robbed, you would understand. If it wasn't nailed down, it was getting robbed, you name it Blazing Squad stole it. Now I'm not just talking cans, bottles and food and stuff, I'm talking all sorts. DVD's and toilet signs saying wet floor would be taken; even blow up dolls would be robbed. One time I remember one of the lads coming back with loads of magazines. Nothing wrong with that you may think, he didn't take anything like FHM or Nuts, oh no that would be too simple. Nope he came back with magazines on gardening and cake baking. With no less than a 10 page step by step guide to making the perfect birthday cake. I said to the lad "why the fuck have you got these you can't bake, and you have no garden" to which he smiled and emptied his pockets, to show me possibly the widest selection of chocolate you will ever see. One thing's for certain, nobody ever went hungry on our away days. The most memorable thing robbed would definitely have to be a cow. Not a real cow obviously but I am sure if there was a real cow knocking about, they would have given it a go. A toy cow you know like a cuddly teddy bear, only this one was a cow. That's just another example of the daft shit that was pinched. You can imagine everyone's faces back on the bus pulling out all the stuff they have robbed and one lad pulling out a cow from under his jacket. We all quickly grew fond of her, oh yeah we decided the cow was a female and named her moo moo Kippax. Moo moo the noise cows make and Kippax after Kippax Street, at the old ground in Moss Side. Moo moo the cow went on to have her own facebook account and everything.

On one of the rare times that I went on a little graft. I completely filled my pockets with all sorts, mainly beer and food. There was a dead awkward moment in there, I was happily helping myself to what I wanted and the staff caught me red handed. Oh for fuck sake the last thing I wanted was to be caught shoplifting, like some little smack head. It was one of them weird moments, I suppose she pretended she hadn't seen me rob stuff and I pretended that I hadn't seen her, seen me do it. And that was that, the bird was proper fit as well, red hair and green eyes, right up my street.

Anyway back to West Ham, we were in contact with them all the way down and were aware where they wanted us to go. They were like "are youse deffo turning up yeah?" I don't think they fully trusted we would. I think they thought we would either not show or turn up with like 50 older lot in tow, which wasn't our style at all. I like to think we are always honest and straight with everyone, I think it's the best way to be, honesty is the best policy so they say. Shame all firms didn't do it that way because they don't, many are sly and can't be trusted. We had finally made it to London, but had hit traffic big time. We were now just 15 miles or so away from where we were going. Now there were 18 of us on this mini bus, but 5 had tickets to the match itself, which left just 13 of us to fight West Ham on their "manor" as they call it. For all we knew there could have been 50 of them, maybe even 80 of them but we were meeting them that day regardless, nothing was going to change that. We finally come off the motorway; it felt like we had been on it forever. West Ham had told us to get off next to a park, not too far from their ground, so we did just that. So we all jumped out 5 lads going towards the ground and us 13 were going in the opposite direction to Barking to meet them.

We really didn't know what to expect at all, whether we were being set up, or if they were going to even be there at all. West Ham's reputation at the time was right up there with the best, so you've got to say, there are not too many firms that would go out of the way to meet them, with just 13 kids. It's dead easy going to away games with tickets, in big numbers like 100 handed walking about, and seeing what happens. Or in United's case making loads of noise to attract police attention and get escorted but that isn't what we are about. No safety in numbers, out of the way on their turf, no police and no place to hide. We were walking down this main road proper taking everything in, not knowing if they were just going to run out from nowhere or what. We were given directions of how to find West Ham, they said it was a proper spot to have it and well out of the way. We made our way towards Barking, crossed over the main road and down the side of some shops, still not knowing what to expect at all. We bunched up fairly tight and made our way round the side of Wickes. Nobody was really talking much, I suppose you could say we were "in the zone". I personally was shitting it a little bit, not even going to lie about it. Had visions of going round the corner and there being 100s of them cunts waiting for us and knowing how daft we all are, we would have stayed and took a right kicking, sooner than run. My heart was proper going, felt like I did the night before walking to the boxing ring.

West Ham were right about one thing though, it was a perfect spot for a scrap. There was a path; I suppose a thinnish path, with patches of grass on either side. On the left hand side was a car park, on the right hand side a river, well that's how I remember it anyway. On seeing the river I just started laughing, "Carl what the fuck you laughing at?". "That river there must be the same one you see at the start of Eastenders". To which we all laughed. and then they took the piss out of me for watching Eastenders. We knew we were roughly in the right area, but still no sign of them lot anywhere. West Ham was nowhere to be seen. The path narrowed for a few metres, then bent round a corner, and widened once more. I would describe it as the kind of place that you would take your dog for a walk. The plan was smash West Ham down here, fuck off out the area rapid, before police had chance to do anything. But still West Ham was nowhere to be seen. We edged closer a few more feet round the corner, we thought this is just getting daft now, let's get the phones out and bell them. Then what happens so many times, happened once more, we heard them before we seen them. I think they had been waiting round the corner and had heard us lot coming. Cries went up of 'ICF! ICF! ICF!' like something out of a film. We all looked around at each other but nobody said a word at first but everybody knew what needed to be done. We all started to jog further around the path, bingo there they were, there was West Ham. This is what we had just travelled all the way from Manchester for. They were still around 50, 60 metres away from us.

Those few seconds jogging down towards them, felt like minutes. That for me is the worst part of fighting, those few agonising seconds before hand. You know you're about to fight but it hasn't started yet. For me as soon as the fighting actually starts I am fine, well more than fine, I am in my element. All the nerves go, adrenaline takes over. West Ham had a lot more lads than 13, that was pretty clear to see from the start. But to be fair they had kept their word, not turning up with crazy numbers or owt like that. Was a good 20 of them though, maybe even 25. Remember having a good look at them, they were all pretty smartly dressed, a few of them had the same Lacoste polo's on but all in different colours, so they looked like a fucking rainbow. Another thing I noticed was they had bars and stuff in their hands, well turns out they weren't bars but planks of wood, plus the odd one had bricks. 'YOOF! YOOF! YOOF!' our infamous youth chant went up. This was it, no messing about now, no eyeing each other up and bouncing about, which so often happens before a fight at football. We both pretty much just ran into each other, like something out of the film 300, only minus the swords of course. We steamed straight into them, which I think took them by surprise a little, with them having superior numbers to us. I was in my own little world for the next minute or so. It was a proper battle, full on, nobody backing off one bit. One of our lads had I suppose ran too far forward into the middle of them. A few of them quickly circled him and were half punching him, half trying to drag him to the floor. Well we couldn't allow that could we, at once everybody charged forward all at exact same time. As we have pulled the lad back to us, I've somehow ended up facing the wrong way. Just as I was turning round, I got a good few cracks all on the back, and side of my head, even got one on my back. Who goes round punching people in their backs?

I've now fully turned round to see 2 or 3 of them right in my face. "come on you cunt" one of them yelled at me, as he bounced up and down in front of me, as if he was on a fucking trampoline. His pal at the side of trampoline boy took a swing at me, but it was a wild swing and he put himself off balance and fell towards me, pretty much into me. Fuck off bang, nutted this kid good and proper, and he has gone stumbling back. Not really sure where it came from, as I'm not mad into head butting. The fighting continued all around me, at this point I would say it was 50/50, nobody really getting the better of each other, and certainly nobody wanting to back down. "Come on West Ham, fucking come on then" we ran into them once more. I was at the front but on the very far left hand side of our lot, fighting with these 2 lads, trading punches with them in the corner. Now either I've gone too far forward, or the rest of City have been backed off, because I've ended up with a fair few of them swarming around me. I had some big black coat on, with a big fuckoff hood. The hood was soon pulled down over my head, and I was being whacked all over by the lumps of wood they had and booted to fuck as well. This pissed me off, because parts of me were still dead sore from the boxing fight about 15 hours earlier. I put my hands up to try and cover my head the best I could, I was then yanked back hard by my hood, nearly fucking pulled me over. It was a couple of City lads rescuing me and pulling me back. So it went on. Punches being traded back and forth, the odd shout of ICF and east London went up but while we were by no means battering West Ham, I think we were starting to slowly but surely get the better of things. With every charge into them, whereas before they didn't budge, now some of them were beginning to take a couple of steps back, every time. From experience we knew that was how it starts, first a few back off, then it turns to some full on running. That was case a lot of the time anyhow. Lads on both sides seemed to slow down, probably tiring. I mean we had in reality we had been fighting for a guess a couple of minutes but to us it felt like a couple of hours. It's like we had done it the wrong way round, the fight first then the bouncing up and down, and eyeing each other up second. There were lads with cuts and marks on both sides. I suppose it was as if somebody had blown a whistle for half time because for a few seconds nobody did or said a fucking thing. Bit of a mad moment to be honest, looking back. Bit of an awkward silence.

Then one of their lads, slightly out of breath started to laugh and said "What is that it you Manc cunts?" we just all looked at each other laughing. One of our lads said "you're supposed to be West Ham aren't you? Throw down your tools and fight us then". At that moment one of our lads took off his shades and threw them to the floor. Why he did this, I have no idea, maybe more to the point who the fuck fights with shades on to start with! We ran into each other again, this time with real intent, whoever got the better of these first few exchanges would have the momentum and more than likely go on to win the fight. I definitely felt it was ours for the taking. West Ham was ours for the taking. They were starting to split up and were no longer nice and tight. We would now begin to pick them off; some of them were falling over each other to get back. But at the same time, some of their lads at the front were still trying to give it a go. I smacked some kid a couple of times, proper smacked him caught him mint and to be fair to him, he didn't even budge at all, hard little cunt. He backed off back with his lads. Then to our amazement they shouted "shit police, run, run" or words to that affect. We all instinctively turned around, we didn't see any police. No police was there from what I could see, we turn back round to face West Ham, and we couldn't believe our eyes. To our amazement they were running away. Shouting 'ICF' and 'east, east, east London' as they were running, taunting us to follow, well we didn't need much convincing, we ran off in pursuit.

Now I'm not sure if one of their lads got caught running off or was being a game cunt and carrying on fighting us but he got caught anyway. He was getting a right good kicking as well. I'm all for one on ones and big groups on big groups, not loads on one kid though, it's not about that is it, do you know what I mean? So me and another lad Raz pulled people off the West Ham lad and helped him up. He slumped down against the wall at the side of him, not far from the river. His nose was broke; it was a mess, blood all over him and his eyes were glazed over. I said to him "you alright mate?" To which he smiled and replied "sweet bruv" and shook my hand. I helped him on his feet properly and said "right fuck off that way then" and that's the last we saw of him. We continued to run after West Ham, who were now pretty much in two separate groups, the ones who still wanted to fight and the ones who clearly had had enough and didn't wanna know anymore. We chased them further down the path and to a bridge going over the river, where there was a stand off again. This time they all had bricks in their hands but at this point it didn't matter, we were there to finish them off. We started to come over the bridge towards them, I think some of them lost their bottle and threw the bricks a few seconds to early, and then they all began to run off. They ran onto this estate, still funnily enough chanting 'East, East, East London', and for us that was that. Don't get me wrong you could see some of them didn't want to go anywhere and wanted to carry on fighting but I suppose you're only as strong as the people around you. One of their lads, he's a good kid; he had a black eye for almost a year after this fight courtesy of Tom.

God knows how it stayed bruised for so long, but it did. So that was that, job done, we had done what we had set out to do, smash West Ham on their own patch, and we had achieved this with just 13 lads. 9 out of 10 firms wouldn't even entertain meeting another firm with numbers like that. The joy on every one's faces was evident to see. Huge cheesey grins, shaking hands, hugging and kissing, the lot. Congratulating one another, telling stories of their part in the battle which had just taken place, for me there is no feeling like it, it's euphoric, we felt on top of the world. We felt unstoppable and untouchable, we are fucking Man City, and this is what going to the football was all about for us. 'City, taking over your town, again' rang out, as we made our way to the nearest tube. High on our own success we arrived at East Ham tube station. We got on the underground, made our way to Euston, which is where the mini bus driver had arranged to pick us up from. Euston is central London, we were in the East End so we were a fair bit away anyway. So we was on the tube which by the way I fucking hate. You have to go through these daft gates to get on it; none of us had a clue what we were doing, so we all just fucking jumped over them. Plus there are just far too many lines, so it's just impossible to work out where you're going. Give me the Manchester Metrolink any day of the week.

The tube pulled into a station and we were met with a wall of noise. It was like the scene of Rise Of The Foot Soldier where they pull into a station and Millwall are waiting. We all went silent and looked at each other as if to say, well what the fuck is going on here then? The platform was completely jam packed with 100s and 100s of people. They started banging on the tube chanting 'Yids! Yids! Yids!'. We moved closer to the doors, ready for anything that my happen. It seemed to be a mixture of Spurs lads and a lot of just normal shirted fans also. The tube we were on started to move again, and I'm sure the doors never once opened for anybody to get on or off. Now how mint would that have been to have done two London firms in the space of half an hour, although the numbers weren't looking good, so maybe it's for the best it didn't happen. Around an hour had passed since the scrap with West Ham and they were now ringing us back wanting it again. But for us we had done what we had came to do and had no intention of mooching back across London to have it again, why should we? All that would have happened is that there would have been even more of them waiting for us. Like the little kids that we were, we went to McDonalds, and got shitloads of scran .We made our way back to the mini bus and back up north. So we had gone to east London and done West Ham, and we had robbed a cow... I mean what more could you ask for in an away day?

The final match of the 2010 season was West Ham away. The last away game generally pulls in big numbers and this game was no exception. It had been just over a year since the fight at Barking and despite several promises, they had not repaid the favour. By repay the favour I mean come to our place, like we did to theirs. I think at one point we had played them at our place a couple times, in a week or so. One time being midweek, so I don't really blame them for giving that a miss. Another time they said they'd fucked up and booked the coach for the wrong date and another they were at a boat party, whatever the fuck that is. I personally think West Ham had seriously underestimated us at Barking, the year previous. Or maybe they just didn't realise how good we were. Either way it was irrelevant now – what happened, happened. We knew this time they certainly wouldn't take us lightly and would have everybody out for us. All of whom would be no doubt seeking revenge, big time. We travelled down by mini bus once more. But there were enough City lads going down by train or coach. The plan was pretty much bang on as the year before, same place and everything, which was fine by us lot. We couldn't have been past Birmingham yet, and already one of the lads was doing my fucking head in. The kid was pestering me to death, ringing every 20 or so minutes, seeing where we were. 'Somewhere in the midlands, a bit vague I know but that's the best I can do, anyway somewhere in the midlands' I said as we pulled into the services.

I went in had a piss came back and there were about 7 of us there waiting outside the bus for the rest of the lads to return. Then around 100 metres away this 52 seater pulled up filled with lads. Now we didn't have the foggiest idea who it was. It could have been literally anybody going anywhere. They all quickly started to pile off the coach, some from the front door, and others from exits at the side. They were all massive fucking geezers. All with dead tight tops on, as if to exaggerate their size even more. They all came bouncing over towards us. Oh god well what the fuck do we do here then, there's only 7 or 8 of us, we still at this point didn't have a clue who they were. Their accent soon gave it away though.

A strong Welsh accent at that, we soon clicked oh shit, it's Cardiff. They had Leicester away in the championship play-offs. "Who are you" they shouted over, "we're Man City" we replied. They sort of looked at each other and shrugged, then I suppose nodded in approval, like we were ok or something. I was staring at the lad next to me who shouted we're Man City, it was little Wizz. Now little Wizz is only small, but he is fucking mad and I was just praying he wasn't going to run over and start fighting with them. We started walking over to them, still a little unsure how the whole thing was going to play out. I think they respected the fact we all walked over to them. They told us they were Cardiff lads from the valleys and there were another 4 coaches en route to Leicester now. Poor fucking Leicester. They told us they quite liked and respected City but hated United, nothing new there. We told them we we're off to West Ham; they seemed even less keen on West Ham, as they did with United. One of their lads went into his pocket and pulled out a blade. Not in an aggressive way or owt, he held it in an open palm. He turned to one of our smaller lads, who was from down my end, and said "there you go little one" and handed him the knife. "There's a present off Cardiff, make sure you use it on West Ham for me". I suppose it was an unusual present to say the least, but a present nonetheless. I suppose they say it's the thought that counts! Maybe it was a good job most of our lads were inside on the rob because if they had been there, I reckon it would have gone off. I think we would have taken a good hammering. We shook hands and said our farewells to the Welshman bearing gifts and went on our way but not before I had rang a Leicester lad I knew and told him how many Cardiff were coming his way…

Anyway we continued on our way down to east London. Like I said, the plan was pretty much the same as last year. But this time we were going to make sure we had a lot more lads with us because sure as hell there would be more of them. We finally made it down there, for some reason this year felt like it had taken a lot longer to get there, not sure why. We come off at a roundabout and it was, if I remember correctly, a left to like Barking and Dagenham, and a right to East London and West Ham's ground. We went left and jumped straight out, same as last year. Only this year the police were waiting for us. There were only about 6 of them at this point but we knew that could all change in seconds. Police are like immigrants, one minute there's a couple of them, next there's 100s of the cunts. There was no point in trying to run past them, all they would do is follow us. So there wasn't much else to do, but walk the opposite way towards the ground. Which I am guessing is what the police wanted to happen, they followed us down, whilst on their radios, no doubt calling for more officers to attend. Lads tried splitting up, going down various side streets off the main road but they were soon picked up by the police. So we continued to walk up Barking Road I think it was, into East Ham. The road itself was a fairly busy main road, with shops most of the way down it. Off the main road were streets with rows and rows of back to back terrace housing. We eventually arrived by their ground at a boozer called The Denmark. The pub was already completely rammed with City, so we all just stood outside it. I was hungry as usual. On the way down I did eat, I went to a Wimpy at the services and paid about 6 quid for a burger, which was the size of a fucking chocolate digestive. So I went and got a sausage butty and then a Greggs, and bought a couple of pasties, so was happy once more. I returned to The Denmark and in the short time I had been gone a lot more City lads had turned up. There were well over 100 City there now, with more apparently on their way – brilliant!

We told West Ham what had happened with the police so we couldn't get down there and told them to come to us. They said it's too tricky them coming to us because of the bans. I thought well surely there has to be still enough lads that aren't banned that can come around the ground and would have been down there anyway. Now the police was mixed with West Ham footie intelligence, Man City football intel and just normal police. They were not for letting us go anywhere. So we decided to try and peel off in groups no larger than 3, hoping they wouldn't really notice us leaving. We managed to get around 30 or so of us away in dribs and drabs. We came to a pub called the Vic, we had heard it was one of their pubs. No sooner had we got near the pub, police just appeared from nowhere and pushed us back away from the pub and towards the ground. We were pushed back to where the rest of City was outside the away end. An awful lot of lads had tickets, and went in the game, we all tried to jib in, some made it, and some didn't. There were now about 8 of us left. Not a chance did I want to go and meet them with just 8 lads after last year there was going to be loads of them.

We walked back to the Vic and a few other pubs around their ground looking for lads but the pubs were pretty much dead to be fair. We told them, look we're not coming all that way to meet you with just 8 lads, that's just daft. But we will tell you exactly where we are and then you can come to us. At this point we were by Plaistow tube station, they insisted they couldn't come to us due to banning orders. Breaching of a ban carries 6 months imprisonment so I could see where they were coming from. That being said if the shoe was on the other foot, we would have been down like a shot, I know because I have done it. We got on the tube and went to Kings Cross, drinking round there for a while. Now we knew this certainly wasn't in their banning area and after saying they would come down to meet us there, they then said it was too far and declined to come. I later got told off another London firm that that day West Ham had a nice firm, 60 handed in Barking waiting for us. It was always going to be hard for this trip, to live up to the one the year earlier. Everyone expected a huge fight with West Ham but it just wasn't to be, just one of them things I suppose. After the game that day all the City lads apparently took the piss round there and took over their pubs and there are supposed to have been a few scuffles but nothing major.

At the very start of 2014, West Ham made the trip up to our place. It had been almost 8 years since I had seen any West Ham down at our place, so I think the trip was long overdue. It all came about pretty much out of the blue to be honest, we weren't expecting them to travel up, especially not for a midweek game. I sorted it out through text initially and then on the phone with one of their lads who was also banned. He said their lads coming up would be a mix of banned and not banned and mainly proper old school lads in their 40s and even 50s. With a handful of youth lads like himself as well. We both agreed Stockport would be the perfect place for all concerned to have the meet. It's not too far from town but far enough not to come under banned areas, for them and for us too. So a nice meet out of the way with West Ham, sounds bang on doesn't it, but there was just one problem, half my lads couldn't fucking make it. It was driving me mad, there were lads who work away during the week, lads who finish work late during the week and then lads on tag so couldn't leave their houses in the evenings. So then I was left with a real dilemma, do I just take what I can to the meet anyway, and risk taking a beating purely because of numbers, and have people like, why the fuck did you go there with that few lads Carl knowing they had loads? Or do I tell West Ham look we just can't pull enough numbers to meet you midweek, and then look like complete fucking shit bags? People would be like we should have met them anyway, regardless of numbers. They had a good 40 lads they told me but will that mean 40 or as is the case so many times does it mean more like 50 plus. Either way it looked like we would be scrapping 20, if not somewhere in the teens, we had enough lads missing that's for sure. Also another thing I had to think about is, do I want to damage our reputation by going into fights so heavily outnumbered, with most key lads missing? This really wasn't the fight for bringing loads of new kids, all 15, 16 year olds but it looked like we had to for the numbers. Hindsight is a wonderful thing and it's very easy to look back and think why the fuck do we do that, when you know what the outcome is going to be. For me it came down to this, could I sit there knowing a firm had come to Manchester to fight us and we didn't meet them due to poor numbers? That didn't sit easily with me at all, I'd rather have a go and if worst comes to worst, come off second best, than have a firm come to our place untouched, making us look soft.

This West Ham game came only weeks after are possibly greatest fight and greatest win at the football. We went down to Deep South Birmingham, proper into their area, on some mad estate and had it with them. Them Zulus are the gamest lads I've ever come across, it was a top fight and we had won it. Everybody was buzzing over that still weeks later and it would have put a real downer on things going from that, to getting done at home. But if West Ham wanted a fight, then I was going to make sure they got a fight. All our lot arranged to meet at the Footage on Oxford Road. Then from there we were going to head off to Stockport, to meet them. Our numbers weren't very good but I expected as much anyway because it's midweek and very short notice. When you're able to think of like 15 lads off the top of your head that can't make it, it's just very annoying indeed. We're not exactly a big firm either, so missing 15 lads, hits us very hard.

West Ham were already in Stockport and were constantly belling my phone, wanting us to come down. I just wanted to hold out a tiny bit longer before setting off and get another few lads who could only make it after 6. If I went down there with what we had and we got done, knowing we would have had an extra few lads if I had waited half an hour, I would have felt a right cunt. It's not like we were trying to match their numbers or owt like that, we didn't even have half what they had. West Ham had been only the second firm from down south after Chelsea to come up here and want it with us. They wanted a fight and I was only too keen to oblige. We all said right another 10 minutes and we're off with whatever we have. It wasn't so much the numbers, well the lack of numbers, that was doing my head in; it was the lack of main lads that couldn't make it out. But shit happens and it is what it is, so it was now time to stop playing for time and to go and have it. Just as we were finishing off our pints and going for a piss before we head off, GMP turned up. With all my worrying about our numbers and stalling for time so more lads could make it, I had forgotten all about the police. It seems they certainly hadn't forgotten about us though. The police kept us there giving us Section 27s and just being as slow as they could about things, as if somehow they knew what was about to happen. They picked their fucking timing spot on anyway. As I've sent a text to my West Ham pal explaining about the police, I almost instantly got one back saying pretty much the same thing, police were all over them and nothing they could do.

Well it looked like that was that then, or was it? The majority of their lads had tickets to the game, but a small handful didn't, because they were banned. They had come up just to have it with us, out of the way basically. Them doing that straight away made me have a lot of respect for them. I said to them, let all your lads go to the game and all our lot, meet down by the ground, but let us banned ones have a little meet in Stockport now. He seemed up for it and said there are only 4 of them left though, I said "nah that's perfect mate". Everybody else had fucked off to the game, or fucked off home, after the police come. There was me, my brother and little Aaron left out, so I rang Blood and explained to him what was going on and he was bang up for it. I suppose you could call this making the most out of a bad situation, but if truth be told I was more excited by this little 4 on 4, than I was for the big fight with all of us. So Blood picked us up and we were on our way to the Red Bull in Stockport, which is where they said they were. I was proper up for this; I thought I bet I could probably smash 4 of these on my own, never mind with these 3 with me. I thought there's literally no chance us losing this one now. Started to bell his phone, to tell him that were almost there, but it was going straight to answer phone. This wasn't good at all but maybe he's just on the phone, or you know what it's like in some pubs, the signals sometimes wank. I rang and rang and rang and still nothing, I was started to get pissed off now. I even text other West Ham lad, to ask them do they know who the lad was with, so I could find out where they were. Well there was nothing for it then, just go in all the pubs in the area where they said they were. So there we were walking round Stockport the 4 of us, in the pissing rain, going from pub to pub looking for West Ham. I was still trying his phone but with no luck, after going in around 5 or 6 different pubs, we decided to call it a day and head back to the car. Why was his phone suddenly turned off? Is all I wanted to know. There's nothing more we could do anyway now.

It turned out that the West Ham kids got nicked for not leaving the area and fucking off back down south. Not only did they get nicked just before we got there, they drove past us in the back of the police cars and actually saw us. We were gutted and so were they, there was no winner that day, apart from GMP. There was nothing more we could do, and nothing more they could do, just one of those things I suppose. After they came up here out of the way like that and wanted it, I think there's a good chance we will be off down south to repay the favour sometime soon. So that's definitely something to look forward to.

Many people claim that West Ham aren't as good as they used to be and are just living off past reputation. But then again you could probably say that about an awful lot of mobs. As far as I am concerned they're good kids, on the whole they're sound to talk to and game for a fight. West Ham away is still a naughty place to go and West Ham had proven they're willing to meet firms out of the way and have it. That fight in Barking will always be one of my favourite fights at City ever, and from that fight I will always have respect for West Ham.

EVERY SAINT HAS A PAST,
EVERY SINNER HAS A FUTURE

I CAN'T EVER REMEMBER thinking I wanted to be a football hooligan, it just sort of happened. Growing up it wasn't anything I aspired to be. My first memory of anything to do with football violence, as I have said, was West Ham at home back in 2006. However it wouldn't be until the summer of 2007 that I was bitten by the bug and fell in love with football violence and all that goes with it. I'm from Whitefield which is north Manchester, roughly 5 miles from the town centre. While it's true that the majority of this fine City is blue, the area I am from is defiantly red. When I was around 10-11 I decided I wanted to be a City fan, just to be different. All them years ago City were not one of the best teams in the world, in fact we weren't even in the Premier League. Like the song goes "we were here when we were shit" I can honestly say I was there when City was shit. I grew up in a poor, working class family, what I would call fairly normal to be honest.

Although there is nothing normal about my family, then again what is normal? For example on my 2nd birthday I received a knife, not a toy plastic one but a proper blade. Although after a few days it was taken off me, because they thought I wasn't old enough. So I got to laugh when I see these teenagers thinking their hard because they're bouncing around with knifes, come on mate I was doing that before I was old enough to start play group. While I wasn't brought up to hate the police or owt daft like that, from an early age I knew not to answer the door to them. My first memories of the police was seeing them coming in and arresting someone, for whatever reason. Even as a 4 year-old I knew if it was the police at the door, nobody bangs on the door like GMP. The first time I myself would feel the force of the long arm of the law I would be around 10. I had been playing football and these kids were cheating, so I had a fight with this lad and his brother and twatted them both. They went off crying, anyway turns out their dad was a policeman. And to cut a long story short he wasn't impressed with what had taken place, his 2 gay little kids getting beat up. Now bear in mind I was only 10, not only that but I was a small kid, so could have easily passed for an 8 year-old. He come bowling over screaming and shouting going fucking mad. This pig was quite a big bloke as well, easily 6 foot and 16 stone. He was a giant to me anyway, he lent down pressing his head against mine. I just started laughing but if am being honest I think it was more a nervous laugh than anything because I was a little scared but I wasn't going to let him know that, or the handful of mates with me. My laughter clearly infuriated the off-duty policeman. He threw me to the floor, "You think you're hard! Fight me then!" he shouted. I was thinking not only is he GMP, he's like 35 years old, he isn't allowed to do this is he? I jumped back up to my feet, the cunt pushed me again harder, at this point my bottom lip was going and my eyes were filling up. My mates started to boot him and punch him. He just stood there with a blank look on his face, then something must have clicked at what he had just done, he just walked off rapid. From that moment on I had a new found hatred for the police. For that entire summer me and my mates spent it throwing eggs, stones and bricks at any police or police cars we came across. As for the bully boy pig, well as luck would have it I bumped into him almost a decade later. I'm not going to go into detail what happened, I'll leave that to your imagination. Let's just say I did a lot more than just push him to the floor.

I hear people say that people are products of their environments. While that may be true to a certain extent, I believe you are what you are and your nature is in your genes. I'm a fighter from a family of fighters, I'm very proud of my background. My surname Moran, a big Irish name, it means descendant of the great ones, warriors from Mayo western Ireland, you know Father Ted part of the world. As odd and gay as this sounds I often think of myself as a warrior but think maybe I was like born in the wrong century or something. I honestly would have been happier hundreds of years ago with a big fuck off sword on a muddy battlefield, perfect. Rather have that than what we have now, all this modern technology which means fucking nothing to me. For example on Facebook when everybody was first getting Blackberrys, and putting their bbm pins on there so friends could add them, I just presumed they were people's prison numbers to write to them. I remember thinking "fuckinel Carl you've got an awful lot of mates away at the moment".

Ours is a bit of a mad family at times, I suppose like one time I was remanded and taken to court. I was expecting prison but got off without going anyway. Didn't have a bean on me to get home but I didn't have to worry because my dad was in court the same day. Not only the same courts, but even the same court room after me, so I got a lift home. He was up on some daft charge, for assaulting police or something, which he was innocent of, I may add. So I got a lift back with him. My daughter was waiting at home for me, she had not long since turned 2 but I'll leave it a while longer before I give her, her own knife. In fact my dad and his car were becoming rather handy for me. I'm quite hot headed at times to say the least, and any daft shit can make me lose it. One time I just lost it over something daft really. Started head butting the wall in the cellar a few times, after a few times it started to hurt my head, so I decided to refrain from using my head and use my fists like a "normal person". Threw a left hook and put my arm straight threw the double glazing. What a fucking idiot I am! I had cut my arm to pieces, I mean really bad, blood was pouring out of me like a tap and huge chunks of glass were sticking out of me. So being the big hard man that I am what did I do? I shouted for my mum. My mum funnily enough was just leaving the house to taking someone to hospital who had just taken an overdose. So they were going to the hospital anyway. The nurse said that the main cut was that bad it wouldn't have taken too long for me to bleed to death. I got 60 stitches to the main cut and a further 25 stitches to various smaller cuts all over my arm and knuckles. What a retard I felt, I can safely say I will never punch glass ever again. I think my nana summed it up rather good, she goes "Carl what are you doing hitting windows, just punch walls and doors instead".

It's true, fighting came naturally to me, it's like second nature and I just get a huge buzz off it, partly I just love fighting because I am good at it. People tend to like things that they're good at, right. Although I will still insist I am a lover not a fighter, well I am a little of both maybe. Give me a night with a fit bird any day over a scrap. Some lads say fighting at City is better than sex. Bollocks! You're obviously not doing it right, mate. I remember being around 12 years old, just started Second year of high school I think it was. I was then, as I still am now, mad into my boxing. I went to some gym not too far away in Radcliffe. That night I waited outside the gym for about half an hour but for whatever reason the guy who ran it just never showed up. Now this was still a year or so before mobiles became popular and everybody had one, so I never had one. So I couldn't bell anybody to pick me up, it was proper pissing it down. So I thought, fuck it I'll walk, I can remember mulling it over in my head what's best to run back or walk, like which would get me less wet. It was while I was pondering this when crack!; I had been punched in the back of my head. At first I didn't really know what had happened. I turned round to see this black guy stood there. He was dead tall like 6 foot 3 maybe more but was painfully thin. He goes to me "give us your money kid before I fucking stab ya". I remember I froze at first, I thought well do I fight him or just run away, cos no way was this smack head catching me. While I was stood there like a mong still deciding what to do, he punched me again, caught me on my ear. My ear starting ringing. Something just clicked then because without thinking too much about it I was smashing fuck out of the clown. Had him on the floor in some big puddle, I was lent over him repeatedly punching him, until my arms were too tired and heavy to punch him anymore. At this point he was just slumped fully on the floor flat now and wasn't really moving much. I suppose the right thing to do now would be to walk away and leave it at that, but bollocks to that. This horrible little smack head hasn't even robbing another man, he had picked on some little 5 foot, 6 stone, 12 year-old child. So I booted him a few more times, then smashed some pavement slab one him. Well I say a pavement slab, it was like a quarter of a paving slab, that was all piled up at the side. His face was unrecognisable to seconds previous, but fuck him, the little cunt deserved it. So I jogged home in the rain, with a big grin on my face because I couldn't wait to tell all my mates at school the next morning what had gone on.

Throughout my teens and early 20s I would have numerous fights for money, in and out of the ring. I just saw it as a very easy way to make money. But fighting wouldn't be the only way I would make money as a kid growing up. By just 14 I was up to all sorts and I do mean fucking all sorts, planning and doing my own armed robberies. By my 15th birthday I had done three armed robberies. I used to wear my school pants and shirt, because I thought it would give the appearance that I was older than what I was. In reality I must have just looked like a school kid in half his uniform but on a Saturday. One time I was so close to being caught red handed it was untrue. Police vans and armed response turned up but because I was just a kid they didn't even give me a second glance. I really did think I was some kind of boss but I mean who even knew I was even there.

Robbing dealers also became an easy way to earn money for me and a couple of my mates, even a couple of times we robbed them and sold them their own gear back, that's how cocky and arrogant we were. Unbeknown to them that it was us that taxed them in the first place. We would be out robbing cars, even robbing alloys off cars, anything to make money. To me it was just a huge laugh and a buzz, we were too naïve to realise what dicks we were being, ruining people's lives with certain things we did. Anyway every saint has a past, and every sinner has a future. Little did I know it yet but mine was going to be as a football casual, a Man City hooligan.

STOCKPORT COUNTY

BELIEVE IT OR NOT, our first big main rivalry youth wise wasn't with United, it was with Stockport County. Like I said the rivalry was more a youth thing, than City on the whole. There's a well watched video on You Tube between City and County, from a fair few years back. There were prison sentences and lengthy bans as long as 10 years handed out for the fight, which funnily enough took place in the Gay Village. What made our rivalry with County strange was the fact we weren't even in the same league, so it wasn't like we even played against one another. Stockport itself is in greater Manchester, it's like around 6 miles or something daft like that south of Manchester City centre. Quite a big City area as well to be honest, a good portion of our lads came from there, mainly south Reddish, top lads. We even had a lad that lived literally right by their ground as well. The first fight we had all together was against Stockport County. We weren't even playing them that day, in fact we didn't even want to meet them that day, we had bigger and better things on our minds – Millwall. The 'wall were playing at nearby Altrincham, so we saw this as a perfect chance to smash them and make everybody sit up and take notice of us. For us young kids, we were aged 15 to 18 at this point, this was perfect for us. Although we may have been dead young, we feared nobody, we were just eager to get out there and make a name for ourselves.

Before this day there had been Doncaster away. Now at

the risk of offending anybody reading this, I am sorry but Doncaster has got to be the biggest shit hole I have ever seen in my entire life. Their stadium, the Keepmoat I believe it's called, opened in the summer of 2007, and City were the lucky team to play the first game there. The ground itself was alright, the only nice thing in Doncaster. This away was the first time I met many of the younger lads properly. I had seen a lot of their faces about and knew them to let on to but that was it. We came out of Doncaster's ground there were probably about 40 of us if not more walking down. We were walking through some estate, with big dirty tower blocks dotted about. The place was just full of smack heads and fat women with more tattoos than me and less teeth than a 2 year-old. They were throwing stuff out of the flats at us down below, classy birds. Well we had seen the locals, so god only knows what their casuals looked like. As we got closer to their town centre we heard shouting and chanting something like TDO or MDO one of them. There were around 20 of them. They would bounce forward as if to say come on then, then turn and leg it. It was more amusing than anything though.

We stayed around Doncaster for another hour or so, nothing happened so we got off because we were really keen to bump into Millwall and have it with them lot. There couldn't have been much more than 15 of us out this day but we didn't care, numbers meant nothing to us. Young, naïve and fearless, we just didn't give a fuck. Still, there were still a lot of people unsure of each other at this point. So we spent the best part of the day in Altrinchham but the only Millwall we saw were a bunch of kids that threw something at us, then got off. Obviously it wasn't Millwall, just a bunch of dicks. Now I am not quite sure if County rang us or if we rang them but anyway the call was made, and we were off to Stockport. Think by the time we actually made it there we only had about 13 lads and that was it. We made the relatively short trip to Stockport, got off at the train station and made our way on foot to Edgeley. At this point I didn't have a clue where we were or where we were heading. A couple of the lads seemed to know the area pretty well, so I was just following their lead. I didn't have a clue how many kids County would have out but rest assured it would be miles more than fucking 13. We were walking down Edgeley High Street and round the corner to a pub, which County were expected to be drinking inside. The mood between us lot had gone from having a laugh and messing about, to a little more quiet and serious. Like people knew it was about to kick off and were getting ready to go into battle. Two lads said they would run in the pub and tell County get outside because City are here. I waited anxiously outside the pub with the others, part of me thinking "what the fuck are you doing here Carl?" There are only 13 of us, most are little kids that will probably just run off or not do owt. All these thoughts were running through my head at the time. The lads returned not long after, shaking their heads and just said "nah" meaning there was no County in there.

We carried on to another known County boozer. As we came closer to it we could see a couple lads stood outside the entrance, one of them stood out a mile in his bright orange jacket. We cautiously approached the pub and words were exchanged between us and the two lads. Turns out they were County older lads. They said it's nothing to do with them, it's between us and County's youth and they will stay out of it, which I thought seemed fair enough. A call was made to County, we set off and made our way to where they claimed to be. Still not knowing where we were, or where we were heading, I was just a passenger along for the ride. We came to a point where we were at the top of a hill and followed the walkway down it. It was green on either side of it, where the grass levelled out at the bottom there they were, there was County, and as I suspected, there weren't fucking 13 of them. Now my heart was proper beating like mad, because this is it. We all kept together nice and tight, if anything maybe too tightly. The County kids shouted "not here not here, there's a park on the next street go there and we will follow you down". I'm guessing the park was nice and out of the way if they wanted us to go there, either that or they had loads of bottles and bricks and stuff stashed there. It was a very fucking awkward and strange moment getting to the bottom of the grass, and having to walk right past County, to get to this park. I am sure most of the others thought it was just going to go off there and then but to my amazement it didn't. There was a lot of eyeing each other up and staring each other out, trying to portray an image of confidence to our rivals. Why we didn't just run into them and smash them there and then, I don't know to be honest. We were now all walking up the street, not all together holding hands like queers, but us lot, then about 40 metres back them lot. I would say their numbers were around 25, no doubt well over 20 anyway. Pretty much double the amount we had out. One thing I will say for County is they all look smart and dress the part.

I can't remember who but one of the lads said "why the fuck are we doing what they tell us to? Let's just fucking do 'em now". With that we all started laughing and all nodded in agreement. The street we were on wasn't a main road more of a side street. On one side of the road were terrace houses, and on the other were high rise flats. We all started to slow our walk down, so that they would catch us up. Well this was it, fuck walking to some park for them; we should come to their part of Stockport, for them already. We all stopped walking, turn round and just put it on them "Come on County, youse fucking wannit yeah?" with that we sort of half bounced, half jogged over towards them. They followed suit, and within a few seconds we had clashed in the middle of the street, much to the delight of a handful of spectators watching from the flats.

Just the same as a boxing bout, as soon as you're actually fighting, the nerves completely go and turn into adrenaline. I think we had taken them by surprise, I reckon they saw our lack of numbers and thought they would be able to bully us. After just 20 seconds, the fight clearly wasn't going to happen. They had a handful of lads who were pretty game and getting into us, they also had a fair few that just stood back and did fuck all. This gave us a huge lift seeing some of their lads shitting and clearly not wanting to know. The fighting continued, we starting to get the better of them now and were pushing them right back. One of their lads just sort of appeared in front of me in this Henri Lloyd jacket/jumper. We were both just bouncing in front of each other, for what felt like a minute, but in truth was probably only a couple of seconds. I thought well this is a bit gay isn't it, so I've banged him; good and proper, with a perfect left hook. Now I could chat shit and say he went flying back on his arse and was knocked out and all that, but that would be bollocks. He took a step or two back and then starting holding his jaw with his hands, with a look of discomfort on his face. Didn't see him again, he fucked off. To the right side of me was some little old crap Ford Fiesta, it was a horrible brown/copper colour, my mate was hammering some kid all over this Fiesta. I turned to my other side and there were about 15 lads in a mass brawl. So I ran over to that to lend some assistance and offer my services. By this point it had gone from us being heavily outnumbered, to if anything us now outnumbering them. The few remaining County kids were now starting to take a proper beating as the best part of their firm had ran off to the bottom of the street and were watching from a far. Some had just fucked off altogether and were nowhere to be seen. To be fair to County, while most of their lads were just shit bags they did have a handful of good lads who kept having it with us. They were just let down by all their shit bags, all the gear, no idea. I think that pretty much sums County up from what I've seen over the years, not just this day, there are a few game lads but mostly just muppets and wannabes. By this point even their game kids didn't want to know, they were getting booted all over the gaff. One or two of their mates did run back to try and help them, so I suppose fair play for that I suppose but they just get a kicking along with them. Then the fight ended rather abruptly, and in an unusual manner. It wasn't the police turning up or County all running away. A few of their lads just all started holding their hands in the air, you know like they do in films if some ones pointing a gun at them, and they surrendered. They said "we've had enough now, just leave it yeah you've done us". And with that not a single more punch was thrown, by either side. Then a few of us started shaking hands with each other, I don't just mean City, I mean with County as well. Bit of mutual respect after the scrap I suppose you could call it.

Now the feeling at that moment and for the following hour is almost undescribable. If you could bottle it and sell it, you would make millions. I felt on top of the world, we all did. The rush and feeling of ecstasy after we had won the fight just tops anything and I do mean anything. From that moment on if football violence was a drug, then we were all addicted. Any doubts I previously had about a few of the lads just being little kids soon vanished, goes to show you just can't judge a book by its cover. I would even go as far to say I was, and in fact still am, in awe of a few of the Blazing Squad lads, because of how fearless they are. So while for a few of us it wasn't a first fight at City, it was the first fight all us younger lads together as one. So for me personally anyway that day 10th November 2007, was the day Blazing Squad was born. Before we had left the street one of their lads walked over with his hands in his pockets, proper timidly said "have you got my trainer, can you give it us back please". I mean I shouldn't laugh but I just couldn't help it I felt so sorry for the kid. Part of me just wanted to give him a hug, he looked like he was in need of one anyway. Was like off Oliver Twist where he says "please sir can I have some more". Anyway he got his trainer back, and they went on their way. I noticed huddled in there with them was orange jacket man, one of their older lot who said they wouldn't get involved. Bet he felt a right prick now. We on the other hand were filled with pride, although the fight might not have been the best ever, or against the best firm ever, for me it was mint. The fight was all I talked about for the following days anyway. Don't think County were too happy about how it ended, right in their area, by their ground as well. That certainly wouldn't be the last time we would go out of our way to give it them though.

The following year and it was pre-season, who did we get, only Stockport County away, happy days, another chance to take the piss. Some of the lads met up in the Waldorf, near Piccadilly, but I was running a little late, so I just went straight to Sports Bar in the station itself. There were also a few lads in Yates's, well they were until Cliff Lea and the rest of City's FIOs turned up. There were also a few young lads dotted about who were too young to get in the pubs at that time. Now for whatever reason County had said they wanted it after the game and not before. Not sure why that was though, I always think it's best to try and meet before the game, then if it goes wrong, you have always got after the game as well. We all had tickets to the game, for one of only a few times. So we had no bother getting the train from town down, because they couldn't Section 27 us because we had tickets, although this didn't stop GMP still harassing us to fuck. There was about 40 older lot on our train, and about 18 of us young lot. We made the stupidly short train journey and jumped off at Stockport train station. On leaving the station we headed up towards Edgeley. Waiting for us at the top of this road was around 25 police and a couple on horses. But for once we weren't arsed, we have done nothing wrong and have tickets to the game, so fuck them. Not like we were really there just for the match, but regardless we have tickets. The police let the older lads on their way, why did I just know it wasn't going to be that easy and simple for us lot.

It was clear from the outset that they weren't happy with us being there. They asked us if we had tickets, well no, actually first they asked us our reason for being in the area, we replied "for the match". The officers sarcastically said "oh so you'll all have tickets on you for the game then yes?" expecting us not to, because we very rarely do have tickets. So to say they were pissed off when we all whipped out our tickets, would be putting it mildly. They Section 60 us and searched us and finding nothing on us lot seem to infuriate them even more. As there was no City spotters present at that time, they said they had to wait for permission to let us on our way. The whole thing was a load of bollocks, because there was no reason to keep us there in the first place, never mind not let us leave. We were getting very pissed off and restless now, they had kept us there for around 15 minutes for no reason at all. Maybe this was their plan, to wind us up so much one of us would crack them. They then decided that they "feared for the safety of the Stockport County fans" with us in the area, and we are going to have to leave. I went fucking mad and told them this is bollocks and we started to make our way to the game. They quickly surrounded us and a van full of TAU plus a car with City's FIO's soon pulled up. They said now it has gone past kick off time, they don't have to let us in, the little cunts had kept us there so fucking long, the game had already been going a few minutes. Section 27s were issued to us and we were made to leave the area. I went mad again about it all but my mate dragged me away before I was nicked.

The final straw for me was on my form they had written they said I had been drinking and was intoxicated, I hadn't had a drop all day. So a very pissed off set of lads begrudgingly made their way back to town. Some lads were that pissed off that they headed off home shortly after as well; I was half tempted to do the same. We went to a bar in town, just got a beer and chilled out. In there were around 20 older lads, and around 10 of us lot left. When you've been handed a Section 27 and fucked off, part of you becomes dead worried there's going to be a huge fight and you miss out. So selfishly part of you wants nothing to go on, because even though you always want City to smash whoever their playing, you don't ever want to miss out on anything. I could see this day turning into one of them, having said that it was only County, so it wasn't a huge thing. Also with County saying they don't want it before the game, just after, many City lads took that as they don't want to know at all. The City lads that were still down there were ringing us to come back down. I was up for going back at first but most people were just like what's the point, nothing will happen and we will just get nicked. The lads who had gone to the game and were in the ground, said it was just daft, all City's FIO were just stood by them, throughout the duration of the match. The lads who were in the ground left and went to Stockport town centre to meet up with more City that had been drinking there most of the day. Wasn't too long before police rounded the 30 or so of them up, gave them Section 27s and they were escorted back to the train station.

Meanwhile County were on the phone saying don't go all the way back to town, hang around, because they're getting their lads together now. So the 30 or so strong City lads, which were a mix of older lot and youth got off the train in Heaton Chapel. Heaton Chapel is in the Borough of Stockport, but on the Manchester side of it, so you would think it was perfect for all concerned. However County's lads was still whinging because it wasn't in Stockport town centre, and said it was too far for them to go. Which was just daft I mean the lads were still in the borough of Stockport, what more do they fucking want? City stayed in the area drinking, hours went by, even with City telling them exactly what pub they were in, still nothing from County. When I heard all this I thought well I'm not wasting my time going down there and I fucked off back down my end to meet some bird instead. It was now several hours since the full time whistle, the majority of City had left Heaton Chapel and either gone back to town or called it a day and gone home. From the looks of things County had shit themselves and clearly didn't want to know.

Then after every one had given up, they turned up, piling off the bus, mini bus and taxis, all with bottles shouting EVF (Edgeley Volunteer Force). I later found out they only turned up because they knew the majority of City had already gone. City were outnumbered big time, but that wasn't anything new, it's all part and parcel. There were only 7 or 8 City left, and around 25-30 County had now turned up. Bottles were thrown on both sides, none really hitting anybody, just landing around them. Near enough straight away a County lad runs in but finds himself dragged to the ground, getting booted in pretty bad. The fighting went on, with the numbers like 3 to 4 times in County's favour. Maybe County thought the fight would go easily their way, or even City might get off, more fool them, if that's what they were thinking at the start. The mixed group of City were not only holding their own against vast numbers, they were pushing County right back. County's lads were starting to get proper battered, being booted in and that. City steamed forward into the County lads once more but this time County didn't want to know, they turned and legged it with City running after them. In the background they could hear police sirens, getting louder by the second. The City lads got off to a nearby park, which saved some County lads a kicking, who were hiding in a garden, or at least trying to hide. The lads managed to get off to Levenshulme and to a pub. Many of them had County's blood all over them, so they cleaned themselves up and had a couple beers. They then made their way back to town to meet the rest of the lads.

Over the following couple of seasons, there would be several other "incidents" with the County kids. Unfortunately for them, time and time again they would come off second best. One time in pretty much the same place we had it with Everton at Piccadilly under the bridge, we smashed County there and ran them all over. Although it wasn't anything too major, as they all ran off pretty much as soon as it went off. On Valentine's Day 2009, just a few days after smashing United at the Garret, County had for whatever reason, called it on with us once more. So we said ok we will go to Droylesden which is three or so miles from the City centre. The idea behind that was, it wasn't in town so there wouldn't be loads of cameras and GMP all over the show. We had around 20 of us down there, all young lads, waiting for County for a few hours, who didn't even show. County had now decided if we want it with them we have to go to Stockport, bit fucking cheeky when it was them that wanted it with us in the first place. We were all that pissed off with them doing it, we thought you know what fuck it we will go down and smash them for messing us about.

A couple of the lads had to get off home; so on arrival in Stockport there were 18 of us. They had rather foolishly told us what pub they were in. We walked down the road towards where they claimed to be. Now I don't recall anybody ringing them, telling them to come out. They might have just seen us outside and all come out. Either way there was a mob of 30 County, mixed older and youth it were. To be fair to them they didn't all just get off on seeing us, like I expected them to. A few of them came bouncing over "come on then City" and it all just went off at that moment. We just fucking steamed into them, no messing about, no bouncing and shouting, straight into the cunts. It was like for all the times they had fucked us about, and not turned up, or just ran off now was our chance to get our own back, and give them a right kicking. We just started proper laid into them, smashing County all over the road. If it was a boxing match, the ref would have stopped it for sure, it was a mismatch. One of their lads shouted something which stuck in my head "there's too many run, run", what a wanker. They had more lads than us, and half of them were older lads to go with it. So they started to run, some a lot sooner than others I must add. We all ran after them down some cobbled street, one of their older lads, some bald lad, fell while running and smashed his head open. I think he smashed it open on the curb when he went down, it was pouring his head was pouring with blood anyway and he was like semi-conscious. At that point a lot of us stopped running, and everybody said "nobody touch him, nobody boot him". Nobody did touch him, apart from a couple City lads who were helping him up to his feet, because he was in a bad way. I can think one or two other firms, would have crowded round and jumped all over him, but we aren't like that. Most of his lads had run away, but a couple of them came back and we let them get their mate, nobody hit them or owt daft like that. Don't think that lad's bird would be too impressed with spending Valentine's Day with him in hospital, getting his head stitched back together.

A couple more times we would ring County beforehand and tell them we are coming down for them. We would sit in their pubs on match days and they did fuck all about it, quite embarrassing really. They would never turn up, so we soon got bored of doing that and then the whole thing with Bolton started off, so we pretty much left County to it. We used to call County the friendly mob, because they always seemed to be going to games and drinking with other mobs but never seemed to fight. They used to always be with Oldham and I've even heard when Preston play Bury, a few County lads go down with Preston.

One time in town, around Christmas 2008 I think it was, we heard there were supposed to be a few County knocking about town. It was proper freezing cold and icy as fuck, even for winter time. There were 15 of us lot walking through town walking up towards Piccadilly station, where we heard a mob of County had been spotted. Which by the way happens a lot more than you might think, people see some lads in Adidas trainers, and think they have seen a fucking firm. But we had to go and check it out anyway, to see what was what. We went past a pub called the Brunswick and somewhere in between there and Piccadilly station is a Greggs. "There they are look", one of the lads said. I just looked up and spotted one; before I knew it I had ran over and went to hit him. Well I did punch him but at the same time I slipped on the ice and went fucking flying back on my arse. Don't get me wrong it was really icy but that's not the point, I felt like a right pillock. I pulled myself up off the lad's jacket I think it was and punched him again. But then we quickly realised there wasn't a mob of them there at all, more like 2 or 3 of them. So it was a bit naughty of me running over hitting him, maybe serves me right for going on my arse but we genuinely thought there would have been a fair few of them.

Another time we were out looking for United or something like that. I had just nipped in a pub near Piccadilly called the Waldorf, for a piss. I noticed a few lads in the corner having a drink and that but I knew there was a lot of City that drank there so sort of presumed they would be City. Three of these lads followed me downstairs to the toilets, I could hear them outside the door saying "yeah that's deffo him, that's that Carl from City". So I had a little chuckle to myself, and thought well this sounds interesting. I yanked open the door dead fast to see three lads stood there, around 18ish, only a year or two younger than myself. I looked them up and down, paused for a second or two and said "how you doing lads, you alright yeah?" to which they all looked at each other a little confused, and one timidly replied "yeah sound mate". I went to walk off and leave it as that but I was curious to fuck who they were. So I turned to them and said "do I know use?" "Nah mate no," they said whilst repeatedly shaking their heads nervously. "Ok no worries then" and I walked off smiling to myself. I think if I had raised my voice at them three, they would have burst into tears, never mind if I punched one. I would have felt like a bully and there was just me, and 3 of them, so work that one out.

I noticed yet more lads upstairs on leaving the pub, so I

got my phone out and told the lads to come over. Within a minute around 10 lads arrived, with more on the way. Told the lads what had happened with the three kids following me to the toilets saying my name and that. Straight away one of the lads said "that's County, I recognise a couple of them, that's deffo County". There was also another group with them, consisting of slightly older lads. Now these lads were claiming to be City fans but they seemed to be trying a bit too hard to convince us of that. Another 10 or so City had now just arrived and wondering what the score was, and wanting to know what was going on. Even I was slightly confused at who was who and what was going on at this point. Then one of the lads said "look we're Oldham lads, and there's a few County with us, we're just out for a beer and nothing else". Had a quick chat with the Oldham lad, he was alright, he seemed a bit embarrassed by his mates, we just went on our way and left them to it, went off down Deansgate looking for United, with no luck unfortunately that day.

We would host Celtic in a pre-season friendly on the 8th August 2009. The Celtic mob was pretty shit that day, possibly one of the worst firms I've ever seen at our place. Not to say that they're always that bad, I'm just going off what I saw that day. Maybe many of their proper lads didn't travel, God knows but that day they were wank. After we had finished slapping a few of them about, we heard that County's mob were coming through town in an escort. They were coming through Victoria, mint we thought, we will have some of that. Think it was me, Wizz and Raz, we went down to the station to see what was going on and if County actually were there. Sure as anything they were there. About 30 maybe more of them on a train, being held there, until police can get them in a proper escort. We got the rest of our lot together, was a good 20 of us maybe 25. Now we knew they were being taken to Piccadilly station, but we were unsure of the route they would go. We got all the lads together just off the main road, near to Victoria. We then split up into two separate groups and went the two different ways we thought the escort may go. Looking back we should have sent one lad down to see where they were going and it would have been a lot easier. Now half the lads were by the Printworks and the rest were between Shudehill and the CIS building. As it turned out they headed the way I thought and towards the edge of the Northern Quarter. We knew it wouldn't be too long before the police clocked us but we didn't think it would happen so quickly, pretty much straight away. At this point there were only around 10 or so of us, we were still waiting for the other 10 to run down from where they were. We were shadowing the County escort walking down. Many lads just stare over, and try to look menacing and intimidating, me on the other hand I thought it would be funny to blow kisses and wave to them all. You could tell that the GMP officers there didn't really know what to do for the best. They knew exactly who we were but should they stay tight to the escort, and hope there's enough police there, to act as a deterrent to us? Or do they send officers over to us, and risk County breaking out the escort? Decisions, decisions...

In the end they did a little bit of both, with the help of a couple more TAU vans that turned up right on queue. In truth we never actually got close enough to their escort to throw a dig. Now we found ourselves being chased all over town by 25 or so police. There was now more police than there was of us. We all made off in the same sort of direction but with every side street we passed, more and more lads would break off and slip down them. It ended up me and about 7 other lads being chased around the Northern Quarter, just off Oldham Street. The police were not only pursuing us on foot but in the vans as well, and you just know if they could get away with running you over, they would do. At the end of the street we were running down there was a big multi-storey car park, so we headed for that. I made it all the way up to the top floor, which was like the 10th floor or something daft like that. I thought well I've got to be okay here, surely they're not going to run all the way up here, I should have known better, they did. Wouldn't be arsed if it was just GMP, but they had the dogs with them too. Vicious little cunts those police dogs are, seriously. I've seen them bite fuck out of police officers, which they are obviously not supposed to, so I didn't have a clue what they would do to us, if told to go for us. Me and my mate decided we didn't want to find out. So as soon as they told us to come out from where we were hiding, before the dogs are set on us, we did just that. The dogs were going mad, barking their heads off and frothing at the mouth. We were put in handcuffs, and rather than go in the lift we were marched all the way back down to the bottom. To say all the police at the bottom of the car park was looking very smug with themselves would be a massive understatement. You would think they had all won the lottery, not just caught some teenagers in a fucking car park. Section 27s was issued, and nobody was arrested, we just fucked off out of town and that was that for that day.

So on the whole the City and County thing may have been a little one-sided but I suppose fair play to them for sometimes wanting it. It has got to be said they do have a handful of game lads. In the last few years County have been relegated numerous times, and we haven't really bumped into them at all. In 2012 we had them in a pre-season friendly at their place. To be fair to them though they didn't mess us about too much and just said there's no point in meeting us, because they can't get enough lads that want to meet us and that was that. But I will always remember that first fight we had with them back in 2007 because it was our first ever fight, all together as a youth firm.

EVERTON

EVERTON CARRY A NOTORIOUS reputation from back in the day as 'The County Road Cutters'. But unlike many firms today, I think Everton still live up to their reputation. They might not have the best numbers or owt like that but they turn up time and time again and have a go. In recent years I can't think of many other firms, if any, that have turned up in Manchester time and time again, and wanted it like they have. But I've got to say if am being honest, for one reason or another we haven't turned up at their place, anywhere near half as much as we should have, and that is very poor and unlike us. I think not only our firm and theirs is similar numbers wise but the football clubs themselves are similar. Maybe not as much nowadays with all our money but both have loyal fans. Also for most part of the post-war years, we have both been in the shadows of United and Liverpool, well on the pitch anyway, certainly not off it. When I think of Everton's firm, the first thing that pops into my head is the Everton Valley thing with United. This was where Everton's lads well and truly smashed United to fucking pieces. They're good kids Everton, nice lads, I've had beers with them a few times in Liverpool. One time I was in a pub right by their ground called The Brick with a few of their lads, a few years ago now. I was proper pissed out of my fucking head, had been drinking literally all day. I went back to one of their lad's houses, my mate, who was living right by Everton's ground. Like I said I was pissed badly and ended up being sick everywhere, I felt a right knob. But that's a different story for a different day.

There has always been a huge rivalry between Mancunians and scousers. In 1830 the first passenger railway in the world was built between Manchester and Liverpool. The rivalry between the cities has always been there, even then, but got a lot worse when the Manchester Ship Canal was built. Liverpool docks were seeing almost 40 percent of the world's trade pass through their port, and it was one of the busiest in the world. By the late 19th century the Mancunian merchants were becoming pissed off with how much money they were having to pay to import and export goods to and from Manchester. So the ship canal was built to bypass Liverpool, so stuff came directly to Manchester instead. Manchester has continued to grow in size and wealth ever since, directly because of the ship canal.

The first time we went to Goodison Park was January 2008. I actually had a ticket to the game on this occasion as well. Not that I saw a lot of the game, with some stupid fucking pole in front of me holding their stand up. On the ticket it said "your view may be restricted" oh you don't say. But anyway, that day we all met up at the train station, can't honestly remember if it was Victoria or Piccadilly if am being honest. We got the train from one of them to Liverpool Lime Street anyway that I do remember. Not sure how many lads exactly were on the train with us or indeed had gone to Liverpool that day but there were a fair few put it that way. It was mine and a think a lot of the other lads' first trip to Everton. I had heard a few things about them, like they love a blade and that. Also that the scouse police were proper cunts with anybody from Manchester, so I was sure we would be in for a warm welcome and a nice day out. Not sure if it's the trains or the track but the train proper took the piss, in fact not just that day, but in general. It takes 1 hour 50 minutes to London by train right but takes longer going by car. Liverpool is half an hour away on the motorway, yet by train it takes like over an hour, what's all that about? I remember thinking on the way down there, while everyone else was getting pissed, and sniffed up and that. Wasn't a huge amount of us there that day, youth wise, than again there hardly ever is. There were around 20 of us younger lot that had made the trip down there that day. There was around 30 or so older lads on our train as well. At that time I didn't really know any of the older lads that well, just knew a few of them to let onto sort of thing.

The train we were supposed to get had been and gone, we had missed that waiting for a couple of lads running late because they were hung over. We didn't really mind too much because we have all been there. Anyway the train that we missed was supposed to be packed with about 70 older lads on it; however people do like to get carried away when numbers are concerned, and always exaggerate. So the train which what had felt like to me had taken a lifetime, had finally pulled into Lime Street station and there was old bill everywhere. British Transport police, TAU, or whatever their version of that is called, dogs, and last but not least every footie lad's worst nightmare, the Football Intelligence Officers themselves. There were spotters for Everton and City stood together, it was just one big wall of police between the train and the platform exit. It's not as if we're scared of them, but they're annoying little pests, following you around filming all day. They can also really fuck your day up before it even starts. You can try and split up and mingle in with the crowds of normal supporters but our clothes are a dead giveaway most of the time. Not to mention the FIOs, who literally get to know you inside out and know your name and address off by heart a lot of the time. So we thought the ones with tickets go first, and while the police are dealing with us, the ones without tickets could try and sneak through. It worked as well. We were half expecting to be kept there and put in some kind of escort but they seemed happy enough to let us crack on and go our own way. We were given Section 27s, filmed, searched and then let go. We then all met up with the rest of the lads down the road from the station, happy days.

We felt in some way we had already got one over on the police that day. The lads without tickets, which made up the majority of our younger lot, would have been fucked off back home if they had been stopped in the station without tickets. So the 20 or so of us younger lot just went around Liverpool town centre, going from pub to pub. Half expecting to bump into a mob of Everton at anytime but it just didn't happen. Also we didn't see any police at all, which was rather odd in a City centre on a match day, you normally can't move for the cunts and spend your day trying to get away from them. A couple of lads went for a scout about but still couldn't really find anybody. This was January 2008, so just a few months after that I would get to know some of their lads. But at this point we didn't know any of them or even have a number for them. It was getting close to kick off time, so the ones with tickets jumped in taxis down to County Road, by their ground. The rest of the lads said they would make their way down after, so we would all be together after the game. Later on I would find out that Liverpool tend to drink in the town centre and Everton down by the ground, which is why we didn't really find anyone.

We dived out of the taxi a few hundred metres away from Goodison Park, so that we could have a little mooch about, even if there were only 6 of us, so what we were planning on doing if we bumped into shit loads of Everton, I don't exactly know. For anybody that hasn't been to Everton, around the ground its loads of rows of terrace housing, similar to our old ground in Moss Side. County Road, where we jumped out, is a fairly busy main road, with shops running along either side. The whole area was rammed with normal Everton fans going to the match. We had a little walk about then decided to just go to the away end because was only like 10-15 minutes to go before kickoff. I suppose I like Everton's ground because it's a proper old school football ground, again similar to Maine Road. One thing I don't like however is them stupid fucking poles in the ground. So we didn't see too much of the game, from what I remember it was shit and we lost 1-0. With it being just a couple of weeks after Christmas, by the time we left the ground it was pitch black outside.

We left the ground with a few minutes to go as we wanted to get away before the police started wrapping everybody up. We met up with some of our lot and made our way across Stanley Park. Stanley Park pretty much lies in between Everton and Liverpool's ground, separating the two, it's mad how close both grounds are to one another. So we were making our way across the park, towards Liverpool's ground I suppose, to a pub our older lot had told us all to go in after the game. The park was proper dark, pitch fucking black, mad because you could hear people before you could see them. We were half expecting loads of Everton to be waiting there for us. We made our way to the other end of the park, well we had been in Liverpool all day, now and nobody had been "cut". In fact we hadn't really come across their firm at all. Not the day we were expecting that's for sure. We found ourselves on a small car park on the edge of Stanley Park, pretty much across the road from Anfield, well not far off anyway. There must have been a reason why we were all waiting there on that car park, but if I am being honest, I can't fucking remember why now, probably just waiting for a couple more lads or something. I can recall thinking at the time how quiet it was, I mean there was nobody about at all.

There were about 15 of us there, on that empty car park, all dead young, all teenagers and that, we had been there for a good few minutes now, when we heard loads of noise in the distance. It was coming across the park towards us, pretty much the same direction that we would just came from. I looked around at my mates and we all just said at the same time, it's fucking Everton. They were still over 100 metres away, so we couldn't properly see them but as they got closer, we could see there were a good 40 or so of them, if not more. I'm not going to lie and try and make myself sound hard, but I shit myself. I thought we were about to get absolutely kicked to fuck and cut to bits on this car park. We jogged over towards the advancing group of Everton, who all seemed to be older lads. By this time they had noticed us as well, so we were both bouncing towards each other, arms out gesturing shouting "come on Everton". Then we heard dead loudly "come on Everton, fucking come on then you scouse cunts". We were all very puzzled, as to what the fuck was going on here. It was our older lads, it was City. Due to it being so dark we couldn't tell until they got a lot closer. We were only about 10 seconds away from all fighting with each other, now imagine how embarrassing that would have been, if we all got nicked for that. Although I doubt that would have happened, it was a fucking top place to have it. I suppose a lot of young firms, if there are just 15 of them, would have got off if they saw 40–50 older lads coming towards them, we didn't, we all bounced over shouting to them. But like I said, don't get me wrong, I did shit it and think we were going to get smashed all over.

Anyway, we all had a laugh about it and walked down

the road, to a fairly big pub on the corner called The Arkles. There were already a few of the City lads in there, as well as the odd normal City fans and scouse locals. Around 60 City I would say we had in there, it was a nice mob to be honest. Word soon got round that Everton not only knew exactly where we were, but were on their way, happy days. We waited and waited, then waited some more but not a lot seemed to be happening. The later it went on we knew the less chance there was of them turning up and anything happening at all. As time went on older lads started to get off in taxis back to Lime Street to get the train back to town. There were a couple of lads outside the pub looking out for Everton; they came rushing in going "they're here they're fucking here". The pub quickly emptied with everybody piling outside on to the front of the pub. I could see around 12 scouse kids, roughly same age as us younger lot. They were coming close enough to us to chuck loads of bottles and then would turn and then start backing right off again. They clearly wanted us to run after them down the road, shouting to us "we're gunna get cut" and all that. I was in two minds about it all, I thought we're the away team, if they want it, then here we are, I can't be arsed running about after them. Then again another part wanted to catch the little cunts and give it them.

They returned once more lobbing stuff; about 10 of our lot just fucking ran at them. A few digs were thrown and a couple of the scouse kids stood but then soon got off again, shouting for us to come after them. Maybe they wanted us to follow them to a boozer full of Everton lads or something, God knows. They came back up again and got a slap and got off once more. But this time some of the lads carried on running after them and caught some of them and gave them a kicking. Meanwhile police were arriving on the scene and I was dragged in a taxi with my mates, before more turned up. Older lads had been bored of waiting around and had ordered several taxis 10 minutes before which was quite handy because they turned up just at the right time. As we drove past we saw several lads being gripped by the police and thrown in the back of the vans. All in all it was a bit of a nothing fight, wasn't anything really, an anticlimax. Then again the day wasn't a complete waste, as a few of them got slapped and we all had a laugh together, which is what away days are about. We went back to Lime Street and got the first train back to town. The lads who had been gripped by the police weren't even kept that long they said. Although they said the scouse police had a proper bad attitude with them, throwing them about and all that shit, which was I suppose to be expected. Anyway they was all back in Manchester later that night. The next few times that we would bumped into Everton would be a lot closer to home.

The following season, but same calendar year still 2008, we had Everton at our place. Not only did I have a ticket for the game, but even had one in the posh boxes, with free food and drink. I'm surprised they even let us in there to be honest. We met up on Oldham Street that day, as per usual. For years and years and still to this day that part of town is a City area. Not just Oldham Street but the whole Northern Quarter itself would be the area where we would all meet up before and after the game. Very few firms have ever come and had it with us down there, none have any done anything but get slapped about, not since I've been going anyway. The City pub and Dry Bar are the usual spots, also a pub called Gulliver's, that day we met up in Gulliver's before the game. I remember one time being in Gulliver's on Oldham Street playing pool and having some trouble telling the balls apart, the yellow balls were red with blood, it was that sort of place back then. There were around 20 younger lads in there, we heard Everton were coming down by train and through Victoria station. We made our way down to the station, but the police were everywhere. We tried splitting up into smaller numbers and coming from different directions but we weren't getting anywhere near them, and we knew it. We had some fun with our FIOs and the normal GMP on duty that day, giving them the run around. All round town and all down the canal, down to our ground. We had them after us on foot, in the car, even the helicopters out for us. On foot though, with all that shit they have on their belts and the boots, even if they are fit (which they rarely are) they're not catching anybody.

So we made it down by the ground and we're going round the pubs like the Manchester and the Townley. There was a fair amount of City dotted about the place, as you would expect there to be on match day at home. We left the Townley on the estate and set off walking towards the main road. Was a nice little mob of us, I reckon around 25 youth and about 30 older lot maybe more, a good 50 or 60 of us anyway. We could see a firm of Everton, on the main road near the Mercedes garage walking down, in a police escort. Around 35-40 Everton were in this escort but there were more than enough police around them. At our ground it's literally just the one main road which goes from town to the ground, which away fans would use to get to there. Police would have no other choice than to escort the away "risk" element the same way, time and time again, and we were always waiting time and time again, to attack them. So while it's an upside, because we always roughly know where their firms will be to attack them, the downside is it's fairly easy to police, by just throwing sheer numbers of officers down there. The police, ever gaining in numbers, got around 25 of us together, the rest had dived back onto the estate. We were all lined up against a wall, across the road from the Mercedes garage, across from

City's stadium. We were all held there as the Everton escort was brought past us, on the other side of the road. There was nothing either firm could do apart from stare at one and other and think what would have been, if there weren't so many police there. We were all held there until Nobby and Cliff, the two main City intel officers, arrived. The usual stuff, all being filmed and what not, and most of us told to fuck off, or we would be nicked. The police weren't the only ones filming and taking pictures of us all, some fucking Chinese tourists were at it as well, those cunts really do take photos of everything don't they!

We had all arranged to meet up round the back of The Manchester just before the end of the match. So as arranged we all left the ground 10 minutes before the end, to meet up behind the pub, to my disappointment because it was free pints in the posh box. We knew Everton would be kept in a couple minutes after the game, we also knew they would probably be in a police escort once more. So the only option was to hope to find lads not in the escort, or just think fuck it and smash into the police and attack Everton that way. We managed to get around 25 lads together and we waited behind the pub, until we knew Everton were being let out after the game. There were GMP all over the show, like as if it was derby day or something. You couldn't go anywhere without police being there. Before we had even got sight of Everton's firm, never mind attacked them, we were on the run back to town with police chasing us. The amount of time we gave the police the run around back then was untrue. But if a lot of the time football violence is a battle between the lads and the police, then this day the police were winning hands down. We had ended up being pushed right back towards Ancoats, past the Mitchell Arms, where we had more of our younger lot, who had turned out late for the game. By this time we weren't sure how far back Everton's escort was, or in fact even if they had been given one at all. We decided to split up into 3 or 4 smaller groups, shortly after we went across this bridge and looked down, and you could see them walking towards town. We were being boxed in by the police, on foot on one side and by cars on the other. We legged it over and round the car and I do mean jumping over the car, to make it down the steps of this bridge. Everybody got away apart from little old me; I was slammed against the wall there and lent upon so I couldn't go anywhere. I think they were a little wound up with all the running about after us they had had to do all day. The police then proceeded to tell me that Everton were all big hard lads and this and that. Said we were all just little kids, who didn't stand a chance against them. I mean what a fucking daft thing to say to me, after that was said, we would do anything to smash Everton to prove a point, surely the police must have realised that. I was issued with a Section 27 direction to leave order, but the last thing on my mind was getting off home.

I bumped into some of the lads, and we made our way back to town to meet all the others. Unbeknown to us at that time it had already been going off between City and Everton. It was nothing huge, just more like little pockets of skirmishes all over. We made our way back towards Oldham Street where we had started from a few hours before. On our way back there we went round this corner and bumped into about ten lads and I do mean bumped into them. Next thing I am looking these lads up and down and looking at my mates to say fuckinell after all this running about we have walked into them. "Use fucking wannit, lad" said one scouser and bang, he hit my mate. So any questions of what was going to happen there and then went straight out of the window! So we all starting fighting and we were getting battered. Well maybe battered is a bit too harsh on us, they were getting the better of us, put it that way. Although they were a few years older and they had more lads than us, but either way, we were taking a bit of a slap. I cracked some kid in a Barbour jacket and he fell back against the wall, dead chuffed with myself I was until I felt a big smack on the side of my head. I say smack because it felt more like a smack, than a punch, right on the side of my face. The fighting went on until they backed us off more and then there was a standoff, police sirens were now in the background. Straight away an unwritten truce was agreed and we all went our separate ways. We missed the police and evaded capture by seconds; I managed to get down a side street and into a pub and that was pretty much it for that day.

The next couple of times we tried to go to Everton, for one reason or another it fucked up. One time we got the train to Lime Street only to be gripped by police. The second we stepped off the train, and we was fucked off back to Manchester on the very same train. I had spent the last couple of weeks on the phone to Everton sorting that day out, so I was well pissed off. They told me not to go to Lime Street but I didn't listen, so completely my fault the fuck up that day. We haven't turned up at their place like they have at ours, there is no denying that and that is poor on our part. It's just one of them things, every time I go to sort something out for Everton away, something always goes wrong and fucks it all up. In 2013 we had Everton away so I told them we were going down with 25 youth. The week before we had Barnsley at home and not only does it go off but around 15 lads were arrested for it and given bail conditions – typical it should happen a week before Everton. We would have things at our place with Everton a few more times but police would be on top of things, on the whole.

The next two times we met we wouldn't even be playing

each other. In January 2009 we would entertain Nottingham Forest at home in the cup. Now this was back when City were still shit and we lost the game 3-0, which pissed a lot of us off. It didn't piss us off because of the score line so much as because the FA Cup was a chance of mad away games against lower league sides. We had heard Forest's older lads were supposed to be decent and we were expecting a lot of them to turn up. We met up at Dry Bar about 4 hours before kickoff. However it was just one of them days where the police are all over us. Our spotters were in the pub before many of our lads had even turned up, that's how bad it was. This started many lads off with their paranoid theories of there being a grass. How do the police always know where we are going to be? Well from my point of view it's fairly simple, if you drink in the same pubs, on the same street, week in week out, the police would have to be fucking retarded not to check them for us. So we knew this was no good and split up and headed slightly different ways to a pub called The Athenaeum.

This pub would be no stranger to City's lads, it was once City's pub, and the police had it closed down for just that reason. We had our usual 20 or so youth lads out, which was pretty standard for most home games. There was also around the same number again of older lads in there with us, plus apparently 30 plus more City in the Waldorf. So there was a fairly decent number of lads out for this cup match against Forest. We stayed in The Athenaeum for a good hour or so, until we heard that Forest had got off the train and were "bouncing" around town. So rather giddily, anticipating a big fight, we all piled out the pub, and made our way towards Piccadilly station. We split up into loads of small groups, like 4 or 5 handed and headed for the station. That way you're still all together walking down but to the police maybe driving past you don't stand out like a sore thumb, as 50 lads walking as one would. As like so many other times in football it would turn out to be a false alarm or they had vanished, either way there were no fucking Forest lads knocking about. We headed off back to a pub called The Bank, to meet a few more lads who were already in there. Nothing much was going on, me Wizz and Raz even fucked off to the food court at McDonald's and chilled there for a bit. We then went to meet the lads who had now moved on to a pub called Mother Mac's. Now Mother Mac's is a weird looking pub from the outside, with big green gates over the entrance and the windows. It wasn't a big pub and was just off Oldham Street down an alley at the side, but it was a proper Man City pub that's for sure. It is a proper old school pub. Anyway we stayed in there for a while until all the police turned up that is, Section 60s and 27s were dished out.

We headed back towards Piccadilly and down the canal to head towards the ground. Takes a lot longer that way, but for the best part of it you avoid the police in their cars and vans. We were going through Ancoats where there are a lot of new houses now but back then it was wasteland and rubble and further down these derelict tower blocks. Now if ever there was a perfect place, close to town to have it, then that was it. We made our way past the Mitchell Arms and on to the main road that leads to our ground. We were still hearing people say "oh Forest have brought a big mob down today" blah blah blah, personally I had seen fuck all of them all day. The best part of my day so far was going to the food court, and eating a couple of big Macs. We bumped into a couple more faces we knew on the way to ground, like half lads, half just normal fans. They just do their own thing and go to the pub and then the game, don't go looking for it, but if they see it going off, they are straight in there. I reckon all clubs have fans like that, not just City. We had about 30, 35 of us now, mixed youth and older lot together. There were police horses and cars going in the opposite direction to the ground, which meant only one thing, their firm must be on the way down from town now. Sure enough around half a minute later you could see them in the distance, a few hundred metres away. They had a big police presence around them, looked to be a good 70 Forest there, all their older lot by the looks of things, well the majority definitely were anyway. Was like an army of high vis jackets around them, a good 30-40 police on foot, then a few cars, about 3 horses as well. We made our way marching down towards them. The police must have seen what was going on and sent the horses into us. Both us and Forest tried to get to each other but it was a little half hearted from both of us, if I am being honest. Both groups tried to look like they were trying to get at each other, but deep down we knew nothing was going to happen, with far too many GMP in the middle to do anything.

Lads started to get off onto the estate, which was behind us, and on the opposite side to Forest and the ground. Around 15 of us were being bullied against the wall, by the horses, and the ever growing number of police on foot. Once again the usual happened, kept there until Nobby and Cliff turned up, and told in no uncertain terms to fuck off, or you are all getting nicked. So did we all get off home? Did we fuck, we went back onto the estate and kept our heads down until the end of the game. Then we would try again to have a pop at Forest. Some lads even swapped hats, scarves and jackets with one another, so at first glance, the coppers might not recognise who they are. Before the game had made it into the second half it was dark outside and fucking freezing too. After the game it was just a shambles, the organisation was a bag of wank, even by our standards. There were enough City down near the ground, as there always is on match day, but everyone was split up, in to too many small groups. Myself and around 12 other youth was at this shop on the estate, that's just set back from the main road. A police TAU van pulled up alongside us, while the van was still moving, the doors flung open and they started to jump out. I thought I'm not getting arrested by these tossers, I fucking hate the TAU me, they're just a bunch of cunts that think they're hard when there's a lot of them. So as the doors were opening of them van, we were already on our way, nobody said run, instinct just kicked in, we were off. The usual monthly, if not weekly game of cat and mouse with the police resumed. More City lads were turning up, and not really knowing what was going on, just seeing us being chased and running off with us. I saw a couple of my pals thrown to the floor and nicked, I managed to get off and it ended up with 4 or 5 of us jogging down away from GMP.

We made our way back from town, and what we thought was away from trouble. I saw lads in the distance and I suppose just presumed they were City, until we got closer and realised we didn't recognise a single one of them. Shit these must be Forest's kids then, not City. These weren't youth lads like us, they were big fucking blokes. There were around 20-25 of them walking down and only like 4 or 5 of us. I just looked at my mate and we both started laughing saying, "we're gonna get fucking battered here now". The Forest contingent were congregated just further on from where the main road forks out, after the Mitchell Arms, heading from the ground back to town. At this point they hadn't noticed us; we were walking behind them, both in the same direction, so it would have been fairly easy for us to fuck off, without them even knowing we were even there. We could have put our tails between our legs, and shuffled off a different way but that wasn't us, we're Man City, and to be honest it didn't even cross my mind to do one. But at the same time if we run at all these Forest, then we're going to get smashed to bits. So we walk over "are use Forest yeah? We're Man City, use wannit yeah". The look on their faces was half shock and half a wry smile, like are these kids for fucking real? They said "fair play for doing that, yes were Forest, but we're not having it with youse with these numbers, we're not dickheads". It was true, with the numbers there would have been no point, it wouldn't have been a fight, just us getting a slap, but we didn't want to lose face. They all shook our hands and numbers were exchanged, said give us half an hour to get our lads together and we will sort it out, we then both went our separate ways. But as far as Forest were concerned that day that was it, police were all over them, and put them on a train and fucked them off shortly after. They could have done what United would have done, battered the 4 or 5 of us and said yeah we done City and all that, but they didn't so fair play to them, they were proper lads.

It was now around 7pm but seemed a lot later because it had been dark for several hours already. Most people were either heading home or thinking about doing it soon. We were on Oldham Street in Gulliver's, 20 youth it was at the very most. All the older lads had either moved on to a different pub or got off home. With it being the FA Cup 3rd round weekend and Manchester being situated where it is, an awful lot of firms would be passing through Piccadilly and Victoria. Manchester is a changing point for so many trains, going from north to south and vice versa. This would prove very handy for us over the years and today would be one of those days. So there we were, sat in the pub with a few beers between the lot of us, because as usual we had all ran out of money, well I say ran out, none of us had any to start with. We used to joke about and say we were the poorest youth firm in

England but looking back I bet we deffo were. Luckily there were always a couple lads who had money, who looked after the ones who didn't so it was sweet. We were trying to ring all the local firms, seeing if anybody wanted it, but it just seemed to be a waste of time. Then someone said to bell Everton, because they were away to some shit team, and would have to change in Manchester, to get home. So I belled one of their lads that I knew, he said he had to get back to Liverpool because he does the doors there. He passed my number on to one of their older lads and we went front there. Everton seemed up for it as they always are, said they have around 20 lads, mainly youth and would meet us near Piccadilly if we come now because they're not messing about waiting. It all sounded fair enough to me anyway, so we all set off around to Piccadilly station to have it with the scousers.

I didn't expect to be going to meet Everton when we had Forest at home but there you go. At this point we didn't have a clue how many Everton had, they could have lied and been loads. I suppose they could have been thinking the exact same about us, with us being at home that day. Having said that firms seem to pull more for away days than standard home league fixtures, well I know we seem to anyway. The walk down from Oldham Street is relatively short, not even 5 minutes I would say. I remember marching down the back streets and it being dead quiet, not the streets, I mean between us lot, nobody was talking, and nobody said a fucking word. Everybody knew what was about to happen and went into fight mode, it wasn't a time for having a laugh or messing about. Everton rang me asking where we were, I told them we were literally a minute away from them now. At this point my heart was beating like mad, I could feel the adrenaline pumping all around me. You get like tunnel vision and become oblivious to anything else going on around you,

you know what's going to happen, and you know what you have to do. At that moment nothing else in the world matters. As we neared the station, me and a couple of the other lads turned to the rest saying "let's smash these scouse cunts, let's send a message to everyone what you get if you come to Manchester and let's show them who City youth are".

As we approached the station I couldn't see them at all, not a fucking thing. I rang them and said "where are youse, we're here now", they said there right up the ramp to the station, which straight away I thought sounded daft. Why would they be right outside the entrance to the station, are they fucking mad or what. So me and three other lads made our way up Piccadilly Approach which has shops running along down it, it's basically just a big walkway up to the station. Ran up there and still couldn't see any Everton, we were starting to get really pissed off now, it seemed they was giving us the run around and messing us about. There's a bridge next to the station – I had a look down puzzled to where they were. Everton had only been hiding in the darkness, under this bridge against the wall. The second I looked down it all just started going off big time. Lads were getting laid out over cars, it was chaos, and by the looks of it, we were getting a good hiding. I put my hands on the rail and leant back, and was about to jump off the bridge to get down below. My pal gripped me just in time and went "you fucking mad Carl it's a 20 foot drop". So rather wisely instead we sprinted down, faster than I think I ever have before. Besides I would have looked and felt a right nob, if I jumped down and broke my leg, I wouldn't have been any help to anyone. So we were sprinting like fuck the same way we had come up, to get down. It was fucking annoying because we had to run back on ourselves to get under the bridge.

There were lads on both sides getting stuck in, but also

it's got to be said that were some lads on both sides who didn't appear to be at all. 'City! City! City!' we shouted as we ran down, I was going that fast I skidded into 2 of my own lads, and sent them flying. Us 4 running down chanting City like that gave the rest of the lads a big boost and we got it together and steamed into Everton, again and again. Everton fought back and the fighting went on. We started to back them off and they started splitting up, they weren't nice and tight anymore and their frontline was thinning out. "Stand Everton stand" their lads at the front turned round and shouted in vain. "Come on City they're backing off, they don't wanna know, let's finish them" someone shouted. With that we piled back into them once more and to their credit a handful of them stayed, as the rest ran back. The handful of lads that didn't budge at first, now had little choice, but to get off with the rest of their lads. They ran through the tunnel under Piccadilly station, with us lot hot on their tails. The cry came out from us lot "Yoof! Yoof! Yoof!" and it echoed through the tunnel and sounded fucking mint. With the echo it actually sounded like there were about 200 of us, not fucking 20 if that. A few other firms do the Yoof chant now, but before that day I had never heard of anybody doing it. So as far as I am concerned the 'Yoof' chant is not only a City thing, but a Blazing Squad thing, it was our battle cry. From that day forward it would become synonymous with us. Like I said a few firms say it, and pass it off like they have always said it, bollocks it's our thing. We can hardly put a copyright on it can we?

Anyway me and Bez carried on running after them, but we lost them. Within minutes they were on the phone to me again, saying they wanted it, but there was police flying about now. As far as we was concerned it was job done. We did spot one of their lads though on his own, in a nice green quilted

Barbour jacket. We went "you Everton yeah", with a strong scouse accent he said "nah mate I'm not like", so we said "yes you fucking are" and chased him up the escalators into Piccadilly station. We were all dead chuffed with ourselves to say the least, we had just done and ran Everton and Everton are no muppets.

The next time we would come across Everton, yet again we wouldn't even be playing them that day. They would be away to Bury in a pre-season friendly. So about 12 of us went down, with a few of the Bury youth lads we knew, to see what's what. Between the thing at Piccadilly and this pre-season friendly at Bury, I had got to know a few of the Everton lads a lot better. I know it must seem pretty fucking mad to some people reading this thinking, well they're friends one minute, then we kick each other's heads in the next but that's just how it is. It's the best way to go about things. See with a lot of football violence people may be surprised to read that there's not actually hatred for the other firm you're fighting a lot of the time. However certain games like United for example, after the fight it doesn't go away, it builds and builds, and the hatred for them just grows and grows. Between City and United, that is real hatred.

Back to Everton anyway, we were due to play them at home second game of the season but because of a European tie, it got changed. We were now playing Sigma Olomouc, whoever the fuck they are. So we saw the friendly against Bury as a perfect chance to meet Everton instead. July 10th 2009 was the date of the game; they made the journey on train to Manchester Victoria and then taxis down to Gigg lane, as they were running late if my memory serves me correct. Now at the end of the day this was Bury's fixture not ours but we weren't going to pass on the perfect opportunity to meet them, without police overkill, like it would be for our fixture with them. So with that in mind we didn't bring shit loads of lads, only about 12 of us, if that. We arranged to meet the Bury kids in a pub called The Waterloo, which like so many other pubs has now shut down. The Waterloo was situated on Manchester Road, the main road that runs directly from Bury to town (Manchester). The pub was a prime location for the Bury lads, bang in between their ground and the town centre. With a park at the back of it which is in a multicultural area shall we say, so whenever they weren't firms to fight, they would always go and fight round there. We got there a couple of hours before kickoff, was like 25 Bury youth there so mixed with our lot was just under 40 lads, was a nice little set of lads to be honest. We stayed at the back of the pub for the time we were there so as not to attract police attention that were constantly flying up and down the busy main road. The plan originally was to get there fairly early, have it with Everton, and fuck off back to town. But it soon became apparent that it wasn't going to happen before the game, they were running late. Now if that had been another firm I would start to think they were shitting it or fucking us about but I know Everton were good kids and aren't like that. We moved on down the road to another Bury pub The Pack Horse, yet another pub that's gone. It was nearing kick off time, so most people were going to the game. On Gigg Lane itself a few lads bumped into a few Everton, and it went off there. A few punches were thrown but it was soon over with the arrival of police on horses.

So the game finished and I am sure Bury won it, fuck knows, anyway the police were trying to keep all Everton's lads together, to bang them in an escort. By now we were all mobbed up together, waiting for them lot. Everton text me saying police have pulled 25 of them to the side and are escorting them back to Bury town centre. Well this was shit;

because I knew as soon as they got them there, they would be put on the tram back to town. Surely the police can't fuck our day up, even when we don't have a game. Bury lads told us the police escort firms the same way every week, so we got on this park, just set off back from the main road, and lie in wait. There's loads of trees and bushes so we tried our best to blend in there and wait for Everton then attack their escort.

We could now see them coming down in the escort in the distance, only one problem, they were on the wrong side of the road. The plan of steaming into them and taking them by surprise had now gone out of the window. The main road at that point has at least 4 lanes and was fairly busy with traffic. There was now no point in hiding in wait in the park and as soon as we came out police saw us and got on the radios. We all split up into smaller groups and we were now being chased all over the show in different directions, it must have been amusing to watch as a motorist passing by. We knew the police would want them on the Met and out of Bury asap. The thing I learnt about the police over the years is they really don't give a shit about us fighting each other, just as long as it's not in the areas they're supposed to police that day, so it doesn't make them look bad sort of thing. If it happens miles down the road, they don't care, just makes it look like they have done their job of policing their area – stopping the 'hooligans' from fighting and keeping the general public safe. GMP realised where we were heading, the interchange, and headed a slightly different way with Everton, also sent more police vans after us lot. But it will be a sad day for football violence when we're out smarted by the police. The way I saw it we now had only two options, go down the escalators and steam into the lot of them. This would have been fucking mint, but let's be honest, would have ended in a crazy amount of arrests, if not there and then, then at a later date. Or get out of the area and fuck off for 10 minutes, let the police put Everton on the tram, and just text Everton to tell them what we are doing, that we will be getting the next tram after them. Would have been fucking top going for the first option, which is what I wanted to do but I got talked out of it, we all decided the second safer option was the best one to go for.

The tram station was camered up anyway, having said that, back then we didn't care much about that, after all the youth of today was "the stars of CCTV". So we fucked off for a little bit and came back to get on the tram after them lot. A fair few of the Bury lads, well the vast majority of the Bury lads, chose to stay in Bury, and not to come town to have it with Everton. Even though it was Bury that were playing them but there you go. I would say around 4 or 5 of them came with us 12 or so City, so we had roughly about 17 lads in town, in fact a couple more City lads met up with us, so we had getting on for 20. The trams are normally like every 5 or 10 minutes, now when we wanted one to hurry up there was none to be seen, suppose like buses, none, then 3 come at once. Now I can't fully remember why or how this happened, but we weren't all on the same tram. A handful of us were on the first tram with me, the rest of them was on the one behind us. So as we arrived at Victoria station, me and my mate went to meet Everton on our own to buy us some time and say give us 10 minutes, then we're good to go. I suppose it was a little weird, meeting them there and shaking hands and being all friendly, having a laugh and a joke, when we were about to hopefully have a big fight and kick fuck out of each other. There were only around 8 of them that met us, they said the other 15 or so lads were very close by. Half the lads there were dead smartly dressed, the other half just like scallies in trackies; they must have just been up for a scrap with Mancs. So the next tram come in, we got everyone together a little further on from Victoria station at Shudehill. I then made the call to Everton, I just said to my mate "we are here now".

Whether it was the adrenaline pumping, or the fact it's all downhill I don't know, but we all started running down to Victoria. "City! City! Yoof! Yoof! Yoof!" the war cry went up, and echoed around the surprisingly empty streets of Manchester. We only saw about 3, maybe 4 of them near the front entrance to Victoria station. This straight away made me think well where the fuck is the rest of them then? By this point I had pretty much stopped running and was now looking all around me scouting for their lads. One of their lads who was there is stupidly tall, one of the younger lads with us launched a bottle, it smashed against a lamp post a couple of feet away from him. I'm glad it didn't hit any of them to be honest, because he is a sound lad, but as the bottle smashed, everybody just full on charged at them. The outnumbered Everton lads retreated back to the station. Now either one of their lads got caught running, or turned round to have a go, I wasn't close enough to see, I was still wondering where the fuck the rest of them were. Anyway this lad got pulled to the floor, and was getting a few kicks and digs of several lads. It's not about that, so I continued my good Samaritan routine like I did against West Ham, Bolton and years later against Zulus, and helped the lad and pushed everyone off him. This had taken place just in and around the entrance to Victoria station, with horrified shoppers and commuters looking on in disbelief.

We could already hear the sirens, 10 out of 10 for response time, gold star for GMP so we all split up and scattered all over the show, running in different directions. I was being chased on my own, by what has got to be not only the fittest, but the most persistent bobby in the whole of Greater

Manchester police force, I mean this cunt really wouldn't give up. He chased me from the side entrance of Victoria station, down past Manchester Cathedral, down Blackfriars and into Salford, then all the way back on myself to Deansgate. I ended up on Whitworth Street West, outside where The Hacienda was. I stopped to catch my breath because I was fucked, and looked round and he was still there, about 20 metres behind me, what a fucking mad bastard. Finally I either lost him or he gave up, was something like a 10 minute chase if not longer, like something off the fucking Bill. I was expecting some half-hearted chase from him, not a middle distance run. So anyway, while I was being chased by Mo Farah, the rest of the lads had gone their separate ways as well. Like 3 or 4 City had ran straight into the path of all the Everton lads, a few digs were thrown and the City lads got off, with the Everton lads chasing them all through the Printworks, from Waxy O'Connors, all the way to Market Street. Well at least if one good thing would come out of today, we would all be a lot fitter! Police were now all over it, there was no chance of us getting it back together again and mobbing up, besides I think Everton had had enough and wanted to fuck off back home anyway, before any of them got nicked. It's a shame it didn't go off proper that day, the way it should have. I later found out that when we ran down and most of them weren't there, they were at a car park just at the side of us. We literally missed each other by a few seconds; only thing I can think of is when I said we're here, they thought we would be there in a minute, not actually that second. It's shit that it turned out that way, because I am sure that would have been a cracking fight, regardless of who would have come on top, I suppose we will never know. By the time I got back to meet the lads, Everton were already setting off home, that's how far that fucking bell end had chased me.

A year or so on, and they turned up at our place yet again, around 20-30 of them. We tried everything we possibly could to get to them before the game but police were all over us like a rash. We even met up down Oxford Road way for this game to avoid them, even this didn't work though. A couple of games we even went down the edge of the Gay Village to avoid the police. Oldham Street and that area was still our area but it didn't hurt to keep Nobby and Cliff guessing from time to time did it? We always seemed to pull alright numbers for games like Everton and Stoke, because you knew there was every chance of it going off. We had about 30 youth in the pub and around 20 older lads; with more on the way, and of course there would be plenty of lads down near the ground. It's quite handy near the ground because one minute you could have say 20 lads and within a couple of minutes lads empty out the pubs and there could be 70 of us. I didn't see any of their lads at all before the game, but there was suppose to have been a little 10 on 10 thing, that broke out between our older lot and there's, near the ground. The police were quickly in there though, don't recall anybody being nicked, think it was more a telling off and pushed on their way. Down south if a fight broke out like that they would have probably been arrested and banned and maybe even sentenced. You hear stories of lads going to prison for just being there, never mind actually doing much. Suppose that's alright about GMP, a few times we've had fights, and they don't even bother arresting us, even if it's right in full view of them.

The game itself was now coming to a close, as it was a midweek game, we had darkness on our side. We got all our lot together down the side of The Manchester just when the game ended, a nice 25 youth, more than enough. Couldn't care less how many they had, we had a top 25, so I was more than happy with that. A few more lads joined us so we now had a good 30 lads, that had been there and done it all before. We had people by the away end who would let us know when Everton were coming out, if they were in an escort, and how many they had and all that shit. We waited out of sight from the main road and tried keeping our heads down and going unnoticed. Easier said than done when you've got 30 lads, many of whom have been on the beer and sniff all day. We got the call saying Everton are on their way out of the ground now, around 30 handed in an escort. We made our way through the various side streets and alley ways in the estate, until we got to the final houses before the main road. There's a small entrance that leads out onto a bit of green, near enough opposite the Mitchell Arms. Nowadays the tram runs through and there's a Met stop around there, but this was years before they were built. So we lay in wait, 30 handed behind the back of the last houses before the main road. All trying to be as quiet as we could without looking on top, fuck knows what residents of them houses would have thought if they looked out of the back windows, to see 30 of us all there. It felt like we had been there for fucking ages, lads were starting to get restless.

We then saw the high-vis jackets in the distance of the first police in the escort, this was it, they were fucking here now. Without making a sound, we stealthily made our way out from behind the houses in double file, once we were all out we then spread out and made for the main road in front of us. Everton were now square on in front of us, about 30 of them like we had been informed, fucking mint. Would say there were touching 20 GMP around them but one good thing was there wasn't a single police horse, hate them horses at the match, proper nuisances they can be. A couple of their lads sort of nudged each other and pointed and nodded their heads towards us, they now knew we were there. Shouts went out "fucking come on Everton, City are here, Yoof! Yoof! Yoof! Yoof!", we charged at the escort. The officers that were at the far side and back of the escort, now rushed to the side we were on, to try and get more police in between us and Everton lads. Several of them drew their coshes and screamed "get back", which made some of us hesitate a little. Then bang we crashed into them, I ran so hard into the police I sent some of them flying, one who took the brunt of my charge went flying back into the Everton kids behind him. I got whacked on my back and arm by the coshes for my troubles. It hurt a bit, but then I got smacked right on my elbow and that proper killed because it was right on the bone. The same as so many times we've attacked escorts, the police never know what to do, push you back or stay tight to the escort. This indecision played right into our hands and after initially being backed off by the police and their coshes, we had now got back together and once more steamed back into the escort lines. The police lines started to split, ones having tit for tat battles with us lot, some stuck to Everton, and ones in no man's land stood scratching their heads, as if to say "well we we're never saw this in training". A couple of our lads managed to get round the police and give it Everton, who fought back. You could see several of their lads trying get to us but I've got to say I really think on the whole they could have, and should have done, a little more. I never even managed to get to Everton, was busy having fun and games with the police though. This went on for maybe a minute, in the middle of the main road.

GMP were now doubling in numbers and it was definitely time for us to go. We darted back the way we had come from, back onto the estate with the police in pursuit close behind us. "STOP POLICE" and various other daft shit like that were shouted at us. I'm fairly sure the police make a special effort time and time again, just to apprehend and detain me. I could literally slip off on my own and half the police force would just follow me. That being said, there were a couple of lads who they really had it in for and they would make little or no attempt to hide that. Most people got caught and were given Section 27s and some were arrested and thrown in vans.

The following season Everton would come down on a mini bus and park it on Asda car park, which isn't far at all from our ground. It's pretty much the opposite direction to where most fans head though, which would be back towards town. I wasn't even about for this game I'm not going to lie, not going to make some excuse up for where I was either, I'll just be honest, it was fucking chucking it down and freezing and I couldn't be arsed at all. After the match a couple of lads were making their way home, I'm guessing they came across the scousers on the car park, and words were exchanged shall we say. The 2 lads went back to the pubs by the ground and got more lads together then returned to Asda car park, to their surprise Everton's lads were still there. Now like I said I wasn't present or even out that day, but from what I've been told it went off proper, even numbers and City fucking smashed them all over. Since then though there's not really been anything worthwhile mentioning between us and them. With the banning orders and bail conditions of certain lads, it's been pretty hard to arrange meets, whether that be home or away. But as I have said, there's no two ways about it, we haven't turned up at their place as much as we should. No excuses for that, it's poor of us. The similarities between City and Everton are there to see, whether that be it about the fans, or the firms. Everton are good lads and always seem to have a go, so that's Everton "laa".

UNITED

WHEN I SAT DOWN to do this chapter straight away I thought, this is going to be by far the hardest to get down on paper. Not because of the lack of incidents with them over the years, far from it, more because of my general feelings and opinions about their mob. Instead of maybe a biased one-sided chapter highlighting how crap they are, and just slating them, I'm just going to try and take a step back, and be perfectly honest; I mean there would be no point at all in the book if I was anything bar that. However there really is no escaping the huge rivalry between us and United, which at times it would be fair to say, is nothing but pure hatred. Hate is a strong word and I don't use it lightly but it's the best word to describe the feelings between us and them. The massive rivalry isn't just there twice a season, or whenever we play, it's 24/7. For years and even decades now City has lived in the shadows of our neighbours United, well on the pitch that is. The Manchester derby is always a massive affair. Now with our improved squad and both teams challenging for the title, the wider football community has a bigger interest in the derby than ever before. For me personally I don't think there's any other derby in England that compares to it but I'm sure every lad feels the same about their respective derby matches. While there is a huge police presence at games, this doesn't always mean they can quell the violence. There have been some epic battles won and lost by both sides over recent years. One time in 2012 after being arrested at the league game at our place against them lot, the arresting officers told me that there's more police on duty at the City/United game than any other fixture in England. Also in 2012 City and United topped the football banning order league table in 1st and 2nd place. There have been loads of fights between Blazing Squad and their 'rats' over recent years. Oh yeah that's another thing, you've got to really think about what sort of lads would take tremendous pride in the fact their called 'the rats'? Personally I think their name just about sums them lot up. Now it would be so easy to just give 10 examples of us smashing them lot all over, and running them out of town. Would be very easy to just make out how good we are, and how useless they are and that we have never been done by them. That would be just utter bullshit though, and there's one thing I am not and that's a liar. Obviously there's been times United have done us, obviously there's been times United have ran us. But I can hand on heart say that we're a better firm and we have the better set of lads and more often than not that's evident to see. So here are a handful of stories and my take on their firm. Like I have already said there will be times where they come out on top, because as every casual knows... everybody gets done sometimes.

Now United's mob not only in recent times but for decades now, have always been known to have huge numbers, and there's no getting around that, they do. Whereas City is the Manchester team, fans and firm alike come from here, United are a little different. United's huge numbers can be chalked down to the fact they come from far and wide, many United firm and fans don't even live in the north of England, never mind live in Manchester. As an outsider looking in another thing that has struck me as a huge difference between us and them is the bond, the closeness, the unity. It seems that half of their lads don't even have a fucking clue who the lad stood next to them is. Whereas we will go that extra mile for a friend, they don't fucking know the lad stood next to them getting a kicking, so they don't feel compelled to run in and help, as they would if it was a close pal. I honestly think anybody could bang some black clothes on, go round the pubs near their ground on match days with all their lads, spend the day with them and nobody would ask you who you were. You would have to wear black though, because to demonstrate how rough and tough they are, they normally only wear black clothing, scary or what. Now as well as being known for their vast numbers, United are also known for another thing which is attacking what we call "shirters". This is basically attacking normal fans in club colours who clearly don't want any trouble whatsoever, sometimes even women and children are targeted too. Now I know what you're thinking, I'm probably just saying all this to give United a bad name, but I'm not, they are renowned for it. Here is a piece from my football banning papers issued to me in 2012. This is what Cliff Lea (the then head of Man City football intelligence) had to say "at 16:05 hours I was on Chester Road near St George's church monitoring fans on their way back to the City centre. There was a hostile atmosphere, as a group of United "risk" supporters confronted City fans. (risk supporters is polices way of saying "hooligans") I saw a group of around 30 City fans being confronted and had to intervene to stop the situation escalating. The City group was comprised mainly of normal fans, including some females". I think that says a lot about United. Not to say all United lads attack shirters, women and kids but it's clear that some do. As I've said there's been numerous scraps with United since I've been going, some we have won, and some we have lost.

My first ever encounter with a United firm would come back in 2007. We had them at our place, and as usual everybody was exaggerating numbers which really pisses me off. Oh there's suppose to be 350 of them coming, another lad goes "What? Are you off your fucking head it's more like double that". Now don't get me wrong there is fucking loads of them but nowhere remotely near that. But I would choose quality over quantity any day of the week, wouldn't have it any other way. Now the game was at our place, but we all met up in town, knowing United have to come through town to get to our place anyway. There wasn't really just one big group of City together in one spot, annoyingly as so often, there were various groups of City plotted up all over the place. We were in The City pub on Oldham Street a good 50 or so of us. There were similar numbers of City in The Waldorf, then smaller groups around as well. Word now was that United had a good 250 lads in a few boozers all near each other down Deansgate, it's the area of town where United drink on match days. Now with it being derby day it goes without saying that all of town was fucking swarming with GMP.

For a good hour or so there was a car and van parked directly outside the pub watching us and I'm guessing something must have kicked off or they were needed elsewhere cause they just fucked off. So the plan was to go down Deansgate and give it United, smash them all over then get off rapid before the police get chance to do owt. We left the City pub through the back door and made our way through the back streets of the Northern Quarter heading for Deansgate, which was a good 10 minute walk away if not more. So us 50 were on our way, the call was made to the other City lads in other pubs to make their move to meet us. So now everybody knew the plan, everybody but United that is, and we intended to keep it that way. We made an effort to walk in smaller groups of no more than 5 lads, so as not to attract police attention. Nothing more on a Saturday match day would attract police attention more than 50 lads bouncing around town. We were now in dribs and drabs on each side of the road, walking down Deansgate. But it was easy enough to see where everybody was because Deansgate is pretty much just one long straight road. It's very busy with shops, restaurants, pubs and bars along either side of the road. Unbeknown to us at the time there was loads of police and cars around the pubs that United were in. So just steaming in the pubs wasn't going to work with a couple of dozen GMP outside was it? Instead we rang United and told that we were on our way and were near enough outside now. We were still all spread out but this was only around 100 metres if that away from the pub, so if we could see the police, it wouldn't be long before they noticed us and seconds later they did. Now a big round of applause to GMP for their response time, because literally with a minute or so there was police vans everywhere. United then started piling out the pub pushing past the police to get onto the main road. But yet more police turned up, so we all darted down various side streets to get away from them. We all ended up in small groups, I ended up with about 12 or so lads, half of which at that time I didn't really know.

We doubled back on ourselves and ended up back on Deansgate, where we couldn't believe out luck. Across the road were about 10 United older lads, proper old school lads all in the 40s I would say. We all just stopped dead, both us and them, as if our minds were processing what our eyes were seeing. One of the lads pushed past me from behind, sort of knocking me out of the way the little cunt, anyway he barged past me shouting "fucking come on then Munich cunts" and with that we all just ran at them. Now I would love to tell the tale now of some mint toe to toe fight that went on, but it couldn't be further from the truth. A few punches were thrown and they legged it, and I mean they ran like little fucking girls. I was fuming because this fat bald prick hit me and ran off. We chased after them, and most got away, but a couple got caught and give a little bit of a slap but that was it really. We all made our way down to the ground anyway, and after the game we all mobbed up at the crossroads (now The Manchester). Was pretty decent numbers for City to be honest, must have been getting on for 200 of us anyway. But out of that 200 these weren't all proper lads, probably the odd game shirter and muppets who just wanted a pop at United. The police held us back and pretty much had us lot boxed in there for at least 20 minutes, while United were escorted back to town. There were a couple of scuffles later on in town but on the whole the police kept the peace that day. So that was my first encounter of United's firm anyway, even though nothing major happened.

A few months later and it was the away match at Old Trafford. Although it was an away game we actually met up in a pub called The Bank not too far from our ground. There were around 15 or so youth and about 40 older lads in there, it was still fairly early though so more lads would arrive as the day went on. The plan was to stay down there for a while, to keep well out of the way of the police. But it would seem they were wise to our plan. As we made our move to head for town, several police cars followed us, we tried to make our escape over wasteland which is now houses and apartments, but we were soon rounded up like cattle. We soon found ourselves split up into 2 separate groups, those with tickets and those without. It was made clear to all us without tickets that if were seen down by their ground then we would be nicked, end of. Nothing new there though. So now with our numbers even more depleted we made our way to town where we jumped on the Met down to Old Trafford. It was a shambles, just small pockets of City dotted all over the show, with very large groups of United, going round picking them off. Around 8 of us all youth found ourselves in some working men's club down near their ground. Now if ever there was a pro United pub, then fuck me, this was it. There was me, Wizz, Racist Ric, Raz and a few others. Not sure how we had come split off from all the others not going the game. I was just sat there and I started pissing myself laughing, mates are like Carl what the fuck you laughing at, I said how long before one of us says fuck off United or Munich cunts at the telly when the game's on. There's a good 300 United fans in here, we're going to get fucking battered; he just nodded and laughed and said "yeah man you're right, fuck it". Anyway we didn't get leathered in the working men's pub, god knows how, just some very, very dirty looks.

After the game it was similar to beforehand as regards to City being scattered about everywhere not all together. Tensions were running high because it was the 50th anniversary of the Munich air disaster as well. As ever there was an over the top GMP presence, trying to make sure the day went without incident. There were around 10 or so of our lot walking back from the ground towards town. They walked past a United pub, some United younger lot came out shouting over "who are youse?" to which little Wizz arms out cockily replied "were Man City us". With that the boozer just fucking emptied, with wave after wave of United was steaming out onto the street. There must have been getting on for 100 of them, the young City lads inevitably got put on the back foot and ended up with no other option than to run. They ran down by the side of Chester House, one of the lads got tripped up and before he really knew what's happening, had loads of them all booting fuck out of him. He somehow managed to drag himself up to his feet, but was soon pulled back to the deck and filled in by a dozen or so of them. Another example of United being bullies. Fair to say also it's an example of City being naïve enough to think you can walk around near United's ground, with just 10 youth and take the piss. So it would be fair to say not a very successful trip down their place that day.

The next thing I would have with them lot would be an arranged meet with them, and for a refreshing change United would be 100 percent honest about their numbers. We had Stoke away and everybody was bang up for it, but it unfortunately just ends up one of them days where fuck all happens because police are all over us. We met in the station, escorted to some student union bar and put in there, then thrown on double-deckers to their ground. Nothing we could have really done about it. So when a fair few of us were eventually rounded up by police in Stoke and put on the train home we were past caring. It was just the ending to a crap away day, or at least that's what we thought at the time. For some reason they seemed to be far more of us on the train home from Stoke, as on the train down there. That struck me as a little bit weird because if anything it's normally the other way around, because it always ends up with lads getting arrested for various reasons. Now this was around the same time we were having our little thing, bullying Stockport County. Now the week beforehand they had failed yet again to turn up for a meet with us, which they called on in the first place, fucking queers. So this train had to pass through Stockport to get back to town and with County playing at home we thought it would be rude not to pay them a little visit. Not everybody wanted to get off the train prematurely, especially when it was only for them lot, which to be fair I can understand, never the less around 40 of us jumped off the train and sat in a pub in Stockport town centre and rang them saying we're here waiting. County didn't turn up, however their FIOs did and they soon put us on the train yet again back to town. It's a good job me and the lads aren't too sensitive, I mean it could really hurt your feelings nobody wanting you in their town and telling you to go back to Manchester. Looked like it was just going to be one of those days, for every mint fight you have or running firms all over, you have another 3 or 4 shit days like this. Shit days like this though make the good days that much sweeter, makes you appreciate them more and realise it's not a film, fighting in big mass brawls every week, more's the pity.

So it was back to town for a few beers and that before we all called it a day and fucked off home. Slowly the numbers started to dwindle as the majority of people drifted home, when someone rang saying they're still out and want it, it was United. Fucking typical that isn't it, they couldn't have rang us a couple of hours ago when there was a few of us out, oh well. It had been a very long day and a couple of the lads that were still out weren't up to much, they were pissed out of their heads. It was now around 9 o'clock, the crowd in town had changed from the people you expect to see there in the day, to people going out to clubs and that on a night out. We were in a pub called The Garret off Whitworth Street. It was quite busy with students and people on a night out, so we dived in another pub pretty much across the road from it. There were around 17, maybe 18 of us left at this point, everybody else had already called it a day and got off. Going home was exactly what I was about to do before them nobheads rang and said they wanted it but credit where credit is due. Not only did they ring and say they wanted it but said they would come to wherever we are, can't say fairer than that can you.

United said they had 25 lads and were on their way with that, you never know with them though, for all we knew could be 125. I can honestly say that we never have, nor ever will turn down a meet with United, or anybody regardless of numbers. Many firms will say they will meet any firm for a row any time regardless of anything; difference is we don't just say it, we do it. A couple of lads, well I think it was more like 4 or 5 were waiting outside the pub, slightly up the road, in the direction we were certain United would come from. A car drove past with a few lads in then sped off, that was them alright, they love using cars and vans to get about. Moments later they were on their way bouncing down the road. Slinging bottles at the 4 or 5 City lads on the front, the majority of us were still in the pub, at this point still unaware that they were here. United skipped over towards the City lads, one of them arrogantly jumped forward into them, as if to intimidate them. He was pinged and put on his arse but with that all United lads charged at the few City lads outside.

There was a sea of noise, which you could easily hear over the music in the pub, 'United, United, United'. This was when I first realised they were outside. The hairs on my neck stood up, within a second my body was overwhelmed with a mixture of emotions; excitement and nerves being the main ones. I refused to get done off these cunts; they were getting it today, good and proper. I slammed down my j20 bottle so hard it bounced off the table and smashed on the floor, and ran for the door. It was a scramble as we all tried to get out of the door as quickly as we could, we were practically falling over one another. The United chants went silent as we all piled out of the pub and the "Yoof" chant went up. People watching must have thought it was some kind of fucking singing competition or something. Both sets of lads just fucking went for it and smashed into one another, right outside The Garret, and it carried on at the top, near O'Sheas. There were like 2 separate fights going on, not really sure how it ended up like that. Lads were getting dropped on both sides and if they weren't getting pulled up by their mates quickly enough, they were getting booted all over. Fair play to United for once they were actually being bang on with the numbers they claimed to have, they didn't bring more than 25 but I reckon they were starting to wish they had. It was clear who was getting the better of things, United were now getting a good old pasting, up and down the street. Within just a few seconds it had gone from us backing them off, to now us running them all over. But unluckily for United we had been mucked around so much that day, by police in Stoke and Stockport, that United were now going to cop for it. After all the shit we had had that day, we weren't going to let them get off that easily by just running off. This is United, we hate these Munich cunts, why should we let them just run off and leave it as that?

As I said for whatever the reason the fight was like split into two separate scraps. The United lads who ran first seen us chasing and threw bottles back, not realising that half of the lads there were their own lads as well. So to my amusement United were bottling some of their own kids. They now started to scatter in various directions, five or so went one way so me and Tom and another lad went running after them. "Come on there's 3 of us, stop running" we shouted, but these kids were not stopping for anyone. Then we couldn't believe our luck, when we saw two of them dive into a Chinese restaurant, well to be honest it was Japanese, but at the risk of sounding ignorant, it's all the same to me. Maybe we had got United all wrong, maybe they weren't running from us because they were scared, they just had cravings for some fucking rice and noodles. They either didn't think we saw them go inside, or didn't think we would follow them into a posh restaurant and slap them. Well we did see them go in and we ran straight in after the little shit bags. I kid you not one of them were in their trying to hide behind menus the silly pricks, although he couldn't have been that silly because he managed to get away. He got off leaving his mate on his own, not very nice of him was it? So me and my pal Tom spotted the other lad at the far end of this restaurant. Not sure what he was trying to do but he was on top of a table, the little shit booted me in my shoulder/neck, well he's getting it now. We pulled him down of this table by his legs, throwing him about like some rag doll, and then give him a bit of a kicking all over this swanky chinky place. The diners looked gobsmacked at what they were seeing, I suppose it was slightly different to their usual dining experience, seeing some United kid get bashed about.

Loads of the United lads ran off into the Gay Village with the City lads chasing them. Maybe United felt safe in the Gay Village, you know like comfort in familiar surroundings and all that. There was GMP everywhere, cars and vans darting about all over the place. How everybody got away from that without getting nicked I will never know. So after all that it turned out to be not such a shit day at the football after all. The way I saw it once again we had proven this City is ours, and why we run Manchester. We later found out United had around 60 older lads in the pub that they came from, didn't bring them with them, and were true to their word of 25. I think that says an awful lot about their main younger kids in not only doing that, but coming right to us, credit where credit is due.

Not too long after that fight outside The Garret, we had United at our place in the league. From start to finish though the whole thing was just fucked up. We all met up in the Leigh Arms in Openshaw, which is out of the way but if you ask me it's a little too far out of the way. So while you may keep out of the way of GMP and City's FIOs for a while, you're so far out of the way, you might as well not even fucking be out. There's no way United would come down there but that being said why should they, we're the ones at home. It's good for keeping out of the way I suppose, just a proper mooch from the ground. After being in there not even an hour the police turned up, so now we were in this pub a couple miles from the ground but with police with us as well. It's a shame the police turned up though, because we had a nice set of lads in there, around 80 of us anyway, youth and older mixed. We all left the pub and marched down towards our ground. The GMP were walking with us trying to put us in an escort, but it was us walking where we wanted, and them just following I suppose. As we got near the pubs near the ground, lads started coming out of the pubs and walking with us. So there were more like 110, 120 of us. As you would expect there was a crazy amount of police near the ground, more than enough to hold all us lot in one place. An easy way to disperse this mob of City was to first split it up into 2 fractions, those with tickets and those without. The ones with tickets were escorted to the ground, which I thought was a bit daft, all us lot left without (about 50 of us) were given Section 27s. It was made clear as always fuck off or get nicked, your choice. GMP don't mince their words I'll give them that. But this was the derby, we weren't about to go home were we? Yet we'd be foolish to stay near the ground now, we'd be nicked in minutes. So we all made our way back to town and found a pub to watch the game in. We knew United would be coming back to town after the game anyway, so we just thought fuck it, we will just smash them then.

The game had ended, and we were all gutted because it had gone off a few times on the main road by the ground. It's proper shit when it goes off and you miss it, it haunts you for weeks, maybe even months if it's a top do. More lads were on their way back from the ground to meet us in taxis and to go and give it United. Walking about town with 50-60 lads is hard enough at the best of times, never mind on derby day when the place is crawling with dibble. As the police have said to me there's no other fixture in English football which has as many police officers on duty for it, says it all really. You know it means trouble when police drive past at the top of street, then stop and reverse back for another look. Another van was coming from behind us; we were about to get boxed in, fuck that. We had no other option than to get off and split up. Within 5 minutes, the helicopter was now no longer by the ground but hovering above us, and going wherever we went. It was now a game of cat and mouse with the police, with us being chased all over town by them. So I thought before I'm nicked for breaching the Section 27 I was getting off home. So me and my mate set off walking down Market Street and under the escalators towards Victoria Way, to get the tram back to Whitefield. Now this part of town is purely for shoppers, so it's the one place where I knew we would be safe from the police, or at least that's what I thought. Just as we walked past Boots I heard "oi stop", I've got to be honest it shit me up a bit. As I have gone to turn round to see who the fuck it was, I've been grabbed on both arms by 2 coppers. It wasn't Tactical Aid Unit, nor was it Football Intelligence Officers; it was two evidence gatherers with cameras. Well that was a little embarrassing, they said if we had ran they wouldn't even have bothered chasing us. What's even more embarrassing is that there was a delay with the van to take me back to the station, so I was there for some time. So there I am sat outside Boots in handcuffs with people walking past probably thinking I've been nicked for shoplifting some Lynx deodorant or something. I think that was my first ever arrest on derby day and it wasn't even for fighting. It certainly wouldn't be my last anyway.

Another home game against United would reveal their sneaky and sly side. Sometimes with United, meets are planned out in advance but the majority of the time its just a see what happens on the day sort of thing. Whether that be just bumping into each other, or turning up at the pub or area they are in. Youth on youth generally goes out of the window on derby day; it's normally just all City together as one, regardless of ages. So anything from mid to late teens all the way up to late 40s would be your age range. With most lads being in the 20s or early 30s I would say. Another thing I noticed about derby day is the role that GMP plays. If the police are proper on it then they can completely bollocks your day up, before it even starts. On derby day from start to finish the police are all over us like a rash, same can't be said about them with United though, in fact the complete opposite. They just get given free rein to walk around in huge numbers and the police leave them to it. I guess the way GMP see it is right we have two risk groups, do we put police on both of them all day, or should we just put all our police on one group, and that way if we're always with that group, there can't be any fighting. So with City being unquestionably the smaller firm, maybe that's why GMP are all over us, and leave United alone.

Another thing widely thought as to why United have an easier run of things is they're a bunch of grasses. Not all of them obviously but it's rumoured that a few of them are, fuck knows. Like I've already said they do have some good lads, but the vast majority of them are just sly cunts and shit bags. This day at our place would be a prime example of them not wanting a fair and proper fight and just being sly as fuck. There's a good chance that deep down they know that's the way they have to play it with us, because if it's just a proper fight, as history has shown, we come on top more often than not. So this game at our place in 2010 was just another derby day, which consisted of poor organisation, with groups of City not as one and police on us from the start. The FIOs try and stick to you like glue, they're like your shadow and very hard to shake on days like this. To be honest the day was a bit of a ballache and largely uneventful but I wouldn't dream of missing it and missing the chance to smash them red cunts in.

Leading up to the game, for a fortnight beforehand, it's all anybody is talking about, and on the day itself the city comes to a standstill. On derby day you can just sense the tension in the air, the hatred is clear for all to see, not just from lads but just normal shirters. Even the police are on edge, their demeanour is different, it's because they know it's moments away from potential violence. As you would expect, when it goes off, it gets bad, the times I've spent being stitched back together in hospital are testament to that. We had all met up in town, or at least tried to, groups of 4 police on every single street corner, not to mention the cars and vans all over. So we started to make our way down to the ground, some by foot down the canal way, and many in taxis. There was no point being around town with that many police there, so I jumped in a black cab down to the ground. I don't normally bother with black cabs, on the count that they're robbing cunts, I think it cost nearly a tenner down to our ground, which is only about a mile and a half away. Like I said, they're proper robbing cunts those black cabs. Down by the ground there are several pubs that all the lads drink in, not just like one set pub. I was in The Manchester, which is a fairly big pub, I mean you can fit enough people in there; there were about 50 lads in there. Across the road in Mary D's, which is generally more a shirter pub, there were a few lads and then further on the estate in The Townley there was supposed to be a good 30 lads, then there were the lads who still hadn't made their way down from town yet. We expected United to have around double what we had, if not more. This however didn't mean a thing to us, quality over quantity every time. The mood in the pub was good, people having a beer and a laugh, singing songs about the scum and that. I told all my younger lot to come down to the Manchester so that we were all together, the older lads did the same.

As time went on more and more lads turned up, I would say we had well over 100 lads in there anyway, maybe something like 120. It was a top bunch of lads as well. Could see people look around at all the lads there, and give I suppose, a nod of approval because what we had there wouldn't just be a match for United, it would tear them a new arsehole. United were being very vague and keeping their cards close to their chest, giving nothing away about where they were. This to us meant they were shitting it and didn't fancy their chances down at our place. They usually come down in big numbers but in an escort and if they're not in an escort at first, they will make enough noise to attract GMP attention so they get put in one. It was now not that long to kick off time. As far as we were concerned they didn't want to know but if worst comes to worst, we will attack their escort coming from town, or at least try to. Then United made the call, they said most of their lads were in escort, but 50 of them weren't and were near our ground, so get to the Mercedes garage now. Music to our ears, the Mercedes place is a few hundred metres away, right outside the ground. Now obviously our initial reaction was to pile out of the pub and get down there. However the smart thing to do was go out in small groups and make our way down there. I mean how on top would it look to GMP, if over 100 of city's lads came out of the pub at once marching down; they would know something was going on. So going out in group of sixes and sevens, just looked like it was people leaving for the match, as it was nearing kick off time anyway. So that's what we did, made our way to meet them. United were going to get turned over, I mean proper fucking smashed, wasn't a doubt in my mind, I know the rest of the lads shared my confidence too. United aren't going to know what hit them.

As it turned out, it was us that didn't know what had hit us, literally. It never even crossed our minds that United wouldn't be coming from town towards the ground. It never even crossed my mind that they would be coming from the opposite direction. They had been under our noses so to speak for a good half an hour and we hadn't a clue. It was a top idea what they had done, just a shame they didn't have the balls to tell us about it. United knew we were in The Manchester, they also knew that with that phone call, everybody from the pub would head to the Mercedes garage. I'm guessing they had someone watching the pub, because they conveniently left enough time for the majority of the lads to leave the pub, then they appeared just as the last ones were coming out. Sly little bastards, good idea though I'll give them that. They must have been pissing themselves watching us leave the pub, thinking we were going to meet them. If they proper wanted it with City that was their chance but they waited until just the last few were coming out and then took them by surprise.

"UNITED! UNITED!" rang out as the last City lads leaving the pub turned round to see a good 60 odd United coming towards them. There was no time for them to tell the other City lads they were here, it just went off, apparently even the police looked confused to where United had magically appeared from. There were around 15, maybe getting on for 20 City lads at best. The City lads stood there and had it with

United, police soon swarmed in with their coshes out but the fighting continued right up the street. By the time word got round to us what had gone on, we all ran back round, but had missed it all by a couple of minutes. We were all stood scratching our heads at where United were at the Merc garage. To say we were annoyed with what had happened would be putting it mildly, we were fucking fuming with how sly they had been, maybe a little annoyed with ourselves for letting it happen. United had got the better of the little fight there outside the pub but most of our lads weren't even there, they had seen to that. After the game there was fucking loads of us out, in near enough the same spot. I don't even think it was all 100 percent lads, there were a few normal fans mixed in there too. Well over 200 of us wedged between The Manchester and the chippy facing it. But with a crazy amount of police present we weren't going anywhere. The horses were soon brought in to push us back and it worked. I don't recall there being anything else that day, annoyingly.

Now if I'm being perfectly honest, it would be fair to say United turn up at our place more than we do at theirs, no denying it. Although there are one or two reasons for it, such as they're allowed to get about in huge numbers, where as if I go to the chippy with my mate, about 5 GMP will follow us. The vast majority of the time at our place all they do is make loads of noise, to get police to put them in an escort and protect them from us. Another reason is bans, we can't go anywhere fucking near Old Trafford if we play there, in fact not even in the borough of Trafford, yet their banned lads always seem to be in escorts at our place, bit dodgy that. Moss Side and its surrounding areas would be a place we would meet up for United away. Moss Side is where the old ground Maine Road was, so is a big blue area; it's also not a million miles away from Old Trafford so handy in that respect. On numerous occasions we would be around that area. I can think of a few times off the top of my head when we have been around Whalley Range, they said they were on their way and never turned up. It got quite embarrassing the amount of times United would say they were coming and didn't ever turn up. We even had a little joke between us all going "United are here" because they just didn't wanna know. Always the same excuse "the police are all over us" don't get me wrong I'm sure some of the times they were but when you hear the same excuse 3 or 4 times on the trot, it starts to get a little boring.

A midweek cup game in 2010 would see us go down to their place and take it to them. We would meet up at the Whalley Range pub at 6, I was running late though, god knows how though because I had done fuck all that day. Everybody was there before me and my mate, anyway by the time we got there, there were already a stupid amount of GMP there. On seeing all the police, I thought well that's the end of that then, and went in some takeaway to get some food. Got my pizza and made my way over to the lads, could see straight away that we had fucking top numbers out, and my mate said look there's still loads inside. The place was rammed with City, young and old, must have been a good 200 lads there. I thought to myself, if even half that lot gets hold of United, they're in major fucking trouble. There was a mass line of police there, must have been a good 70 of them, wouldn't say the line went as far as the eye could see, but you get my point, there were loads. The police were a bit taken aback with the numbers we had out that day. GMP were trying to get us into two separate groups as they like to do, those with tickets and those without. They wanted to fuck off everyone without a ticket and bang everyone with a ticket in a big escort, and take them down to the ground. There were around 130 lads with tickets that were surrounded by the police and told they were to be escorted to Old Trafford. Me and around 10 other Blazing Squad kids managed to sneak our way into the escort. How fucked up is that though, I mean usually we're trying to break out of the escort, and here we were trying our hardest to get in one. I decided to walk alongside the escort then look shifty and try walking off. Hoping that GMP would see me, think I was trying to get out of the escort, and throw me back in it. Sure enough they did and my plan worked. Now a handful of the older lads had a slightly different approach to getting in this escort than mine. They basically threw the police out of the way and dived in the escort, mingling in with the crowd, before the police really knew what was happening. So there were now 140, maybe even 150 of us in this escort, was a top set of lads anyway. We were to be marched all the way down to the ground but I think the police soon realised it was us lot dictating the pace of the walk and not them. Yet more police on foot and in vans were brought in to bulk up the escort numbers. With the size of this escort we were just walking straight down the middle of the road. For some reason I naïvely thought it would only be a 20 minute walk but it took more like getting on for an hour. The further we got down Chester Road and the closer to their ground, the slower the escort got. The escort would frequently slow down to a crawl, and even stop for the police to make the escort tighter and cram us all together even more. One song/chant rang out all down Chester Road "this City is ours, this City is ours, fuck off back to London, this City is ours".

As we drew closer to the ground the song was sung louder

and louder, the hairs on the back of my neck stood up, every single time it was chanted. We were now less than a quarter of a mile from their ground, we were being escorted past some of their pubs. Was less than half an hour to go until kick off, so going past the pubs there wasn't really anything that resembled lads or their firm, just little tramps that would throw shit at the escort, then get off. That got us lot a bit lively and we started to push the police out and spread the escort out, so yet again more GMP were brought in to contain us. I swear to god there was more police outside the escort, than there were lads in it. We were now literally right by their ground on the forecourt, when I heard what I can only describe as a roar go up from my left hand side. It shit me up big time because it was so loud and it came out of nowhere.

As I've looked over my left shoulder I couldn't believe my eyes it was a sea of United lads, I couldn't believe how many of them were stood there. I was proper taken back by the sheer numbers they had there, 100s upon 100s in a massive line a few deep, the line just seem to go on forever. How the hell are them lot (must have been honestly like 300 of them) allowed to congregate right outside their ground before kick off like that? At our place no way could we stand near the ground with 13, let alone 300, without police jumping all over us. So our initial reaction was fuck me there's loads of them, second was how the fuck have all them lot been allowed to stand there, third was now to get to them and kick fuck out of them. They all bounced over towards us and we all pushed to get to them, with all the police sandwiched in the middle. One of our FIOs, Nobby, whipped out his cosh screaming at United and ran at them, they all backed off. At the same time a few dozen United had managed to get up to the escort to get to us. With a mixture of not wanting to get crushed to death in this escort and wanting to twat these little cunts, a fair few of us managed to break out through the police lines. Anybody would think it was us that had the 300 lads the way they shit themselves. Seeing their faces drop as we got out of the escort and started heading for them was priceless, and I'll never forget it. A few of them stood and had it but most backed right off. It's very easy to act hard when there are lines of GMP in the way to protect you, they didn't seem too keen when there wasn't, that's for sure. The police lines at parts had been broken and there were even police mixed in with the lads in the escort. More police ran over and within seconds we were all back in the escort, being crushed to fuck, it was horrible. It felt like to punish us for breaking out they were now going to crush us all so tight, that we couldn't move. I'm claustrophobic, so I can't stand being in escorts at the best of times, never mind when the police's aim seems to be to crush you to death. I started to proper panic like a little queer, thinking if somebody goes on the floor here, they're going to get crushed to death. A little daft and extreme I know but it really was that bad, for me anyway.

Loads more United came back over to have another go, but this time the police made sure that none of us could get remotely near one another. The trouble died down from that moment on, at least till after the game anyway. I managed to get a ticket for face value £50, which was handy because I had not a penny more on me. Me and my mate got in the ground after I had been searched no less than 4 times. We got into like a bar inside the ground and fuck me it was mad, between me and my mate we must have known every single City fan inside. Not a clue where I was meant to be sat, I just found the bit closest to the United fans and plonked myself there. The game itself ended with them scoring right at the end to knock us out. So here we were in the "Theatre of Dreams" with 70,000 jubilant United fans after their victory and what could you hear United songs? Could you fuck. All you could hear was City songs, 'Blue Moon' rang out from the 3 or so thousand away fans and drained out any United songs. Now there's proper fans for you, that's why Man City have the best fans in the world, just been beat in the last minute by United and knocked out, yet all you can hear is City songs, love it.

Some fat Paki United fan had been pissing us off all game, when he was leaving his seat to go he was mouthing off again. The exit where the United fans nearest to us were leaving, was pretty much just below where we were sat. My mate leant over the metal barriers so far I thought I was going to have to help him up and cracked the fat Paki right on top of his head. This fat prick who had been mouthing off all game, waited until stewards came over, then made a feeble effort to pretend he was trying to get to us. The police and stewards said fuck all to us and dragged him away. Now word had got round to everyone that we would all meet just outside the away end and get everyone together. Once we were all together we would then set off walking back through their area, only this time hopefully with no police escort. The last thing we wanted was loads of little groups of 5 and 10 getting picked off by United and ran off or worse. United would think nothing of 50 of them smashing 5 City on their own, for many of them that's right up their street. That's their idea of doing our firm. As we left the ground I expected there to be similar numbers outside as what we had before the game, I should have known better, this was City and nothing is ever that easy. Me and my mate got out and there were around 20 of us there, where the fuck was everyone else from before? We were all looking at each other and shrugging thinking where's everyone gone? We gave it a few more minutes and a fair few lads came out, we now had more like 50 lads. If we waited any longer it's just asking for GMP to spot us and throw us in an escort. So we decided to make our move there and then and set off walking, not knowing how many United would be waiting for us, as they were let out around 10 minutes previous.

So we were now on our way marching down. To my amazement we didn't see a single one of their lads by the ground or forecourt, or even lurking nearby anywhere. They would be somewhere knocking about; of this I was sure, what is it they say, you're never more than a few feet away from a rat? Our numbers grew the more we advanced, young and old attached themselves on to us lot marching through. We now had about 70 lads in total I would say. The police we went past didn't say a thing, none of them batted an eyelid at us all walking past, we couldn't fucking believe it. If only it could be like this every week... We were bouncing along past their pubs but still no sign of a big firm waiting for us, or of any lads at all to be honest. So 70 handed with no police at all with us bouncing down Chester Road with none of them Munich cunts in sight, this is their area, where are they hiding? This is a big wide road and we were pretty much spread right across it. A few of the younger lads all started chanting "CITY! CITY! CITY!" but were soon told to stop. 70 lads all chanting City is just asking for GMP attention, we're not United; we don't want or need police protection.

Soon after the chants came up of 'CITY!' yet again, this time however it was for a reason. Well there they were; this was where they had been hiding. Bottles, rocks and bricks were pelted over in our direction. It would become all too familiar with United and bricks, but that would be a couple seasons later. They were all coming down this grass verge and onto the main road, all dressed in black looking really scary, as I'm sure you can imagine. We all just fucking ran into them, well I say into them it was more towards them, because after a few punches were traded in the road they all backed off. Nothing short of laughable they were. However around 60 seconds later they appeared yet again, but this time with a lot more lads and this time looking a lot more up for it, game on. Both sides now spread out across this main road, completely filling it. There was a lot of shouting back and forth, as you may expect, gesturing with arms out and all that shit. Two of their lads just came running over into us lot, I remember one was bald, in this black coat that was easily a couple of sizes too big for him. They took a bit of a slap and backed off back to their lads and they all thought better of doing that again, fair play to the pair of them though. We steamed into them time and time again, each time; they would stand and fight us but get pushed back a little bit more each time. Every now and then people broke out of the lines and then going on a mad one and steaming forward on their own. We were getting the better of things and had backed them right back now. Both sides stopped and started to part, which meant one thing – police and to be precise police horses. There were only two horses, but when you have those charging towards you, two horses are enough to make you move right back.

Now one of the police on the horses was a bird, and she was absolutely gorgeous, I mean she was unreal. There were something about her eyes; I just couldn't take my eyes off her at all. She had her cosh out and was trying to smack us all with it; she didn't try and get me with it though. I had now completely lost all interest in what was going on around me, I couldn't even tell you if the fighting was still going on or not, because I didn't give a shit, I was just staring and smiling at this police women. Was this love at first sight? Well if it was it was over before it started, cut short by the arrival of those horrible queers aka Tactical Aid Unit. With the arrival of the TAU United disappeared into the night as quickly as they appeared, nobody saw or heard nothing of them again. We were now held there until more City came and we were all banged in an escort, about 80 of us and escorted back to town. Given Section 27s and all that but by this time it was getting on for 11pm so fuck all else was going to happen that night. Overall I think the day went pretty well, and to a certain extent we proper took the piss down at their place, especially after the game. If we ever had 300 lads out (not that we ever would) and we still got slapped about and ran on our own area, I would be so embarrassed, don't think I would ever go down the match again, but that's just me.

There would be a few more things with United over the coming months. The next big one, that I actually didn't spend the day in the police cells, would occur at Miles Platting. It was a proper bloody affair, literally for me anyway. It was October 2011 and that period would be a very busy few weeks indeed for the Blazing Squad. Many people would have you believe that football violence is dead, or if not dead then at least on the decline. While it's true the police are far more on top of things, not to mention the banning orders, they really can bring a firm to its knees. But the bans only last for so long and there's always a new influx of lads ready to start it all again. But there's no denying it's not week in week out, on the scale it was in the 80s. However this time around October 2011, was a bit of a mad time for all that were involved, with fights with Villa, Napoli and United coming all in the space of 4 weeks. That just goes to show that for Man City youth it wasn't dead, it was still very much alive and kicking. So it was derby day again away at Old Trafford. Many City lads wanted to get a huge mob of us together, and go down their place and take the piss. This did sound good, but in reality all that would have happened is GMP would have been all over us, before we even got anywhere near their ground. We went to the Claremont pub in Moss Side but on arriving our FIOs were already there, so the day was a fuck up before it even started. So we decided to all go down by our ground, with it being an away game the police surely wouldn't be expecting us to head down there. We went in a big pub called Mary D's, more of a shirter pub if anything but we all dived in there anyway. There were about 40 of us in there all without tickets to the game, was a mix of youth and older lads. The plan was to keep in there, nice and out of the way, until after the game. Then try and get more lads down with us and then go and give it United. Simple enough plan don't you think, well this is City, and even the most simple things turn into hard work at times. United weren't for letting on how many they had out, but were obsessed as usual with how many we have. You've got to laugh really, one of the biggest firms numbers wise going and yet they're so obsessed with how many lads little old City have out. I think from bitter experience they know if it's anything like even numbers then they're in trouble.

So there we were in Mary D's by our ground watching the game, and what a cracking game it turned out to be. We didn't just beat them, we tore them apart big time, 6-1 it ended up, 6 fucking 1 at Old Trafford. None of us thought we would ever see anything like that, we were all going mad, hugging and kissing etc. Now this would have pissed the United lads off no end being beat like that. I know it would wind me up to fuck if it were the other way round, makes you wanna take revenge. So the plan was to get more lads down and then go and meet them. But United were proper messing about, stalling for time, so instead of us gaining numbers, we were losing them. It was now a good couple of hours after the game had ended, the day was dragging, I hadn't had a drop of beer and I wanted to fuck off home, there's only so many hours you can sit in a pub, drinking fucking orange j20s, alright for all the others who were getting fucking steaming though. There were now around 30 of us if that, the really annoying thing is there was supposed to be 50 in Rusholme that were supposed to be coming down. The longer it went on, the less likely it were they were going to show. We were never going to back out of the meet due to numbers, not a fucking chance... It did take the piss though knowing how many City were down the road but for whatever reason weren't coming. It's like a tactic United use and we play into their hands every time with it. They keep fucking us about for hours, knowing most lads will get pissed off and think they're not coming again and get off home. Then when they know our numbers are crap, they then want to meet. Knowing full well that regardless how outnumbered we are, we always turn out to meet them. It was sorted for in under an hour's time, yet people were still getting off, it was doing my head in.

We had 25 lads, a mixture of young and old, it was a good bunch of lads don't get me wrong, but would have been nice to have a few more out. The mood between us all just started to change slightly, don't get me wrong not saying we were shitting it, but we just knew it was deffo going to go off. Stuff had been said between both firms and tensions been building up for months now, and today was the day it was all going to spill over. There's a sort of casual saying amongst football lads "a true lad fights not because he hates what's in front of him, but because he loves what's behind him" that saying is true. With United it's a little different, because we do hate them, with United all bets are off, anything goes.

We got everyone together and made our way from Mary D's to go and meet United. We were heading for an area called Miles Platting, which isn't a million miles away from our ground, still a good 15 minute walk though if not more. There were around 25 of us I would say, mix of youth and older lads. Even though the streets were dead and there weren't any GMP around, we were still on the lookout for them, and tried keeping off the main roads just in case. We passed a skip filled with bricks, poles and pieces of wood, many lads grabbed stuff to use as weapons. I personally didn't pick owt up, not really my thing. United said they weren't far away at all and to head for the back of the Navigation pub, there's a big field at the back of it, and that's where they said they will be. It was now proper dark outside, 25 of us mostly tooled up walking through this estate, looking on top to fuck. I was looking all around me down every street half expecting them to be there waiting and jump out. But they insisted they were gonna be where they said, they were on their way from a pub called the Shamrock, I think it was. Now we were just around the corner from where we had arranged to meet them. I'm not really sure why, but I just knew 100 percent that it was going to go off proper and it was going to be fucking mint. I also had a feeling people were going to get badly hurt and as it turned out I wasn't wrong...

We arrived at the boozer and it looked like it wasn't even open, the field at the back of it seemed dead as well. It had a stream running through it with a bridge. It was pitch black so we couldn't see far but we could see far enough to see there was no cunt there. Another minute or so went by and there was still no sign of them at all. Two young kids like 11 year olds or something went past us on push bikes "eyar lads there's about, well there is shit loads of men down there, if that's who youse are after". No sooner had those kids told us that we could now see them, right in the distance, on the far end of the field. Now they were still fairly far away from us, but now close enough to see that there was certainly more

Me (aged 8)

Me and the lads in 80s gear

Me and some of the lads

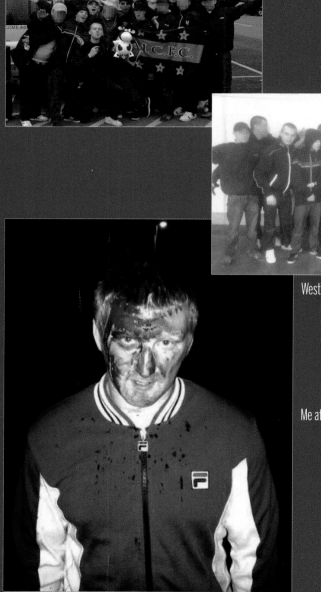

West Ham (away) 2009

East Ham tube, back in 2

Me after United, 2011

A mixture of young and old in Rusholme

Me and a few of the lads

Liverpool at home

Me and Rodgers, Dry Bar, 2013

Irish Paul, Bez, Andy and me in Ratcliffe, 2015

Yates's in town, 2014

Me n Big Ant after our fight at the City Boxing Do, 2013

Me, Rodgers n Blood in Blackpool

Me, Brooke's n Baz 20

Oxford Road, 2013

Wigan away, 2007

On the estate by the ground,
filming for Football Fight Club

Zulus away

Barnsley at home, 2013

Back in 2012. The day we won the league

Tank, me and Niall in Rusholme, 2013

of them than of us, but would we expect anything else? I would say there was a good 40 of them if not more; we were now caught in two minds about what to do. We were on the higher ground, so do we just stand where we are and let them come to us, or think fuck it come on then United let's see how brave you really are, and just run into them. We held the higher ground and all stood there and let them come to us, but would that decision come back to haunt us? It's mad seeing them getting closer and closer to us, knowing that your about to have some big fucking war with them. Needless to say my heart was beating like mad; I can almost guarantee that I would have been the only stone cold sober person present, on either side as well. It's derby day, and this was it, a chance to smash these Munich cunts all over, remind them that this City is ours, and we run the show.

"City get together, come on get fucking together, nobody go anywhere and we will do these cunts good and proper" this and various other comments we said amongst ourselves. Last words of reassurance before going into battle I suppose. United were getting closer, they all seemed to burst out the darkness at once and spread out about 50 metres in front of us. We stood firm holding our position, nobody moving forward to them, just holding where we were. "Come on United use fucking wannit yeah? Here we are" meaning come and get us basically. They pushed on getting closer by the second, the lads who all had the bricks lost their cool and lobbed them at United. I say lost their cool because they threw them too early, if they had only waited an extra few seconds, I'm sure they would have done some serious damage. Instead they landed a few feet in front of United, fucking mint.

Now I bet you can see where this is going now can't you... surprise surprise United picked up the bricks, moved a few feet closer, and returned fire. I saw this brick come flying over, heading straight for my fucking head. Everything just went into like slow motion, it's a mad thing and hard to get across, but time stood still for what felt like ages. Now as you can imagine various things were running through my mind, how the fuck do I stop this from smashing into my face. Do I duck and let it possibly smash into one of the lads behind me? Or do I try block it with my hands, like try and catch it sort of thing. Even side-step out of the way, so which one did I do? The sensible thing, what a normal person would do and do anything to stop it smashing my head. Nah did I fuck, no not me, what I did I do? Well I just put my head down, and rammed my head right into the brick. My mate said he wouldn't describe it as the brick hitting me, he would say it was more like I head-butted the brick. Definitely not the smartest thing I've done but certainly not the stupidest which is a bit worrying. Fuck off, smash I've put one on a brick, wouldn't advise it to anyone put it that way. My head just split open instantly, blood was everywhere. It was like someone had turned a tap on above my head; it was running down my face that thick that I couldn't see at all for a couple of seconds. My brain clicked back out of slow motion mode, and back into real time. Not only was it the brick, it was the pointed edge of the brick as well. It had knocked me a step or two back but it didn't make me go down or owt like that. I felt a shooting pain all round my head, one of my ears started to ring like mad. I went a little dizzy for a split second then had to rest my arm on someone's shoulder next to them just for a couple of seconds, then I felt alright again. I had both arms up to my face, whipping the constant shower of blood away from my ears; it was a battle I was losing. No sooner had I used both my sleeves of my Fila to whip my face and my eyes, the blood had gushed out of my cut and back down my face once more, blocking my vision a little to say the least.

A few more bricks came flying over, a second wave of them, these must have been what they had brought with them I'm guessing, fuck knows. Another brick hit me, this one I didn't see coming at all, and this one hurt a lot more. It had got me right in my fucking balls. I wasn't having a good time of it here at all, a brick in the head, a brick in the balls, and the fight hadn't even fucking started yet! I'm sure they must have been just fucking aiming for me you know. My mates said to us after "yeah Carl we heard you like goo ahhhhh in pain when the brick got your head" nah I said it wasn't that one; it was the one in my balls. The moment it got me right there I sort of crouched down in pain, what made it worse was I had the tightest jeans on ever. I guess the pain in my balls took away from the pain in my head!

We were now only a matter of feet away from each other, through my somewhat impaired vision, I could see well enough to see that some of their lads didn't want to know. Their older lot were at the front turning round to the rest of them pointing and screaming at them to get forward with them. We didn't know it at the time, but that would be a huge turning point in the fight. A United lad later said that if we had all ran at them, then they were off. Yet again we thought we were doing the correct thing just holding our ground, and letting them come to us. There was now a standoff, both sides maybe cautious to be the first ones to go steaming in to the other. I suppose we all just went half way and met in the middle, it was now going off big time, a mass fucking brawl like something off a film. Lads on both sides getting stuck in and proper going for it and also lads on both sides it would be fair to say shitting it and wishing they were sat back in the pub. Not even going to say I was right there bang at the front, first one in blah blah, because I wasn't at all. There were a good five or so City a couple of feet in front of me, they know who they are. I was there or thereabouts anyway, in my defence my balls were fucking killing, plus I was struggling to see properly.

So the fighting went on. The hatred from both sides was just so bad, as gay as I know it sounds, it really wouldn't have surprised me if someone got kicked to death that day. We were doing alright, more than holding our own but after a while their extra 15-20 lads, were starting to show. As it went on bit by bit they pushed us back. Speaking about numbers our numbers weren't what they had been, I don't think we even had 20 anymore, let alone the 25 that we started with. It was fucking carnage, lads in the river, lads on the floor, lads taking a fucking kicking, shouts of "come on" and "stand" and various other stuff, were clearly heard. I'm weird me at times, in fights at City and as well as in the ring, I often find myself day dreaming or just focusing on random shit, and today would be no different. Those two kids on their bikes were back with a couple of their mates watching the fighting, some shouting 'go on United' some shouting for City. A little lad there with ginger hair shouting 'go on City don't give up, youse are winning'. How I even noticed them, let alone could hear them with all what was going on around me, I don't know, but it stuck in my head anyway, but those words rung louder in my head than my fucking ear buzzing. We steamed back into them again, punches were traded, we were matching them blow for blow, and it seemed to go on forever. But in the end there were too many of them and we were pushed back onto the bridge. We knew if they had got on to the bridge and backed us off that it was game over. "Stand City, fucking stand" echoed out, but to some it fell on deaf ears, others didn't need to be told. There were a couple of older lads in front of me trying to hold United off and a couple of my lot near me and the rest were behind me on the bridge. The fighting went on, United coming forward, bit by bit every time. They were now on the bridge with us as well. Trying to fight them cunts and hold them back, while having to keep wiping blood out of my eyes because I could barely see, was no easy task.

United now steamed the bridge about 20 of them at once, luckily the bridge wasn't the widest so you could only get maybe 4 or so across width wise at one time. Pockets of fighting were going on all around us. Rodgers was to one side of me and we were holding them back. Rodgers hadn't had a good time of it either; he had been booted to fuck on the floor and been cut by a blade in his stomach. I had 3 maybe 4 of them round me now, all falling over each other to punch me the most. I put my head down with my arms over my face, partly to protect myself, partly to wipe the blood. I could just see loads of trainers all around me, so I kept my head down and started throwing punches at them. I caught a couple of them and they all bounced right back, for a few seconds at least. To make matters worse there were City lads on the bridge behind me, they were pushing me into United to give them a head start when they turned and ran. Now that really did take the piss, not what we needed at all. It was just no use trying to fight them anymore, United ran at us one last time on the bridge and we all got off. They chased us over the bridge back in the direction we had come from. A few of them carried on over the bridge after us but as we turned back to give it them, they realised they were outnumbered, and thought better of it and ran back over the bridge again.

Nobody really knew what to say, I know I certainly didn't have a fucking clue what to say. We all just looked around at each other in disbelief at what just happened. We had just been done off United. Didn't exactly start counting lads at the end there, so fuck knows the true number left, it wasn't anywhere near 25 put it that way, at a guess maybe 16, 17. Police sirens could now be heard, which was our queue to leave. One of the lads started asking where one of the older lads was, he couldn't still be over there could he? My heart just sank with the thought that one of my mates had somehow been left behind over there. With that me, Brooks and Blood sprinted back over the bridge shouting 'CITY!' I guess hoping they will get off thinking there were loads of us, not fucking three of us. All United got off back the way they had come across the field, however that probably had more to do with the police sirens rather than us three. We were right to go back, one of the lads had somehow been left behind, and I thought my head was bad until I saw his. They had proper booted him in on the floor, his face was unrecognisable. I felt fucking horrible inside, how had this happened to one of us? How the fuck did nobody see him still there? I felt that bad I wanted to fucking cry. I can't find the words to describe how bad his face was, his cheekbones must have been jumped on loads and given way, because his face just had no shape, was just round and swollen to fuck. While we were asking silly fucking questions to him like "are you alright mate?" a GMP van pulled up and loads of them dived out and surrounded us. They weren't football police or owt like that, just standard GMP. They asked us what's gone on to which we didn't really say much and just shrugged our shoulders. They said they know we're Man City, and they know what's just gone on with United. They produced a couple of camera and all started filming us and giving us Section 27s. To which I couldn't believe our luck, I mean if they're giving us Section 27 us they're obviously not arresting us, lucky or what.

There were now police dotted about everywhere. It came through on the radio to one of the GMP officers next to us, that maybe the fight was a little more serious than they first thought. One of them said on the radio "Sarge we have found a finger""I'm sorry can you repeat that""Erm yeah we have found a finger, a United lad's finger, it has been bitten off by the looks of it". The police were a little taken back by this, one person there had a little smile and chuckle to himself anyway, I'll just leave it as that. After being kept there by police for around half an hour we were eventually allowed on our way. One of the lads got a taxi with another lad to hospital; I made my way back towards the ground, where the rest of the lads had gone. I went in the toilets of Mary D's to try and clean myself up a bit. It must have been around an hour since the fighting but my head was still bleeding, although not as badly as before, thank god. When it actually happened, it didn't hurt as much as I suppose it should have, but now an hour on I was in some discomfort. My head was throbbing; it felt like it was going to fucking pop, it was now proper killing.

I hadn't had a beer all day but I fucking needed one now, so we all went across to The Manchester, and I necked 3 or 4 pints rapid. We all had a few beers in there and spoke about what happened, or in other words what the fuck went wrong. Then we all made our way to town, and then got off our various separate ways home. I went to hospital to get my head stitched back together, which was no fun at all. 12 staples I had on my head but before that they had to get all the bits of brick out of my head with tweezers. Now the nurse as fit as she was, was clumsy as fuck, every now and then she would by mistake, push the bits of brick further inside my head, and then have to go even further down with the tweezers to remove them. I wouldn't wish that on anybody, there were enough bits of brick, and cement and shit in my head, that's for sure anyway. I think it was 3 of us ended up in hospital and 2 or 3 of them, with broken ribs and not forgetting the missing finger. Rodgers had been stabbed twice in 2 weeks, so he wasn't having much luck either. Not forgetting Garvey aka David Haye with his broken toe as well. If we had just gone fuck it and full on just ran at them, it would have been so very different. Oh well shit happens and what's done is done, United got the better of us on that occasion. So that was Miles Platting, a fight which we never should have lost...

There have been a few scraps since, there would have been an awful lot more if the police didn't get in the way. Before I was given my radius banning order in 2012, the police and our FIOs had decided they wanted me out of the way. Near enough every single game as soon as they saw me, I would be given a Section 27 and then more than likely would end up being arrested. On derby day this was a frequent occurrence, I think I got arrested on 3 maybe 4 derby days on the trot around then. I was really starting to get the hump with the police around this time, not even so much the FIOs, more them dickheads who jump out of the vans with an attitude problem (TAU). "We're the hardest firm in Manchester, fight us" was a favourite saying of theirs, when there was loads of them and a handful of us. Strange how when there was a lot of us lot, they were surprisingly respectful, and even slightly timid at times but there you go. But the main thing that got on my tits about GMP was how sly there were, buying people with money. Paying people to be informants and grass on their own mates, I refuse to bury my head in the sand and pretend it doesn't happen, because unfortunately it does.

In 2012 we had United at our place, we had a good 80 maybe 90 lads outside The Townley. It was nearing kick-off time, so we all set off down the ginnel, to go find United on the main road and give it them. Although the police had other ideas, me and about 25 of my lot were pulled aside and all filmed. The vast majority, actually I think everyone else, was let on their way, apart from me. I was held there and told I wasn't going anywhere; I was then pulled to one side by Cliff Lea, City's main footie Intel at the time and some high ranking GMP officer with him. I had a rough idea what was coming next, not really sure why or how I knew, I just did. Before a word was said to me I just started laughing and said "listen this isn't for me, just nick me now, or let me on my way." "Mr Moran calm down, you're not in any trouble we just want a little chat". Well this was even worse than I thought, they were talking to me as if we were good mates. I was half expecting him to put his arm round my fucking shoulder next. It was basically put to me as "Carl it's not grassing on your mates, it's giving us information, in fact you'll be helping keep them out of trouble". They wanted me to tell them where we were, where we were going, what we were planning. I just laughed and like I said at the start this isn't for me; you've got the wrong kid. "Carl just have a think about it, there's big money to be earned, we know you've got a kid and you're skint, so just think about it yeah, a grand a month cash, free tickets home and away, free travel etc". Fuckinell they were pulling all the stops out here weren't they. Nah it's not for me, I wouldn't do that to my mates for all the money in the world, let alone 12 grand a year, my mates are more important than money. As cringey as that sounds its fucking true isn't it? It just makes you wonder though, if they did the same pitch to others, would their answer be the same as mine, I would certainly like to think so... They seemed pissed off that I wouldn't take them up on their slimy little offer, which looking back I took great offence at because it's like they thought I was the sort of kid who would grass on his pals for money, cheeky bastards. I was eventually given a Section 27 and let on my way, so I begrudgingly headed back towards town on my own. I soon bumped into a couple of lads, they were going to town to watch it and they blagged me to go with them. Now the pub was right by the ground and it was obvious the police would clock me around there. How I thought I wasn't going to get nicked god only knows. Got in the pub, went to the bar to get my j20 and a packet of Mini cheddars and sat down to watch the game. No sooner had I opened my Mini cheddars about 15 GMP came in didn't they, gripped me and dragged me outside. I asked if I'm alright bringing my Mini cheddars with me to eat in the van, a simple no would have been good enough. Instead they threw my Mini cheddars on the floor and stamped on them, what's all that about? I was well hungry as well.

While we're on the subject of GMP, there was an all too common case of police brutality on big Craig. This took place after we had it with United, well I say had it with, slapping about United would be more accurate. It was another home game against United; I had once again already been nicked a few hours previous. City were at the Leigh Arms, about 70 lads all together. A car pulled over to two of the younger lads outside and shouted "United are coming get ready you blue cunts", then drove off rapid. A good few minutes had gone by but still no sign of United, so people made their way down towards the ground. So the 70 City were on their way towards the ground to find United but it wouldn't be long before the police found them on the estate near the ground. So everyone split up and got off in different directions with the police giving chase. Many City headed for the main road and made for the away end, hoping to bump into United. Turns out their luck was in, about 20 City there walked right into 25 United lads. City lads steamed right into them, after a brief fight back from United, they were already trying to get off. United was getting slapped about and pleading for police protection, which I've seen them do before. There was just normal City fans shouting "go on City smash them" as United were running off. The fighting ended when all United had ran away, United claim they got off because of the police, but the police all ran down after United had started running off. These United lads weren't kids either, all in their 30s and 40s. City were now back on the estate, running down the numerous alleys and ginnels, that we know only too well.

Craig split off from the other lads on his own, in an attempt to get away from TAU he slipped left round this corner, and ran straight into the arms of 2 GMP. Bang on cue a TAU van pulled up, the first one out runs over and knees Craig in the balls. He was then pulled to the floor and held down by a couple of them, while some more GMP took turns punching and booting him. They picked him up off the floor and threw him into a van; the blood from his bleeding face, splattered the side of their police vehicle. They removed his coat and put him in cuffs, the cheeky cunts then used his coat to wipe the blood off their van. More police were now on the scene, coming over giving him sly digs and kicks, as Craig lay slumped against the van, in cuffs on the floor. Now Craig's not exactly the type to start moaning about it, he was laughing going "is that it, is that fucking it, bunch of queers aren't ya" which was probably not the best thing to say at that time. The police then lost it with him even more; they formed a circle around him, blocking the view from anybody walking by seeing what was going on. They kicked him back to the floor, from his slumped upright position. One held his legs, while another dug his knee into his neck, so that Craig couldn't move, his arms still obviously in cuffs. Some police would get his fingers and snap them and try and break them, while others were more interested in punching his face and his balls. All the time being egged on by the rest of the officers, who seemed to be enjoying themselves. This went on for some time. City's football Intel officers arrived with a camera but were quickly told to stop filming, which they did. The TAU booted him a couple more times, then threw him in their van. Listen, when you run around doing what we do at football you can't moan about the odd dig off the police or the odd smack by the coshes, that's fair enough. What they did there though was too fucking far, he said they were obsessed with snapping his fingers and punching him in his balls, shouting out "get his balls" how fucking gay is that!

The next derby day would also see me nicked fairly early on, so I missed all of the fun. There were decent numbers of City out that day, but as always it's the problem of trying to get everybody together. There were a good 50 City in a pub called The Shakespeare, just off Market Street near Primark. They decided to move off and head for Deansgate, which is the United area of town. City dived in a boozer just off Deansgate, but the police were all over, so they decided to move on. As they were moving on, good old TAU pulled up, half the lads managed to get out; the other half got kept there. They moved on towards St Peter's Square, where by chance they bumped into some United kids, the chant went up 'CITY! CITY!' and it went off. There were a few punches traded until United ran off. Now it is worth pointing out at this point, there was more City than United (for a change). City ran after them. Now either Rodgers really wanted to catch them, or the other lad's fitness perhaps wasn't what it once was, but either way he ended up catching them on his own. That's the thing with running after firms, I always try and keep us together, and make a point of not letting anybody run too far ahead, and getting caught out on their own. The last 5 or so United that were running, saw it was just him on his own, and turned round and had it with him.

'CITY! CITY!' rang out as the rest of the lads caught up with Rodgers and United were soon back on their toes. City would soon be following suit as vans of police turned up moments later. Throughout that day it consisted of City bumping into United, slapping them and chasing them off, then police coming and chasing them off. Now I'm not going to lie, United do have some good lads but most are just fucking cowards who would be out of their depth in a puddle. United even took to driving round in a van and jumping out tooled up, until they took a slap and got off again, even that wasn't working for them. Earlier on in the day around 150 United lads were escorted through Piccadilly gardens, around 60-70 City went up to greet them. United's arses went big time, it was supposed to be fucking hilarious and I'm gutted I missed it. There were United lads running and jumping on buses, getting on trams to get away, the lot. There's footage of it on YouTube but to be honest it's not the best, it's hard to make out what's what. You can just make out United getting off, then City being chased by police, through the bus station at Piccadilly gardens in town.

In 2011, we played United in the Community Shield at Wembley. As you would expect there was an awful lot of City travelling down there that day. We were making our own way down about 18 of us on a mini bus and meeting all the other lads down there. It must have taken 4 maybe even 5 hours getting down there and that was only to fucking Watford as well. We then got the over ground to Harrow-on-the-Hill I think it's called, after a lot of messing about, getting off at the wrong stop and having to walk. We soon gave up on asking people for directions, as we remembered this is London and the majority of people can't even speak English, let alone are English. So without any directional assistance from the not so local locals, we finally made it to the pub. It had taken us that long to find this pub, which by the time we got there, everybody was leaving for the match. There was a proper mob of us there, mainly older lads if I am being honest, around 150 or more. The police were trying to get us in an escort, without a great deal of success. There weren't anywhere near enough police to escort a firm of this size. Word was that it was on to meet United at the bottom of Wembley Way, 15 minutes before kickoff. Why the bottom of Wembley Way I have no fucking idea but United said they would be there bang on 15 minutes before kickoff anyway. We would both have to time it right, because just 60 seconds apart could see one firm being escorted 100 metres away from the other. We had 150 easy, I mean I'm saying 150 there were some who swear blind we had more than 200. Either way it was a big firm of City and god only knows how many United had, so if this goes off on Wembley Way, with these sorts of numbers involved, it's going to be fucking mental. I couldn't wait to see United lad's faces drop when they saw our numbers, because I knew for a fact they would. They just take it for granted there always going to heavily outnumber us, 3–1 probably most games, but I doubt they were expecting this many City, together as one firm.

So we managed to get on the same tube and made the short trip to Wembley. We couldn't have timed it any better if we tried, got of the tube with about 17 minutes to kick off, so two minutes before they said they would be at the bottom of Wembley Way. We were all bang up for this, those red cunts aren't going to know what's hit them. We all moved down in groups of 20 and 30, so it didn't look daft 150 of us stopped dead together. A few minutes went by and still no sign of them, lads were just saying these are a joke, they're not going to show and started to head up Wembley Way to the game. It was now about 5 minutes to kick off and the police started ushering us towards the ground, when all you heard was 'UNITED! UNITED! UNITED!'. Yeah here they were, making as much noise as they possibly can, to attract police attention, they really are utter mongs. All day we had been led to believe there was some giant United firm about, of well over 300 strong, and I'll be honest I believed it. They all came rushing down but there wasn't 300, wasn't anywhere near 200, in fact there was about 100 of them, if not less. for the first time ever we outnumbered them. Police now rushed to get in between the two firms, which United practically begged them to do so, with their gay chanting. Which they were still doing like a broken record. All the lads that had turned and gone to the game a minute or so before, were now rushing back in the opposite direction to us. "Come on then Munichs" we cried as we steamed straight into them, pushing them right back and sending a few of their lads on their arses. They went down I think more from the sheer force of us piling into them, you know the momentum of us all running, rather than actual punches at that point. Most of them just started backing right off straight away, some of them were game for it though and made a go of it. All their years of relying on numbers in fights, now they didn't have the numbers, they were even more useless than usual. United were getting fucking leathered all over Wembley Way.

Police had managed to get in between us now and were pushing us towards the ground. We charged at them again and again, backing the police off and United's lot at the same time. The police lines had their backs on United and were solely facing us, I don't recall seeing any of them not facing us. Every now and then lads would break through the police lines and be able to get into United, who just blatantly on the whole, didn't want to know. We were stood there laughing at them, shouting "youse are fucking shit aren't ya" with no reply at all from them. We were only a matter of feet away from each other, with police in the middle. They were proper hiding behind the police and making little or no effort to get to us. This went on; us smashing the police right back and United fucking shitting themselves, in case we all got through, which unfortunately we never managed to do. But the look on their faces was just priceless, the eyes don't lie, and in their eyes you could just see fear. Police horses soon came galloping down and that was the end of that. I don't know what pisses me off more TAU or police on horses, both cunts. After a couple of minutes of getting trampled on by horses and whacked with coshes, we made it into the ground. Not sure how many City actually had tickets and how many just jibbed in but every single City away I've been to there's always far more people, than there are seats. We arranged to meet after the game but them lot were nowhere to be seen. As far as we were concerned we had embarrassed them enough before the game. Even had a text off a United lad saying "heard what went on before game, we had loads a lads missing, but fair play". I was amazed they normally deny all knowledge of anything, "it wasn't our lads" would be one of their usual lines.

We made our way back to Watford, where the coach was waiting for us, well the mini bus, all of us except poor Rodgers, who was nicked for the trouble on Wembley Way. Although we didn't get to proper smash them because police saved them, it had still been a laugh and a good day out. We were still half hoping to bump into some of their lads at the services on the way back. We pulled into some services at Stone or Stafford or something daft, basically near Stoke. One of our lads Jake has got a thing for getting his kit off; he gets wrecked and gets naked. We're all used to him doing it, so just leave him to it. Anyway were all getting off our bus at these services, when this big 52 seater pulls in; it's only fucking United isn't it. We all charged at the coach, throwing bottles and all sorts at it. Lads trying to pull open the doors to get them out, the coach soon changed its mind about stopping, and started driving off, with a naked Jake running after them. Fuck knows what they thought was going on, being chased by a bollock naked teenager at the services, I think that scared them more than the beating they would have got off us. We went in the services, which as usual got robbed blind and went on our way. That for me is what away days are all about, not such much the fighting, more just having a laugh with your mates, nothing beats that.

In September 2013 we would play United, at our place in the league. The match was a 4 o'clock kick off, which I imagine pissed GMP off no end, as it meant the banning orders counted for fuck all, early on in the day at least. You see the bans kick in 4 hours prior to kickoff and end 6 hours after it's finished, so it meant up until 12, we were not breaching anything by being out. It pretty much covers the vast majority of the day, meaning you can't normally go out. As it turned out, I stayed out from the morning till gone 6, that day anyway, out of the banning area, wouldn't breach my ban now would I? We knew there was around 50 City meeting up in the Millstone in the Northern Quarter part of town. But we all decided to meet up in the Fallowfield/ Rusholme area instead because it was rumoured United would be meeting up in neighbouring Hulme. As it turned out United didn't even go there at all, they were on my side of town, in a snooker hall on Cheetham Hill Road. We didn't know any of this until much later on though. Us younger lot met up fairly early on Wilmslow Road in a pub called Ford Maddox, it was only about 9.30am. There wasn't a huge mob of us or owt daft like that, only around 25 but GMP were driving past all the time giving us a good look, so we decided to move on. We moved on to a pub in Rusholme called The Albert. We got a good 30 lads in there and waited for the call off United. Not that we just sit there waiting to see if they call or not, we had rang a few times, they said basically give them an hour to get it together, then they'll call us. They rang back, said they will meet us in Moss Side, well out the way, just give them half an hour, sound we thought, buzzing with that. Well half an hour went by and still we heard fuck all, I'm sure you can see where this is going now. We had 30 in there waiting, and 50-60 in town but nobody had seen United anywhere. It was still around 3 hours to go before kick-off time, so was still more than enough time left for them clowns to get their act together. Two of City's FIOs soon turned up and came inside the pub, well more like outside, because we were out the back in the beer garden. They just wanted a nosey, seeing who was out and what banned lads, if any, were present, which was just me and Rodge, I think. Then had a quick chat with us, told me I need to teach these young kids how to fight. Which was a friendly dig at one of the lads, who was sporting a big black eye from Cardiff a week or so previous. They then fucked off out of the pub and sat in the car outside. This didn't concern me too much because we could always dive out the back and lose them easily enough on the estate. So that left nothing much more to do than get wrecked and have a laugh, so that's what we did.

More time went by and still nothing, so I gave them a ring, to see what the story with them lot was. To be fair to the lad he's a sound kid, not a dick or owt, he just says it how it is, he was just like "Carl we have been piss poor today, there was loads of us out on Cheetham Hill Road this morning but now nobody wants to know, 5 of us have come out the way to meet youse, the rest said they would follow but clearly aren't, so there's literally just 5 of us". Well you certainly can't fault his honesty. Got off the phone to him and told the lads and they were all in fucking stitches, laughing their heads off. United are supposed to be this huge massive firm, can only get 5 lads who wanna meet little old City. I told United just do your best to get more lads together and we will even come to youse, whenever you're ready. More time went by and still nothing from them, most of our lot were now heading off down to our ground. I just rang them back and put it to them, look there's five of youse, I'll bring 5 now and meet what you say? They seemed bang up for it. So the plan was for me and Rodgers to go and meet them on our own, just to make sure there wasn't like 20 of them, then we would get the others and have it with them. As we were setting off to meet them, their phones were going straight to voicemail. I couldn't fucking believe it, we tried and tried and tried but nothing, phones were off. The game itself ended 4-1 to City, we battered them. As I was getting on the bus going home, the United kid rang back and said he's sorry his phone died, and his just had to buy a charger for it now. If it was anybody else from United I would think it was just bullshit, but he isn't like most United, he seems genuine and honest, so I took his word for it. But that was that for that day anyway.

So that's United anyway. On their day with the sort of numbers they can pull, their capable of turning anyone over. It's happened to us in the past, and I'm sure at some stage it will happen once again. But make no mistake we're the number 1 firm in Manchester, always have been, always will be. THIS CITY IS OURS!

STOKE

'YOU'RE STOKE, YOU'RE A FUCKING JOKE', is a song often song directed at Stoke fans at the football. Let me tell you right off though that Stoke's hooligan element, is far from a joke. Stoke are held in quite high regard from the majority of lads that I talk to, from various firms up and down the country anyway. That being said I just can't mention Stoke without bringing up their accent, possibly the least intimidating accent in the country. They seem very much into their clobber, dead smartly dressed, always with daft long floppy hair as well, fuck knows what that's all about. They seem to have fairly decent numbers as well, I've never heard of them taking shit numbers anywhere anyway. Over the years I become good mates with one of their main lads, he's been up here for drinks and I've been down there etc. Overall the Stoke kids are alright, always a bit of "friendly banter" shall we call it between a few of us and a few of them, but it's all harmless fun really.

The first time we had it with Stoke it wasn't with their youth, in fact it was their proper older boys, The Naughty 40. Proper old school lads they were, that carried a very big reputation from years gone by. So it was 2008 and we played Stoke in the league, at our place. Most of the day was pretty boring, mundane, standard stuff, met up on Oldham Street, police came, so we went the canal way to the ground. Fuck all happened before the game, and if memory serves, we didn't even see any of their lads, not a single one. After the game

there was supposed to be a big S
again if there was, I certainly didn
off making our way back to town.
was a proper "can't be arsed today a
Word got round that it had gone o
by the ground, but that GMP were ;
it, the one day I actually don't both
We got back to town and went in
City lads were spread out in several pubs, across the Northern
Quarter. We soon made our way to Weatherspoons, the one
near Piccadilly gardens, which is so often used as an away fan
pub. I can't remember if someone rang us to head over there
or what but we made the relatively short walk down there
anyhow. There were only about 3 or 4 of us walking down
there.

On our way down there we were stopped by some black
guy, he had some mad dreadlocks, he started asking us where
we were going. We didn't really pay too much attention to
him, because we just thought he were a homeless person,
or a smack head wanting change or something. We arrived
at Spoons and I definitely didn't expect to see what I did
in front of me. At the bar and pretty much covering all the
front of the pub, were around 50 lads. Now these lads just
stood out like a sore thumb to me, it was clear they weren't
from Manchester. To me they just looked like a bunch of
farmers, all dead big blokes with woolly jumpers on and daft
hair. A lot of them in Stone Island and Barbour, so I suppose
it would be fair to say they were "casual farmers". A few of
them were looking over at us, none of them said owt though,
probably because there were only 3 or 4 of us. We spotted 2
of City's older lads further down in the pub. Apparently they
had been in there having a beer and Stoke's lads had said
something to them, so they had rang City lads telling them

...ke are in Spoons. Was something daft like that ...I I don't know about the other lads with me but ...in a great hurry to start a fight with all these, with ...umbers we had in there, we would have been killed. A ...ndful of more City lads came in but only like another 5 or so, so there were still only around 10 of us in there. We just sat down more towards the back of Spoons, just keeping ourselves to ourselves, drinking and waiting. Then that black guy, the tramp from outside earlier, comes in and was sat talking to all Stoke's lot, which confused us a little. Anyway turns out the black guy wasn't a tramp after all, he was one of their older lot, in the Naughty 40 book and everything. Funny as fuck that we thought he was some homeless guy asking for change or whatever. Didn't help that he was stood against a wall, where most of the ones begging for change sit. So when he's been asking us where we were going, he must have been trying to arrange something. They had the odd lad in their late 20s and 30s but near enough all of them were well in their 40s, some could have been in their 50s. I was only 18 at the time and I think my mate with me was only 16 so we were only kids really.

With each passing minute, more City came into Spoons. Now we had around 20 maybe 25 lads in there, so it was undoubtedly going to go off and I just knew it was going to be fucking mint. Do we wait for more lads, or do we just kick it off with what we had now? There was only ever going to be one real option. "Fucking come on Stoke" it had started just going off, not too far from the doorway to Spoons. Bottles and glasses were smashing all over lad's heads. The fighting had now spilled outside, so there was now a mad rush to get through the doors. Stoke were already all outside, they were sat by the door, so got out sooner. There was only around 10 City outside fighting with them all, we all ran right out and straight into Stoke, from behind them. So there was City on both sides with Stoke sandwiched in the middle. Blows were traded; digs and kicks were flying left, right and centre. A few more of our older lot came running down and we were now separated into two groups, as you may expect. We were on the Market Street side, with the Stoke lads on the Piccadilly train station side. There was now a small stand-off, or as I like to think of it a breather. Objects were slung at each other, by both sides. Insults were traded as well as more stuff being thrown and after the brief stand-off the fighting resumed, with both sides steaming into each other once more. Not even going to lie, at this point I still hadn't even thrown a single punch; I wasn't close enough to do so. We were all bunched in far too tightly, and there were a good few people in front of me, I suppose I was sandwiched bang in the middle of everyone. This was no fucking good at all, I might as well not have fucking been there, so I barged my way to the side, so I could get right to the front. Just as I made my way to the front I was nearly hit by a big fucking traffic cone, I mean who the fuck in a fight throws a traffic cone? Then from both sides traffic cones and road signs, as well as the usual bottles and what not, were being launched about. Not really into all that throwing stuff me but at least there were no bricks flying about!

A handful of these N40 came bouncing right over, what a surprise they come over in my direction, me being just a little kid. I was mad into my boxing at the time; I had an unlicensed fight the following week after this as well. I was only tiny, like less than 10 stone, so I must have looked like an easy target. Right I'll show these fucking inbred cunts a thing or too, I thought as they came right over towards me, one looking old enough to pass for my granddad. He just stepped forward and bang, I've hit him with a right, just under his eye, on his cheek bone, stopped him dead in his tracks. Bang, I cracked the old cunt again, same punch, same place, fucking top dig. This time he sort of turned away and bent down a little and staggered back, his legs had gone. I was buzzing, like a little giddy kid I turned round to see if my mates had seen me crack him. Before I had chance to turn back round, I've got two of them on me smacking me, so I've started fighting with those two. More City came over, and they backed off to the rest of their lads. We went into them again, but this time I think a few of ours took some good cracks, because we all seemed to back off.

Then all I heard was "they've got one of ours, they've got a City lad" I looked and there was one lad on his own, right in the middle of them getting battered from all other. Instinct now took over, not a word was said, nothing more needed to be said. Every single City lad sprinted forward at once and we pushed them right back. That moment seemed to be the turning point for the whole fight. After that we started to back them off, they had a few lads dropping to the floor. Some of the lads getting back up, others lay unconscious on the floor. "Your too fucking old, now fuck off back to Stoke" I heard directed at one of their lads on the floor. It was only the same guy I cracked a couple of times moments earlier. We were now starting to pick them apart, and were proper getting the better of them. Give them their dues though they were good lads. They might have been backed off but not a single one of them ran off. We were no longer two separate groups; it was just random fighting going off all over. With more signs being thrown about and bottles and glasses too. I didn't see them, but there's no mistaking the sound of smashing glass on the pavement. Then someone shouted, "Get him, get the black bastard" it was only our tramp mate with the locks from earlier. He was slyly whacking lads, then moving on and doing the same again to someone else. But his escapades hadn't gone unnoticed. Just saw him getting set upon by a few City, who were swinging him about by his hair from one side to the other, booting fuck out of him. I pulled my mate out of this mêlée, and we started booting fuck out of this Stoke lad, that had pulled a City lad to the floor. What did I see out of the corner of my eye, the black guy up to his old tricks again? He must have somehow got away from all the lads, who were giving him a proper kicking, just seconds before. He was walking round smacking lads proper sly, from the side and behind yet again. The black guy was grabbed by his daft dread locks and was getting leathered. There were now two maybe three Stoke lads laid out on the deck, proper out for the count. I can honestly say not a single person touched them while they were like that. Another 10 or so City came running down Newton Street, better late than never I suppose. But for Stoke the damage had already been done. Stoke were now all over the place, some were pissing blood and most looking in a bad way. We ran at them once more, "CITY! CITY!" the chant went up. This time they must have just had enough, because they turned and ran.

We didn't have much chance to chase after them, police vans pulled up, on the crossing to Portland Street and Newton Street. They didn't jump out at first; soon more police were on the way, with the sirens getting louder. Now it was definitely our time to leave. Was a really daft place to have a fight, funnily enough a few years later, would be near enough the exact same spot, for another fight with Stoke. Bang in the middle of Piccadilly and Market Street, it's a stupid place for a fight but sometimes these things just happen. Half of GMP were soon on the scene, there were fucking loads of them, but we were long gone. We split up and dived down the various side streets around the Northern Quarter. At the time it was a really big thing for me, and the few young lads that were present. The N40 was a big name, I mean we were just kids, but we had heard all about them, and we had just smashed them to pieces. It was a nice scalp to say the least, I remember going home fucking buzzing my tits off about it. That fight with N40 outside Spoons would be the first, but by no means last fight with Stoke. Over the coming years we would have numerous scraps with them lot, at our place and at theirs.

We made the trip down to their place a few times. Midweek cup games and a few times in the league as well. We usually travelled down by train. Stoke isn't a million miles away from us, it's roughly in the middle of Manchester and Birmingham. Only shit thing about going to their place by train was their police had it pretty much boxed off. They get you all in a big escort at the train station, then march you all together down the road. Round the corner there's a university, they would bang us in the Uni bar there. After you've been there for a while they get loads of double decker buses and put you on them to go down to the game. We always say nah were alright mate, we will make our own way to the grand sort of thing. But we're told on the buses, or nicked, you decide. To fucking top it off, not only are we forced on these buses, we have to pay for the ride as well. So we end up paying for a trip that we don't even want to take. Their ground is fairly new and is in the middle of nowhere. It's so far away, you have to get on the motorway to get to it, we had a nice escort from a few police motorbikes down there. We were only kids so we buzzed off daft little things like that. Police escorts and helicopters out just for us, we loved all that, as sad as it sounds, I still buzz off it now... We were obviously an easy target and sitting ducks, as we pulled in near their ground. There's some pub on the corner, not sure of its name, The Harvester or something daft like that. Anyway not our bus, but the one in front of us got bricked and had all its windows put through. This pissed the police off almost as much as us as they have officers on the buses with us. Every now and then you would hear of odd little things going off by their ground but nothing major. Well I've never been involved in any fighting down near their ground anyway. In fact one time we had been put on them buses, no sooner had we got off them, they realised we didn't have tickets and were sent right back. Not on the buses though, this time in the police vans. Drove right back to the station and put back on a train to Manchester, what a pointless trip that was!

Another time a year later, we managed to get away from the police and made our way to a pub. There were about 25 of us, all our younger lot, we got in this pub not too far from the station, and chilled in the beer garden at the back. This was one of them posh smoking areas with heaters and lights and that. We let Stoke's younger lot know exactly where we were, they said they would be 20 minutes tops. They said they had around 25-30 lads out, similar numbers to ourselves. We were all well up for it but like so many times it just wasn't meant to be. No more than 5 minutes after I got off the phone to Stoke, police turned up in a couple of vans. It wasn't long before more arrived on the scene. They put police at the front and the back of the pub, so we weren't going anywhere fast, that's for sure. They kept us there until they could get one of them buses through to take us to the Britannia. Yet another pointless trip down there, just as we thought we had got one over on the police as well, then they turned up. We were starting to think going by train to Stoke on a match day was just pointless. To have it with them at their place perhaps we needed to be a little smarter about it and go about things a little differently.

There was a time we had it with Stoke, in Stoke, and it went off big time. The funny thing was we weren't even playing them that day, that's what made it even better. It was pretty much a chance meeting, well at first it was anyway. We had Zulus away, so we were off to Brum. Nothing had been arranged with Stoke that day; however I had spent the last couple of weeks sorting a meet out with the young Zulu lot. We had our own bus down, think it was a 26 seater, or 28, was one of them anyway. A few lads had let us down and had not turned up, for whatever reason, so there were about 20 of us. The Zulus had a reputation (they still do) as being one of the best youths around, so we were all well up for this, and had been since the day the bus was booked. So we were on our way down to the West Midlands. One of the lads wanted to meet someone, who was also on their way down to Birmingham, to get something off them. Can't remember if it was drugs or money or what, but this lad was a few miles behind us, so we decided to pull off and wait for him. We weren't too far from Stoke, so we all agreed to get off there, have a couple quick pints round there, get back on the motorway and smash the Zulus, happy days! We got our driver to take us to Stoke train station and just wait there for us, said we would be half an hour, maybe 45 minutes max. So we jumped off our bus and made our way to find a pub.

As we were going past their train station these lads were getting in a taxi. Straight away my mate said they were eyeing us up and down, to be honest I didn't even notice them, I was too busy on the phone to Zulus. "Are you Vale?" came from the taxi, in that daft Stoke accent, Vale meaning Port Vale their local rivals. We all had a little laugh to ourselves, fucking Port Vale. A couple of weeks previous to this we had bumped into a few Vale kids at Piccadilly station in town. We put it on them, said get out the station and round the corner now. Anyway to cut a long story short, they shit themselves and wouldn't leave the station, so we slapped them anyway. Back to Stoke then, we told them "we're Man City, and we are on our way to Birmingham". A very brief conversation was had, basically saying they have just come back from Manchester funnily enough and if they could get numbers together, do we want it? Numbers were exchanged and all that and we went on our way. I thought nothing much of it to be honest, didn't expect them to turn up, not at such short notice like this anyway, I know we would struggle to do it.

We made our way to the pub, the one we had been in previous with the smoking area and heaters in the back. While most of the lads were chilling outside, I took it upon myself to teach a few of the younger lads a lesson in how to play pool. A misspent childhood in pubs, drinking and playing pool instead of being at school, has made me rather good. My pool master class was cut somewhat short however when this Stoke kid rang and said they were on their way. We were all a little taken back with how quickly they had got a firm together, especially when we found out they weren't even playing that day. Obviously Stoke is a lot smaller than Manchester, so their lads would live a lot closer to their town centre. That being said though if they have managed to get a mob of 20 odd lads together in just 30 minutes, then fair fucking play to them, because I certainly couldn't do it. Time went by and still nothing from Stoke. The lad insisted they were only round the corner but he had insisted that 10 minutes beforehand as well. Fuck this lot, they were not showing, we knew it sounded a little too good to be true, getting a firm together that rapid. So we left the pub and made our way back towards the bus, to carry on down to Birmingham. Came round the corner, with the train station and our bus in sight and still nothing, they were nowhere to be scene. We just told them straight, "listen yeah you've got a couple more minutes, and then if you're not here then we're off". A couple more minutes went by and nothing, apart from one lad who walked past us. Now this lad caught my eye, purely because he had the exact same trainers on as me, red sl72s. He didn't look over at us once and for me that was a dead giveaway that he was Stoke. It's like he was going out of his way trying not to look at us. If I'm walking down the street and I saw 20 lads stood there, I would look over, but maybe that's just me being a nosey cunt. Birmingham had been nagging me to leave Stoke and come down to them, rightly so to be honest, I would have been saying exactly the same thing. So we all got on the bus and told the driver to set off. The bus set off and slowly started to pull away, from where it had been parked for over an hour now. Suddenly someone shouted, "That's them, look that's them there" we all looked towards the back of the bus. Through the back window we could see a good 25, if not more lads, pegging it after our bus. Talk about timing, another 15 seconds and we would have been gone and wouldn't have even noticed them.

We all jumped up and made the driver stop, the poor driver didn't know if he was coming or going. We all made for the door at the front of the bus; it was like a mad dash, all clambering over each other to make it out. The way we were rushing to get off the bus, you would think there was a fire on it or something. Only around 6 lads maybe 7 managed to get off the bus, by the time Stoke had caught us up. Worthy is the first one of the bus, he sprints straight into them, and gets put straight on his arse. He jumps back up, Tom, Craig and Raz and a couple more are all fighting with Stoke but there's fucking loads of them, half of us were still trying to get off this bus. If I am being honest I think a couple of lads getting off the bus didn't quite fancy it after they saw Stoke was there around the bus. They were hesitating, in other words shitting themselves. There were loads of us behind waiting to get off, in the end we had to throw people out of the way to get off. Finally after what seemed like fucking ages, we were all off the bus and giving it Stoke. Then from nowhere, this lad had started spraying red spray at people's faces. At the time we didn't have a fucking clue what it was, for all we knew it could have been some spray that makes you blind for a few minutes. Someone shouted "they've got CS gas" and we all backed off. You know what, I'm not even going make out I had that red spray all over me, because I wasn't close enough to the front to get it on my face. Just had the tiniest bit on my jeans, I had only just got off the bus; I hadn't been involved in the fighting whatsoever at that point. Craig had it sprayed full on all over his face and the top half of his body, he looked like a fucking strawberry!

Stoke had now chased us right back to our bus, well now this was nothing short of fucking embarrassing. I nearly fell running away from them as well. I thought what am I doing here, running away, I felt like a fucking faggot. Here I was running back from Stoke, before I had chance to even hit any of them, the closest thing I had had to a fight was barging my own lads out of the way so I could get off the bus. We were now all together, grouped tightly by the side of our bus, basically in-between our bus and the train station. After a few seconds we all realised nobody was coughing or blinded by the spray, so whatever it was, it didn't seem to affect anyone. 1 or 2 pool balls (taken from my favourite pub in Stoke with the heaters in the beer garden) were launched right at Stoke. "Come on City, we will fucking do these now" and with that we all steamed forward right into them. This Stoke kid has just appeared from nowhere, right in front of me, as I've gone to hit him he's sort of turned his back on me and turned to the side. So I got him with a big left hook, which was a perfect body shot in his side, he let out some gay sound, like he yelped. You know like if you've ever stood on a dog's paw or tail by accident, that yelp, well it was similar to that, but gayer. I looked around and Stoke were now getting slapped about all over, it's funny how a fight can turn full circle and completely change in a matter of seconds. Less than a minute earlier we were being ran off by them, although that was pretty much due to that red spray, whatever the fuck it was. I didn't even whack the lad again, couldn't bring myself to do it, I just kicked his arse out the way, he went flying. I had 3 of them in front of me so just dived straight into the 3 of them. I was proper up for this now, felt like I had a point to prove, not to the other lads or owt like that, just to myself. I was that embarrassed about before. Good game lads Stoke but they were now starting to get off, leaving just a handful at the front to take a battering. Well maybe battering is too strong but we were getting the better of them. One of their lads tried getting off to seek sanctuary in a nearby hotel. Two City lads saw him and followed him in and kicked the shit out of him in the hotel entrance. We went to go into them once more before they just turned and ran. Well actually thinking about it they didn't like sprint away, more jogged off. We were in two minds whether to chase after them, or get on our bus and fuck off, before we all got nicked. Me, Tom and Lawler ran after them, "come on there's only three of us" I shouted gesturing for them to turn back and fight us but they didn't. They were too busy shouting insults and mocking Lawler's hat. He had these big shades on, and some mad thick Russian hat. Fuck knows what that was all about, it wasn't even a cold day. Those hats must have been all the rage down Wythenshawe or something, he looked a right tit.

By now the rest of the lads were all back on the bus, I jogged back towards them and noticed a couple dozen or so people outside the station. They must have witnessed the whole thing, by the looks on their faces. But their faces were nothing compared to our driver's face, he looked scared to death. I actually felt sorry for him, he looked that terrified, like as if he thought he were going to all turn on him or something. I don't think he will be volunteering to take us anywhere soon in a hurry.

It was now like a big party on the bus on the way down. We had just done Stoke and now we were going to do Zulus too, if we did these two on the same day, now that would be some achievement. This is what away days are all about. Our bus was rocking all the way down the motorway. We were around 10 miles away now, so I rang them and told them we wouldn't be long. The plan was to get the postcode off them, to where they were, go straight there and have it with them. We got to just past Walsall's ground or thereabouts, when we saw these police motorbikes at the side of the road. One of the lads jokingly said that they're waiting for us, to which we all pissed ourselves. Well no sooner had we finished laughing, we realised that actually the police motorbikes were waiting for us. They made our driver follow them all the way through Digbeth and to St Andrews. We were taken onto the forecourt outside their ground and made to all get off the bus. "So did you lot have fun in Stoke then?" said one of the officers "nah, don't know what you mean mate" one of us replied back. We were all searched and filmed and it was clear we're all going to be arrested. The police assumed that the red stains on several of the lads clothing was dried blood from earlier. The couple of coppers stood by me and Tom were called away to do something, we both just looked at each other and said let's get off. So we started slowly walking away, expecting to be grabbed and dragged back at any time, but it didn't happen. Nobody said shit to us, we just walked away, a couple of our lads seen us getting off and were pissing themselves, how could they not notice us just walk away. Everybody else was arrested and thrown back in vans to be taken to the station, just moments later.

I rang Brum and told them what had happened, and they seemed a bit dubious to say the least. "So you went to Stoke, and happened to bump into them, and battered them, then police motorbikes escorted your bus to the ground, where everybody was arrested apart from two of you, because you both just walked off". Does sound a little daft I must admit, but it was the truth. We wandered about with nothing really to do until the end of the game. We ended up at McDonalds, which is just by an island, not too far from their ground. They kept ringing me asking where I was, I said "look I'm not having it with youse when there's only two of us, and started arguing with them on the phone". Tom was inside in the toilet, so I was just sat outside on the benches on my own. I look round and can see about 40 of them walking past me, whilst on the phone to me. How they didn't see me I will never know, I was happy enough that they didn't anyway. Well it had all been too much for our driver. On seeing everybody get nicked he just drove off, without saying a word to anyone, just got off home. We made our way into the town centre on foot, and met up with more City lads who had gone to the game. Had a couple of beers and that, then the lads who had been nicked started getting released. So we got on the train and headed back to Manchester. Nothing ever came of that do outside the train station with Stoke, although apparently it was in the local paper that the police believed it was Wolves Yam Yam army. Which has got to be the maddest name for a mob ever hasn't it? The Yam Yams, it's a gayer name than

Blazing Squad, and that really is saying something.

★

Now in 2010 Stoke brought a right mob to Manchester, easily 100 lads I would say. We had around 80 lads out that day too, so we hoped for a day of fun and games. We set out to arrange a youth on youth thing before the game, but for one reason or another it just didn't materialise. So it was going to have to be after the game. Stoke's younger lot said they had half their lads in town and the rest in the ground. We had around 12–15 in Eastland's bar, a few in The Manchester and the rest in the game. The match itself had finished and everybody knew the drill. The lads left the game a few minutes before the end, and made their way down to the pubs to meet the rest of us. We were going to do our usually thing off the estate. Get everyone together, keep off the main roads and on the estate, wait for their escort, then rush out and steam right into it. This was tried and tested, we had done it countless times over the years. Was normally just us younger lot that do it but today we had loads of the older lads with us. We decided now was the time to make the move and get everyone together from the pubs and get onto the estate. Our numbers were gaining nicely, the further we walked onto the estate, it's like the more people started to follow us. We went down the side streets and waited in one of the ginnels, waiting until their escort was on its way. We had a good 60 lads if not more, waiting for Stoke to come our way. It was mainly made up of older lads; I had text and rang all the other young lads, telling them to hurry up. Some of my lot aren't exactly the easiest to get hold of; several of them don't even have mobiles but have an uncanny knack of just knowing where to go to find us.

Word soon got round the lads near the ground that

Stoke's escort was on its way. It was said there were around 80 of them in this escort, but apparently they had enough police around them. We marched up towards the main road, to where there's a couple of gaps in the metal fences, which leads you onto a grass verge then the main road. I gripped Craig and said come on we'll go to the next opening about 30 metres down, and loads followed us down. Everyone steamed out of the two gates simultaneously, right into GMP. If we had timed it better and gone maybe 30 seconds later, we would have gone straight into the middle of Stoke. As it turned out we had ran into the front and back of their escort. I mean what are the chances of that. Don't know who was more shocked, us that had somehow timed that so wrong, or GMP that had just had 60 City run out at them. We pushed the police back, which in turn pushed Stoke round. What it did was mean all the police charged over at us with their coshes out, horses the lot. There was now pretty much no escort, the police were more concerned with chasing City back. We weren't one big group of City, a few of us was on the town side, and most on the ground side of the police. A fair few lads had been chased back onto the estate by GMP, who were now smacking lads with their coshes for fun. Stoke's lads were on the town side of the police and the side of the road where the ground was on, with City on the other side. While loads of City lads were being chased off by the police, the rest were fighting with Stoke on the main road. I would have to say there were around 70 Stoke but at that point only about 20 City, or something along them lines anyway. There were just too many of them, they were swarming round the City lads, attacking them from all angles. Everyone seemed to part, from two separate factions and little random fights broke out, up and down the main road. Me and a few others managed to push past police and get down there. Well I would actually say it was more run round the police, than push past them.

It was just utter carnage everywhere. There were people getting laid out over cars, dropped on their arse, rolling about on the floor fighting, the lot. I saw one of the older lads having it with a good 5 of them on his own. The 5 or so lads fighting him looked more scared of him, than he was of all them, and with good cause to be as well. This lad, we will call him "Big A" is as big and as hard as they come. When I first started going City, he was one lad I looked up to, he is fearless. Not only is he a big hard cunt but he like isn't a bully with it at all and I think that made me respect him even more. I ran down the banking at the side of the pavement, and ran into a few of their lads, who were fighting with "Big A". Running down from the banking and onto the cycle lane part of the road, where they were fighting, I almost fell over. I think it was the drop from the pavement to the road; I must have lost my footing or something. So I half ran, half fell into the Stoke lads, used them to break my fall, well to stop me from falling. The impact sent a couple of them hurtling back into their own lads, one of them, some fat cunt, who went down rolling around on the floor. There was this big monster of a man in front of me, not so much muscle, I think just more naturally huge. He must have been well over 6 foot and like 20 stone, I thought you're getting it, I want it with you. The big monster kicked me in my shin; I mean who the fuck does that really. How would it even pop into your head to do that, it's unnatural to go round kicking people in their shins, the fucking puff. I thought you're defo getting it now, so I proper planted my feet and caught him sweet, with a big right hander. The fat fuck stumbled a couple of steps back. As I've gone for him again I've been yanked back that hard it nearly pulled me straight over. I turned round to see half of Man City's FIOs round me; Nobby, Kelly, and Horton, "fuck off now Carl or you're getting nicked" one of them screamed at me and then pushed me in the direction of town. They pushed me once more up the pavement, not like hard enough to make me go flying, more like encouraging me to move on. They then ran into the middle of the road once more, to where the fighting was still carrying on.

There was now a good 25, 30 of us on the banking and pavement. We all ran down once more into Stoke. A few digs were thrown back and forth and the fighting was pretty even to be honest. On the whole, Stoke did get the better of things on the main road. But that was more at the start of things, when City was heavily outnumbered. The fighting towards the end was pretty even I would say. GMP finally got their act together and made a line of officers, bang in the middle of us and Stoke. We all got back on to the estate to have another pop at Stoke further down. Stoke were trying to claim some kind of victory, as if we were getting off from them, which just wasn't the case. We both couldn't get to each other at the point and it would have been daft to try with the amount of police and horses in the middle. We had about 25 lads on the estate, all pretty much youth with a couple of older lads. We wanted to make our way down towards the Mitchell Arms, the plan was to beat the police and Stoke down there and rush out into them.

The helicopter was now out for us, flying overhead in fairly tight circles above us. See we could lose the police on cars, horses and foot fairly easy on the estate, can't lose the helicopter though. We got to the Mitchell and tried having another pop but it was a half hearted effort from us. We didn't so much attack the escort, more just stood there like come on Stoke, we're here if you want it sort of thing. There was far too many police for owt to happen there though. The police ushered us lot towards town and put a few police walking along side us. There was also some of our FIOs driving around in their unmarked car, a silver Vauxhall Zafira. They used the same cars every single week, so it couldn't have stood out anymore to us.

With all the fun and games down by the ground, I hadn't had chance to get my phone out. When I checked it I had numerous texts and missed calls off them Stoke kids that were in town. It's funny how some things just work out, I mean what were the chances these Stoke lads were in a bar, on the same street we were on. Not only that, it was Dry Bar, our pub we always used for meeting up in, the cheeky cunts. I belled them and said look we're on Oldham Street now, we will be walking right past Dry in about 60 seconds, so be ready for us. Now remember there was police walking near us, I think they were under the illusion that they were escorting us but we were just walking where we wanted to go, and they were tagging along. Now by luck something happened, must have been going off again somewhere, because these police got something through on the radio and some of them got off. There weren't enough of them before to stop a big fight, never mind them doing it now, with less of them. Think there were only a couple of them, just walking at the back of us. We were now just metres away from the entrance to Dry Bar. Dry didn't just have like a door, and then you're on the road, it was set back a little, with tables and chairs in front of the entrance. I was just staring at the front of the bar as we were approaching it, waiting for god knows how many of them to come rushing out. I made sure I was at the front on the far left, so was closest to Dry Bar, so I was right there for when they come out. We were all still buzzed up and high on adrenaline from the fighting down by the ground, just minutes earlier. The second these set foot out of the bar, they wouldn't know what had hit them, we were gonna fucking waste them. We were now just a few feet away from it and there wasn't a huge mob there outside at all, just a couple of indie kids having a cig. Now I was really caught in two minds what to do, Dry Bar is the type of place where people looking like that would go, now I'm only saying they were just indie kids because of their hair but that's how lads have their hair in Stoke. So do I just drop one of these kids now, on the idea that they are Stoke, or leave them, because why would they be just two of them stood there having a cig. I stared right through the glass doors into the bar and couldn't see a large group of lads, I was perplexed and pissed off, where the fuck were they, lying little cunts.

Me and the lads continued walking staring back at Dry Bar, shrugging our shoulders at each other. We must have made it about 50 metres further down the road, towards Piccadilly Gardens, when we heard loads of noise from behind us. I turned round to see around 15 lads bouncing up and down outside Dry Bar, shouting stuff to us. Well it was a bit fucking late now, why didn't they do that a minute ago. We've gone to run over to them, but got boxed in by the police in between road works, with metal fences round them, and the wall of a shop. Our FIOs pulled up out of nowhere, in their not so unrecognisable unmarked motor. Nobby jumped out the car and ran at the Stoke lads screaming "aarrrrggghhhh" at them while doing so. Was one of the funniest things I've ever see, the lot of them turned round and ran in the opposite direction. Was only Nobby on his own and they fucking legged it from him. He loves it Nobby though, like outside Old Trafford on the forecourt, he whipped his cosh out and backed fucking loads of United lads off, on his own. Anyway we were all rounded up and given Section 27s and Stoke were rounded up and put on the train and fucked off home. A few days later I was speaking to my pal from Stoke, who was present in Dry that day. I said to him "why the fuck didn't youse all just run out when we was there, why did you wait, it would have been mental if you lot rushed out, when we were outside". He seemed slightly embarrassed by it all. He went on to say when he told the lads we were nearly here, half of them went down stairs to the toilet, all at the same time. By the time they had all come up, we were where we were down the road. Make of that what you will. The next thing we would have with Stoke would be not an arrange meet but bumping into one another in town.

It was nearing the end of the 2012 season and we were in town for one of the older lad's birthday. We met up in The Shakespeare; well that's where I met up with everyone, I think everybody else had been out for most of the day. There were about 50 of us in there, old and youth alike. I think we might have had a home game that day but can't remember who against, it wasn't Stoke anyway, they had Wigan away. A few of the lads had been out all day and were just getting off home, just as I was turning up. So they were off making their way through town towards Piccadilly station. They must have been gone 5 minutes before Brookes got a call saying there's loads of Stoke kicking off with Blood and a couple others, near Piccadilly. So all the younger lot in there, which was about 12 or so of us, left the pub sharpish and jogged up towards them. I just thought this was going to be a load of bollocks and a complete waste of time. We made our way up the top end of Market Street, went past Spoons on our left and we could see a large crowd of people and it was going off. Funnily enough in pretty much the same spot as we smashed the N40 4 years earlier. Before I had a chance to say or do out, Wizz and Brookes were sprinting off well ahead of me and steamed straight in there. The rest of us ran down after them. "YOOF! YOOF! CITY! CITY!" chants went up, as we were running down. It was all going off pretty much in the middle of the road. There were from what I could see around 25 Stoke, 15 City, now us 12 on top of that. Outside Massimo's there were lads rolling about on the deck from both sides. Brookes was having it with this fat guy, he must have hit the guy a good 5 times and he hadn't budged him. I stepped to the side and pushed in front of Brookes, took a swing for this kid and caught him clean on his chin. Straight away his legs went funny on him; his legs were like jelly, he went all floppy, and sort of flopped to the floor. I turned to Brookes and gave him a little nod and a cheeky smile, I still wind him up about it now. Although he insists his punches must have already softened the fat lad up...

All traffic at the busy crossroads was now at a complete standstill. There was also a fairly large crowd gathered watching, consisting mainly of City fans making their way back to town after the game. Remember this is the middle of town near Piccadilly Gardens, yet again we have found ourselves fighting in one of the most on top areas. The fighting went on, a few of them started to turn and run off, they didn't want to know anymore. One of our lads had been cracked round his eye, and it was a fucking mess. I grabbed him and told him to fuck off before the police get here, as he had not long been out of prison. A few of the lads ran into Stoke again and chased them off. I didn't bother, in fact I kind of hardly felt like I had been involved, I had only punched one person once. Hadn't even been punched myself or owt like that, I suppose that's what happens when you turn up towards the end of a scrap. For once not only was there no police on the scene, we couldn't even hear any sirens. Which given the area we were in and the length of time the fight had been going on for, was quite a surprise. Now, while there might not have been noise from the GMP sirens, there certainly was noise from a lot of the bystanders watching. "CITY! CITY! CITY!" a few were chanting, and applauding, one even patted me on my back as we were jogging away. Now I don't mean one or two people were clapping us, and chanting City, am talking like around 100 people. Not sure about the rest of the lads, but I was certainly a bit taken back by it all anyway. We soon returned to the pub, and was telling everyone what had gone on. About half an hour later it all started kicking off in The Shakespeare, bottles and pints going all over the show, people punching each other. I was at the very far corner of the pub, so didn't fully see what was going on. It soon spilled out into the street outside. Apparently a few of them Stoke lads we had just battered had returned to the pub to have another pop I suppose. This time GMP were fast to respond and was on the street rather sharpish. We all disappeared rather quickly, and that was that.

In 2013 we had Stoke away in the league. Due to all the bans and that there wasn't a big firm of City down there. I told them well in advance that I doubt there will be anyone going down, so they knew not to expect us. Things seemed to have quietened down between us and Stoke in the last few months anyway. One of our lads Posh Daz went down to the game; he was with a couple of kids. After the match had finished they were followed by loads of Stoke lads who smacked them a few times. It was very fucking cheeky and extremely out of order. Many lads lost all respect they had for Stoke after that day because we thought they were better than doing shit like that. What comes around goes around and all that. Stoke haven't been to our place in the last couple of seasons, that being said we haven't been to theirs. The banning orders will obviously have a large part to do with that. They are good, very game lads on the whole, always up for it, similar to Everton I suppose. I am pretty sure we will bump into each other at the football someday, sooner rather later I hope.

HERE, THERE AND EVERYWHERE

BOHEMIANS – Bohs and Shamrock Rovers is a fixture first played almost 100 years ago. The two Irish clubs are both from the capital Dublin and originate from opposite sides of the City. Shamrock Rovers from the southside and Bohs from the northside. Not only is this fixture a derby, it's the biggest fixture in Irish football.

It's no big secret that I have mates at Shamrock Rovers and have gone over to several of their games. There is no link between City and Rovers or anything like that, more just a personal thing with me. One of my best mates is their main younger lad Paul, I go over to see him and he brings me out to their games. A handful of them would go over for Bury matches and I would met them then too. I would fly over to Dublin as often as I could. A fixture that I would try and get over for would be Bohs and in particular Bohs away. Bohs ground is called Dalymount Park and it's in Phibsborough in the north side of Dublin. Now their ground, the best way I can describe it is old school, it's a proper old school ground. The ground would be similar to say English lower league grounds in the 70s or something. The place is falling apart, I mean proper falling apart, it's a mess. Even though it's such a shit hole, truth be told I rather like it. The contrast from Dalymount Park and the state of the art modern Premier League grounds is mad. It looks like it's been abandoned and left derelict for a decade. If it was in England, no doubt health and safety people would be all over it and it would have been torn down years ago. Two of their stands have in fact been closed down. It's known as "the home of Irish football" but like I said it's seen better days. Their ground is situated around a mile north of O'Connell Street, which is the centre of Dublin.

I've been with Paul and the Rovers lads to two Bohs away games. The first of which was back in 2013, I think it was. Now the games in Ireland are mainly played on a Friday night, which I think is cool. It makes a change from the Sunday and Monday fixtures over here. There were around 30-40 of us in a beer garden in the centre of Dublin. It consisted of mainly youth and under 5's with a few older lot. There was talk that Bohs wanted to meet on O'Connell Street, which was just stupid, with that being the main street in the centre of Dublin. When it got to around 45 minutes before kick off, it was time to make our move. Another 15 or so older lads met us outside the bar and we all made our way towards Bohs ground. There were a good 50 odd of us now. No sooner had we left the bar on our way, the Garda (Irish police) started to follow us. To my amazement they weren't following on foot, or car or van but on push bikes. That made me chuckle anyway, although I'll be the first to admit I am fairly easily amused. So me and the 50-60 Rovers lads walked towards their ground in the northside. Closely followed by them silly cunts on push bikes, think there were 3 or 4 of them. The push bike police was soon joined by Garda riot vans, GMP's equivalent to TAU I'm guessing. On the way to their ground, the area had a few sets of flats but mainly these 3 storey Georgian looking gaffs. Wouldn't say the area looked dead rough or intimidating, or anything like that. There were various shops and pubs dotted about too. One thing that did catch my eye was the infamous Mountjoy prison.

The closer we got to their ground, the more you just got

the feeling it was going to go off. We knew that they were nearby "they" being Boh's firm. They knew exactly which way we would be walking, so we were expecting them to rush out at any moment. We noticed a large Garda presence, up the side of a street. We could hear Boh's lads, but still couldn't see them. They couldn't have been more than 100 metres away but with Garda and houses in between, there was not a lot we could do. We were ushered towards the away entrance of the ground and that was that. Don't remember much of the actual game itself. I do recall one lad going mad when Rovers scored. Now the first couple of levels is actually not far from being eye level to the pitch. With a wall covered in anti-vandal paint, separating the fans and the pitch. When Rovers scored everyone went mad, trying to get over this wall, and on to the pitch itself. One lad did make it over but was quickly lobbed back over, by the Garda and the stewards. His face and clothes were now black from the anti vandal shit. Anyone who has had that on them will know it's a cunt to get off.

The game ended and similar numbers as before the game got back together again. We tried making it into a couple of their pubs near the ground, the Garda soon moved us on though. There was a much larger Garda escort after the game, as there had been before it. They weren't going to leave us alone either. It was now a good hour after the game and I was fucked. I wasn't pissed, just tired. Was on the first flight over in the morning, so had been up since like half 4. So I was eager to get on the Luas (tram) and back to my hotel, so that's what me and Paul did. We didn't think anything would happen anyway. It was midnight now, me and Paul was at Mcdonald's, when he got the call to say it had gone off. It had gone off between Bohs and Rovers near Christchurch. Bohs had crossed the bridge over from their area and come into the southside, Rovers came down the hill to meet them. Rovers had around 30 lads, Bohs with getting on for 50 or so lads. They both clashed on the main road, stopping cars in their tracks. The fighting was pretty much even, with Garda soon steaming in, eventually chasing the Rovers lads off. We were both fuming that we had missed it. It's just one of those things though, nobody can be at everything al the time.

It would be 2014 before I was next over in Ireland. This time I would be accompanied by the BBC and this time me and Paul wouldn't miss it, neither did the BBC.

March 21st 2014 would be when I was next there for Bohs away. Was a bit different this time however, I had the BBC over filming me. For several months prior to this they had been with me, pretty much week in, week out filming for a documentary called "Football Fight Club". This, if I remember correct, would be one of if not the final day of filming for it. We bumped into a handful of Bury lads in the airport who were also going over for the Shamrock Rovers game. We got the first flight over, got to our hotel, got some food, the usual shit. We didn't end up meeting Paul and the rest of the lads till much later on. We did bits and bobs, here and there filming, more to pass the time than anything. Think it was around 4 when we met up with the lads. We first met up with everyone in a place called International Bar. Soon after we walked to Trinity College, then all got taxis to the next place. We soon moved on to the next pub Caulfields, which is on Dorset Street in the northside, Bohs area. Now Bohs have links with Celtic and Wrexham and the talk was that they would be over for this game, as they often would be. The Alliance they call themselves. So there we were, in the boozer in Bohs area, about 50 handed numbers wise. At this point there were none of them tits on push bikes knocking about, in fact no Garda at all, which I found surprising. A Bohs lad came to the front of the pub, said they would text when they are here. So we could all get out of the pub and meet them. None of the Rovers lads was tooled up or owt, apart from a few with umbrellas. I thought was a bit mad, these kids with umbrellas, as it wasn't even fucking raining. Anyway turns out in Ireland people use them as a weapon, which had me in stitches, because I thought they were taking the piss. So be weary of Irishmen with brollies. We went into the beer garden at the back of the pub, with the BBC and did some filming. Then once that was done, went back inside drinking. I would say a good half hour easy had gone by, with still no word of Bohs. Was a bit mad how 50 of us were sat drinking in Bohs area with no Garda anywhere to be seen. The whole thing was a bit weird, as regards to being out filming with the BBC but knowing it could go off at any minute. Normally it's either filming or being out with the lads, not both. Also I was a "guest" over there with Paul, so you could say it wasn't even my fight. That being said though, going over to Ireland a few times, I had grown fond of Shamrock Rovers. Not that I would class myself as being a full blown supporter, because I'm not. I'm from Manchester, so City is the only team for me. Nevertheless as my fondness for Rovers grew, so did my hatred for their rivals Bohs. No better way for me to word it than I can't fucking stand them.

A bit more time went on and I went for a piss, and was talking to some bloke in there. Always found it weird how people talk shit to each other while having a piss but I was doing the same thing. I've come out of the bog or "jax" as the Irish call it, walked out into full on carnage. I only went for a piss, came out and it's like a fucking war zone. How I didn't hear anything from the toilet is beyond me because it was loud as fuck. Bricks, chairs and stools were coming through the windows at the front of the pub. I could just see a mass of bodies in front of me. Unbeknown to me, fighting had already been going on, in and around the entrance to the pub. Bohs had turned up and were smashing fuck out of the windows. Rovers lads had been scrapping with them, around the doorway and just outside. There were lads trying to push their way through, to get outside. I'm not going to lie, there was a small number of Rovers lads backing away and keeping to the back end of the pub, away from the trouble. There was also the odd innocent bystander if you like, caught in the middle of it all. I've started darting past people, and chucking them out of my way, to make it outside. I managed to push my way to the front, there was a lot of throwing pint glasses and chairs. We steamed out of the pub, about 20 of us, and right into them Bohs cunts. Minimal punches were thrown, before Bohs shit it and backed right off. I found myself in the middle of the road, ahead of most of the Rovers lads and bouncing towards Bohs. I felt something hit the back of my head, didn't know if it was a pint, or bottle or what. Turns out it was a fucking chair from the pub. It came from behind me and struck the back of my head, so must have came from Rovers lads behind me, trying to hit Bohs. Which turned out to be the case, was just a wank shot that hit me.

The sirens normally start dead quiet in the distance and get louder as the police get closer but there were no sirens at all, then as they arrived, all the sirens went on. Several Garda vans all skidded to a halt at once around us. The doors seemed to simultaneously fling open, as dozens of Irish police steamed towards us. These lot weren't for the softly, softly approach, it was coshes out and hit everyone in sight. The BBC cameraman was moved off and they didn't catch the vast majority of it. It just looked on the programme as if the police came, hit a few people and that was it. In truth it was a lot worse than that. Some lads were unconscious on the pavement with Garda swarming round them, whacking them and stamping on their heads. The Garda were now coming from both sides of the road. There was this one Bohs kid that I could see. Give him his dues I couldn't see the rest of his lads near him but he didn't seem to back off or owt. Paul cracked him and yet more Garda came. One of them has grabbed Paul on his arm, I've punched the copper's arm a couple of times and yanked Paul's arm free. I've then felt a crack on my forehead, it made me go a bit dizzy for a couple of seconds. Ears ringing and buzzing to fuck, it was one of the Garda, he had whacked me with his cosh. He was a fat bloke, with a massive potato looking head. I think it hurt me because I didn't see it coming. I thought, well I'm not just standing there letting you do that, you're getting it you fat cunt. I've gone forward for him, he has stepped well away from me. A few Garda rushed me from the side and basically rugby tackled me to the floor. Then gave me a bit of a slap with their coshes. Tried to put my hands up, to cover my head the best I could. That's how I ended up with a broken finger. There must have been around half a dozen bodies laid out in the road and pavement. None of which was caused by anybody but the Irish police.

While I was receiving my warm welcome back to Ireland, pockets of fighting continued up and down the main road. However by this stage it was more against the Garda than Boh's lads. One or two got nicked, most of us went on our way. I made my way to Bohs ground and found the BBC. Still pumped with adrenaline, gave a quick interview on camera, about what had just taken place. Then we went in the match itself. The rest of the day went relatively peaceful after that.

Neither side managing to shake off the Garda presence.

Aston Villa – Villa have shown up at our place several times over recent years, with mixed success. Well the first couple of times I never had anything to do with them, they were nothing short of laughable. Back in 2007, they came up to our place. Now earlier on in the day, a few of them had got a slap in town but nothing major. Later on in the day down by the ground, we ran them all over. They were so intent on getting away from us, that they ran and hid in... wait for it... Asda. They all ran into a fucking supermarket to get away from us. Maybe they had forgotten to do their shopping before they came? Or maybe all that running away from us had made them hungry. We were in stitches laughing at them, we just thought fuck it and went back to the pub, and left them hiding in Asda. A couple of years went by and they were only at it again. I swear they come up for a fucking big game of hide and seek. This time we chased a few of them down Oldham Street in town, round onto Great Ancoats Street. There weren't any supermarkets for them to run into but that didn't seem to bother them, as they soon found a hotel to run into. They must have dived straight in the lift, or through some doors, because they just vanished. First it was Asda and then a hotel, whatever next for these hardcore shoppers. I call them hardcore shoppers, as they call themselves Hardcore youth...

In 2010 it was if I'm not mistaken, yet again they travelled up to our place, although why they bothered I was really starting to wonder. This time I had one of their main kid's phone numbers for their younger lot. So hopefully this time something could be sorted out and there would be none of this hide and seek shit. The lad I was talking to on the phone was alright, you could tell straight away he was a proper lad and not a gimp. Same couldn't be said for his mates constantly shouting shit down the phone like little kids, I mean these weren't teenagers, and these were well into their 20s. It was now during the game and we had just about 6 of us that hadn't gone in. They said they had around 20 in the Crown and Anchor in town but said they didn't want it till after the game, until the rest of their lads are with them. I said "look mate there's only 6 of us, you've got 3 times our numbers; we will come and meet youse now with this". The lad seemed fairly happy with that and we set off on our way to meet them. Walking to the pub there, heart pounding like it does, having second thoughts thinking, there are only 6 of us, what if about 40 odd of them come rushing out. I soon pushed those thoughts to the back of my mind, if 40 odd of them did come rushing out, so be it, shit happens. We approached the pub now, geared up for war, waiting for loads of them to come rushing out of the pub doors. But it just never happened. Went to the windows and looked through, and there certainly wasn't any lads in there. It was one of them really, I was pissed off that they weren't there but also at the same time maybe slightly relieved, as there were only 6 of us. I belled the lad's phone out several times, with no answer. I left it a few minutes and thought fuck it, I'll try him one more time, this time I did get through. He went on to tell me their just getting on the train home now, I was like "what the fuck are you going on about?" He seemed pretty embarrassed by the whole thing, even sent me a text saying he is sorry, all the lads he as with wanted to get off. So to clarify, they had come up to Manchester and set off home, before the match had not only finished but before it was even half time. I really don't know what else to say about that to be fair. In my book, that even tops the whole Asda thing a few years previous. I spoke to a couple of my Zulu pals and told them what went on, they said it didn't surprise them one bit. Told them the name of the lad I had been talking to, and they said yeah he is one of their top boys. So as you can imagine, after all that, Villa aren't exactly rated by any of us. In fact we would piss ourselves every time we heard their name mentioned.

It was now nearing the end of 2011 and Villa yet again made their way up to our place. What was to take place next was shocking and embarrassing. Was it a case of underestimating someone and us becoming too arrogant or were we just set up big time and there was nothing we could have done? I'll let you make your minds up about that one at the end. If ever there was a fight at City that I sat down afterwards and said "Carl you should have done more" then this fight with Villa was definitely it. Villa said they had loads of banned lads coming up so didn't want to go in town or by the ground. So we suggested meeting in Stockport and everybody was happy with that. We met up in the morning at a pub called The Chestergate in Stockport town centre. It was all youth there but a mixture of new faces and lads that have been there and done it all before. Now the week leading up to this all Villa had been saying is they wanted a 15 on 15, youth on youth, with no tools. We said yeah whatever that's fine with us lot. On the morning they rang and said look will be honest there are 20 of us, not 15, but same applies to everything else, about weapons. We thought well fair play to them for being honest, but as far as I was concerned, I couldn't give a fuck how many lads they had, we were going to tear them apart. In all honesty, I wasn't expecting much of a fight from them at all going off past experience. I just thought we will get right into them and they will just run. I recall saying to Rodgers that it's good for the new lads, that today we're meeting Villa and not anybody good. After all these are the hardcore shoppers, not exactly up to much are they? As I say, I was far too cocky, far too complacent...

We stayed in that Chestergate for another half an hour or so, then we got ready to go. There were 17 or 18 of us altogether there, all proper up for it, and eagerly awaiting the chance to smash these cunts all over. Villa said they were in a pub called The Wheatsheaf, according to our lads from Stockport it wasn't too far away, so we set off. On our way down there on this main road, some of the lads managed to get into an argument with a van driver, still not a clue what it was all about, I just carried on walking. The lads soon caught up with us and we were now just seconds away from the pub. We could now see the pub at the bottom of the street. There was no need to ring and say we're here, as there were two lads stood outside who, on seeing us, darted back into the pub. We now all started bouncing down to the pub. It was all a big laugh and a joke bouncing down there; it was something which I haven't seen before or since. The mood certainly wasn't one seconds before a big fight, everyone was just having a laugh. It's like nobody was even arsed about fighting Villa, nobody thought they would even put up a fight, never mind have a chance of winning. We were now just metres away from the pub and Villa now started piling out and that's when the mood changed. That's when it hit me; we have just been well and truly set up, big time. 15 on 15 youth on youth, no tools, yeah right, the cheeky fucking bastards! There were loads of them, more and more and more just kept coming out the pub, onto the front. All with bottles, glasses, pool balls and pool cues, and god knows what else. We had been set up proper here, but what can you do? We did the only thing we could, which was try and dodge the pints and bottles coming our way, and steam into them. You know the film 300, well the part in that where he says "our arrows will block out the sun" well it was like that, only with fucking pints and bottles coming our way.

Like clockwork Craig's in the doorway fighting with them all on his own at first, you expect nothing else from that mad cunt. The rest of us were fighting all across the main road, just outside the pub with them. At first I would say we were holding our own, if not getting the better of things and I was thinking maybe we will win this fairly easy after all. But they just kept coming out of the pub, more and more of them, it was relentless. I looked at the size of the pub, and it didn't even look big enough to hold that many of them inside. They were coming out of a side door now, as well as the main entrance at the front. There must have been getting on for 60/70 of them or something like that. I could see Craig still by the doorway fighting with them, Rodgers a few feet in front of me doing the same. I wasn't too far away from them, just next to the pavement on the road. We were getting separated from the rest of City, who were on the other side to the entrance of the pub. Craig and Rodgers were over the railing in between the road and the pub; I was on the other side of the railing, trying to get over it. Which is easier said than done, when there was Villa coming at me from everywhere. I should have just dived over the railing right at the start, like they did. Not just stand around waiting for Villa to come to me like a mong. Lads were getting bottled and dragged to the floor and booted in, it was a right mess. There was just too many of them, some of our lads started to get off. I turned and screamed "CITY, STAND!" I think it was a bit too little too late for that though. Curly haired Brookes wasn't too far away from me, I could see another 4 or 5 lads by him as well, then there was me and them 2 over the railings. At this point it wouldn't have been an exaggeration to say it was getting on for 10 on 1 in their favour. The annoying thing is even with these ridiculous numbers, we were still doing alright and just about managing to hold them off. You know when it's bad though, when you're fighting 2 or 3 lads in front of you, while at the same time being punched and kicked from behind as well. They kept pulling me into them; there wasn't even any room to throw punches. I was just basically head butting them, just ramming my head into their faces, and they soon backed off. They were now all around us, and that's when we knew we were fucked. Lads were getting whacked by pool cues and balls, well more by the cues to be fair. The horrible little cunts put a pool cue right through Rodgers' cheek, leaving a big hole, you could see right through it. We were now getting backed off big time and taking a slap. They must have known with even numbers they didn't stand a chance, that's why they set us up and came with so many. Our cocky attitude, "oh were man City we do what we want" just played right into their hands.

We were now running down the street being chased off by them. They were chasing us shouting stuff, couldn't tell you what they were shouting, with that accent they just sounded depressed. You would think they would have sounded happy wouldn't you? Me and Rodgers were being chased by loads of them and we got off down some side street. Meanwhile unbeknown to us, two things were going on. Craig was still in the doorway fighting with them, although by now Villa had had enough of him and were leaving him to it. Also Gaz Manchester had been caught and tripped up trying to get away. The hardcore shoppers proper started booting him in, and dislocated his shoulder. They then decided he had had enough and helped him to his feet. More Villa lads arrived and wanted to jump on him again, so they all started arguing and fighting among each other about it. GMP were now everywhere as I'm sure you can imagine, me and Rodge were just trying our hardest to get away without being nicked. We managed to get away and ended up back at the pub we all first met up in, the mood wasn't the best.

Listen, everybody gets done sometimes, we have before, and we will again. It was just the sly way they went about it, setting us up like that. We heard they were now in a different part of Stockport. Half fuming and half just plain embarrassed about 12 of us went down there to have another go. They had loads of police with them though, so not a lot really we could have done. It confirmed what we already knew though, that there were shit loads of them. Their buses were outside the pub they were in, yep buses, plural. It looked like they had a big 52 seater and then a smaller 20 seater or something daft like that. Now Villa would have you believe this was a fair fight, a 30 on 30, which is nothing short of laughable. But there was no getting away from the fact Villa had done us and Villa had ran us. Yes they did set us up but it will teach us for thinking we're a lot better than what we are and thinking we will win every fight, regardless. Lesson learnt I suppose, I would like to think we won't be making the same mistake again. As for the hardcore shoppers, set up and numbers aside, they ran us that day but we look forward to bumping into them again sometime soon.

Tottenham – The Yids, the self-proclaimed "guvnors of London" so their main kid always tells me. Although I'm not too sure about that myself, I know who my money would be on for that title, and they play in blue and no I don't mean AFC Wimbledon, although the Yids firm have got a reputation of being one of the better firms in London, and the south, there's no doubt about that. It was the last home game of the 2011 season and it was mid week. Now in the time I've been about The Yids have never really brought much to our place. Like many southern firms, I think they get scared to come north of Watford, as hardly any of them ever seem to do it, bar Chelsea and one or two others. Chelsea came up to our place right out of the way without tickets to the game, purely just to meet us. GMP somehow were there waiting for them before they even arrived at the pub, still fair play to Chelsea for doing that. West Ham in the last season or two have started travelling also. But by and large, southern firms will not come up north. Anyway back to the Yids and if there was an award for the gobbiest firm in the country, then it's got to be them, they win that hands down. I don't even mean their youth, although their man lad, as sound as he is, could talk all day long, I mean their older lot. In their escort they were shouting shit, in and around the ground they just wouldn't shut up. You could even see the police getting pissed off with them. At the football, at our place especially, you get what you come for. Keep your head down, keep yourselves to yourselves and chances are you'll be left to it. But spend the day mouthing off, acting hard behind the police and sooner or later you're going to get it and after the game they did.

After the game their older lads came out, about 30 odd of them. We had a fair few of us waiting for them and we just fucking hammered them on the spot. They were getting battered and looking for the police to protect them but the police seemed happy enough letting it happen. There were Yids being put over car bonnets, this black lad in pink was getting booted around this lamppost, literally from one side to the other and back again. Don't get me wrong, some of their lads were bang up for it but most either ran away straight off, or soon wish they had. Remember being in fucking stitches staring at this flat cap on the floor, just lying there. It had fallen off one of their lad's heads, he ran off as fast as he could to get away. I really don't think them Yids will be in much of a hurry to come to Manchester. They're best staying down south where it's much safer for them, after all they do say it's grim up north.

Yids away is a fixture I've long wanted to do but for one reason or another it just never materialised. A lot of the time it seemed to fall on a Wednesday night, certain fixtures just time and time again, seem to be midweek fixtures, just one of those things. At the start of 2014 the Spurs away game once again would be a midweek fixture. My ban would stop me from going, although to be honest I'm not sure I would have fancied going all that way and back on a school night. A few City lads did fancy the trip though, in fact a fucking shit load of them did. There was supposed to be around 50 lads that had made the trip down to north London. Now that might not strike you as being a huge amount but with all the bans and on a midweek game in London, 50 lads is fucking loads. The 50 was comprised mainly of older lads, although there was a few fair youth that had made the journey down. Around 25 of the lads made their way from Seven Sisters station, down the long road towards White Hart Lane. Out of pretty much nowhere appeared 15-20 lads, chanting "YIDS YIDS YIDS" They were on the opposite side of the road, making their way towards the City lads. The City lads made for them, 5 or so of the Yids lads bounced forward, the 2 sets of lads clashed. Digs were traded and a couple of the Yids lads were laid out on the road, the rest soon started to leg it up the road. They were chased off and that was that. Not exactly the best fight by any stretch of the imagination but you can only fight what's in front of you I suppose. I'm not saying this was Yids main lads either but they were certainly lads nonetheless. I know at the time their main man was away and from what I hear when he is inside, them lot are pretty much a shambles and don't know what they're doing. It would be nice to arrange something proper with them, with all their proper lads present and then we will see what's what. Banning orders on both sides make this fairly difficult at the moment, but I'm almost certain it will happen over the next couple of seasons.

Oldham – this little scrap with Oldham wasn't at a game between our clubs, in fact it wasn't really at the football, or anything to do with it. It was at a Twisted Wheel gig at the Academy on Oxford Road in town. A few of the City lads had gone to it, half way through they heard loads of shouting, so listened to try and make out what it was. 'OLDHAM OLDHAM OLDHAM' was being chanted by around 25 lads in the place. There was a few City in there but at that point they were all dotted about in small groups and not all together in one place. The handful of lads that heard the chants just bounced over to Oldham and put it on them, "we're Man City do youse wannit yeah?" And it just went off big time from that moment. The crowd of people separated as City and Oldham went at it. Digs flying in from all angles, at this point City, still heavily outnumbered, with less than half what Oldham kids had. They get pushed back and separated, leaving a massive gap at the front of the venue. More City then realised what was going on and ran down. Oldham was getting backed off more and more with every wave of City attack into them. Security was now involved trying to stop the trouble but they ended up getting filled in, along with Oldham as well. By this point Oldham didn't want to know, they had had enough, they were getting smashed to bits. Loads of them ran off and headed through the fire exits, leaving some of their mates behind to get battered. In the end all of Oldham ran off and only 2 of them would come back inside. One of the lads was bleeding and had some big fuck of bandage wrapped around his head. They admitted their lads were shit and they got done, although it would have been pretty hard for them to argue anything otherwise.

Towards the end of 2013 Oldham's younger lot had called it on with us lot. Why they did this I've no idea, didn't bother us though, we told them we're here anytime they want it. Now they said they were coming down to us on the Saturday, which worked out alright seen as we were all out that day anyway. We were in The Albert in Rusholme, just off curry mile, for a do for one of the older lads who isn't well. There must have been a good 80 or 90 of us down there anyway. Around 25 of that was youth, so when Oldham came down, the plan was to get them on this park nearby, and just us younger lot go and smash them. Oldham were with Hibs and it wouldn't have surprised us if a few County kids were down with them as well. We just thought it would be piss funny doing them all at once. But Oldham were messing us about saying they weren't coming down to us. They called a meet on with us, then said they don't want to come down, what's all that about? So we tried arranging it for town but in the end they wanted us to go all the way to Oldham, fuck that. If I call it on with a firm I will turn up wherever they want us to, whether that be on their estate, their pub or whatever, I wouldn't call it on and them tell them to come to me. This pissed us all off no end. It was largely down to the frustration of that day that I rang the Zulu lot and said in a couple of weeks we're coming to have it with youse, wherever you want. Which turned out to be the best fight that I've ever had at football, the Zulu lads said the same as well. Still, I would hope that sometime in the next season to two we would bump into each other, us and Oldham that is.

Burnley – 2009 it was and Burnley had won promotion to the Premier League. We were supposed to be going to their place but something happened a couple of days beforehand which fucked it up. It was a shame really because it would have been a right laugh going up there. Would have definitely been something different, that's for sure. I've heard people describe going to Burnley away as like going back in time a few decades. Burnley Suicide Squad, their firm, were well known, so I'm guessing they're supposed to be fairly decent. With Manchester only being 30 miles away if that from Burnley, we were expecting them to bring a fair few down. Plus bear in mind, it was more than likely going to be their only season in the top flight. We expected them to be making the most of it and taking huge firms all over. I spoke to some of their younger lot, they said there coming down and bringing a fair few of them. Buzzing, this was just what we wanted to hear. To put it bluntly they fucked us about, had us going here, there and everywhere on some wild goose chase. We weren't impressed one bit, this wasn't how we liked to do things at all, it's not about fucking people about. We were used to talking to firms, arranging a meet and having it. This lot were just pissed up idiots, mouthing off on the phone. Maybe we had just been talking to the wrong people, because I had been told they were fairly decent.

We had another number for them which we got off another firm, which was a fairly common thing to do. Most Saturday mornings my phone would be going off non-stop with different firms up and down the country, ringing asking for various firm's numbers. I felt like the fucking yellow pages at times. Anyway this lad's number who we got passed was at the time one of their main youth faces, he's a nice lad as it goes, so we gave him a bell. We rang him up and said where are you lot because there are 40 of us here waiting. He said he is in work, so we said okay then can you do us a favour and get hold of another number for us and pass it on. He said yeah he will do in a minutes, he's just in McDonalds. "Hang on a minute you're in a McDonalds? You just said you were in work a second ago". He said "yeah I work in McDonalds", to which we all pissed ourselves laughing at and so did he. Still wind him up and have a laugh about that today. Not really sure why it was so funny at the time, at least he had a job I suppose. Now they had all turned their phones off. The last thing they had said was call me a "ginger steroid freak" and called Craig a "fat Manc cunt" which made us laugh as they hadn't even seen Craig, just by his voice they must have guessed he was a fat cunt, which he is. Anyway it was clear they didn't want to meet us, the three numbers we had for them were now all going straight to voicemail. A lot of the lads were now thinking maybe it was time to call it a day and head off home, me included. Then near Piccadilly train station purely by chance we bumped into them. There were only around 10 of them and I would say there was 20 City. Burnley lads straight away said look we're on our way home there's only us here, we don't want it sort of thing. A couple of their lads seemed nothing short of disgusted with what they were hearing. "Course we fucking wannit we're Burnley, come on then" fair play to them I suppose. They came forward and it went off and the Burnley lads although well outnumbered, were game for it. In the end it ended up with the Burnley lads getting done in and even a couple of them being spark out on the deck. Can't help but wonder what a top fight it would have been if it happened a few hours earlier on in the day. When there's a cup draw, Burnley is one team I always think would be a top to get away. So fingers crossed one day it will happen, even better if it's when I am off this stupid ban.

Napoli – Napoli was a game I almost missed because I was hungover to fuck and had barely been to sleep or out. I stayed over in Brum the night before with one of the young Zulu kids who I'm good mates with. My head was banging, I just wanted to go home and sleep it off, the last thing I wanted to do was go to the football. All the lads were like "nah you've got to come Carl, it will be top" and they eventually talked me into playing out and I'm so glad they did. We knew that Napoli were hated all across Italy and they loved using a blade. A Roma lad told me that a stabbing below the waist in Italy is okay and just classed the same as punching someone in the leg, as long as it's below the waist that is. So basically they all stab each other in the arse and leg, by the sounds of it, as it's classed the same as giving someone a dead leg, a bit strange but it is what it is. Besides being hated and known for stabbings, they seemed to be begrudgingly respected throughout Europe. But if these Italian cunts thought they could come to Manchester and take the piss then they were in for a massive shock...

It was a Champions League game, so was obviously a midweek fixture. Midweek fixtures always tend to be a bit shit because of lads working and finishing at different times, so it's a ballache for meeting up. We got to town just about 12 of us and we heard a train full of Napoli were coming into Piccadilly from the airport. So we made our way to the station, hoping to follow their escort from town to the ground and get in touch with the rest of the lads and ambush them somewhere along the way. We sat in one of the bars in the station, sitting on the balcony to see their train come in. On its arrival we ran down the stairs to get a bit closer, just to get a better look of them. We were merely going to have a closer look at them and for whatever reason the police shit it, thought we were trying to attack them, fuck knows what gave them that impression. Loads of GMP ran over to us waving their coshes about and throwing us against the wall.

It was all a little bit over the top, seen as we were still a fair distance away from the Italians. We're not just standing there being hit with coshes and thrown about, so we pushed them all back and told them to fuck off, all we were doing was stood there. They said if we are seen anywhere near the escort again then we're all nicked, dickheads.

It was fairly difficult to see how many lads they had brought over, there was around 300 but many were just normal fans. We certainly spotted a fair few mixed in there though. They all had them sleeveless Stone Island bubble jackets on, if you know what I mean. Another thing I noticed straight away is many of them didn't even look Italian at all, looked a lot darker like Turks or something. We couldn't be arsed walking down to the ground, so we jumped in a couple of black cabs down there. Going past The Mitchell on the way to the ground we went past about 15 lads, some dressed like scallies but others dressed like casuals. We didn't recongise any of them, they clearly weren't Napoli as a couple of them were black, so we just thought they were kids off the estate. We got out at The Townley and there was around 30–40 City there already, with a few more said to be in Eastlands Bar and The Manchester. People were fucking about drinking and that, who would have thought it, lads drinking in a pub. But there was no time for any of that, Napoli were here and I just wanted to smash them and get off home to bed. Around 20 of us just Blazing Squad went walking about looking for Napoli before the game. Now I've no idea what the police had done with them but they had vanished, we couldn't find them. We must have somehow missed their escort, how we managed to do that I don't know. Anyway most of the lads had tickets so got off into the ground, as it was nearing kickoff time. A few of us stayed hanging around the away end, in case any of them were late coming in. If we saw any latecomers we'd just smash them, then get back on the estate before GMP knew what happened. As we were waiting around the away end on the front, those lads we went past in the taxi before walked past and they were scouse. To say we were a little confused would be an understatement, what the fuck were scousers doing round here? As they went past us Rodgers heard them say something about Man City and Carl Moran, now I really wanted to know who the fuck they were! I knew it wasn't Everton, well at least I didn't think it was, because I knew a fair few of their lads and I didn't recongise any of these lot, so it must be Liverpool.

"Who are youse?" we said to them, the lads then proceeded to tell us that they are Liverpool, and they didn't want any trouble with us, they're here for Napoli. Napoli had stabbed some Liverpool lad a year or so before, so there is big hatred between the two. Now this was certainly a strange situation to be in, do we just say fuck it and twat them, or do we just leave them to it? With them being scouse, the lads wanted to twat them. I thought they must have some huge hatred for Napoli to come down to Manchester looking for them, so I was happy to leave them to it. Loads of GMP ran over anyway, I think they thought it was kicking off or something, which it wasn't, and the scousers got fucked off back to Liverpool, all but 3 of them. I don't think the 3 scousers fancied staying round near our ground on their own and they disappeared off somewhere. We went in Eastlands Bar around 10 of us, and just chilled and watched the game in there. A few minutes before the end of the game we made our move, leaving the pub to get ready for when Napoli left the ground.

We made our way down the main road by the ground, gaining in numbers all the time. There were now around 25–30 of us, all younger lot. We bumped into them 3 scouse kids again, I went over and shook their hands and said "you're fucking brave coming down here" but told them they would be alright with us. Told all the lads nobody touches them cos there's only 3 of them, after all we're not United, we are not bullies. So we got off the main road and back onto the estate and planned to do what we have so many times before, come off the estate and smash them. We knew there were more lads down at The Manchester, who said they were going to come up but by that time it would probably be too late. Napoli had already been let out of the ground, so it would be any minute now that they would be passing us. We were expecting a good 100 of them, in a big police escort, because the lads in the ground sat near them said there were loads of them, all sat with each other. Then we saw them coming down, it was definitely Napoli, around 40 of them, and not a police escort in sight! We couldn't believe our luck, we knew we needed to time it right, and not give them chance to know we are there. Hit them with the element of surprise and all that. When the time was right we poured out of the estate, through the gap in the metal gates and fucking smashed right into them. They literally didn't know what had hit them. random shouts of "City" and "fucking come on Napoli" went out. We had taken them by surprise big time, and they were getting twatted up and down the main road. Not long after that they turned and ran back towards the ground. A handful of them got caught and tripped whilst running off, and filled in on the floor, only to find one had a London accent. I later found out that it was a few Millwall lads that were with them, seems Millwall and Napoli have some link. It would certainly explain the London accent anyway. So not only had the Blazing Squad just slapped and ran Napoli, but some Millwall too. Not bad going, glad that I came out after all.

Pockets of fighting continued up the main road, GMP soon got wind of what was going on and were quickly all over it. Police ran down in our direction with their coshes out and we all split up and scattered with most running back on to the estate. Me and Garv ended up surrounded by about 15 GMP, annoying little pricks with attitude problems these ones were. They were telling us to fuck off and walk away, so every time we went to walk off, they would run up pushing us. One ran up and kneed me in my back and whacked me in the leg with his cosh, not a clue what for. I'm guessing to make me lose my temper and smack him, then I would get fucked for it. Poor Garv got thrown into some bushes by them and then thrown into a doubledecker bus. He did go down rather easily though, like Ashley Young trying to win a penalty. That fucking idiot pushed me again, I was losing my temper with him, I threw him back and thought if he pushes me once more, then I am just gunna kick fuck out of him, not arsed what happens to me. More City lads came running down, which was probably the best thing for all concerned. It saved the GMP officer from getting a slap and saved me from the beating I would have got from the rest of TAU after it and from having to explain the whole thing in court. I've seen the policeman a couple of times after that, I'm always dying to crack him, he is one annoying little prick that's for sure.

We went back on the estate and walked round to the next ginnel leading back out on the main road. I saw a large group of lads in the distance and just presumed it was City, remember it was night match so pretty dark. Turns out it wasn't City, it was Napoli. Not only was it Napoli but it was only the same ones we had slapped and ran a few minutes earlier. There were only 4 of us as well, well there was 4 until one of the young lads seen how many Napoli there were and got off, now there were just 3 of us. Now one of their lads looked the spit of Super Mario, he goes to us in broken English "are you Man City hooligans?" with that there was a pause, then I half heartedly shouted back "yeah we are City yeah". With that Super Mario started to take his belt off, I have to say I was a little worried and confused to what was going on here, wanted to know what Mario's intentions were. Now the smart thing at this point to do would be to turn and run, there was a lot of angry Italian lads here, who wanted to fuck us up for before. There was only 3 of us, and a good 20 or so of them, so the odds wasn't looking too good, there was more chance of David Moyes' United winning a trophy, than us winning this scrap. As they got closer to us, we didn't run, but we didn't move either, just sort of stayed where we were, a little unsure what to do. Too proud to run off, or maybe just too stupid. Super Mario wacked us with his belt buckle and a couple more of them followed suit. One or two of them pulled blades out, I thought well this isn't going to go well at all and that's when we started to run off. Well we got about 10 foot away till we realised they had cornered Jake and surrounded him. God this was one of the only times you actually want the police to turn up and they're nowhere to be fucking seen, typical. I got smacked off the buckle of the belt in my ear, let me tell you that isn't nice at all, it fucking killed.

We started to give it them back and they didn't like it one bit. See where we were, there just wasn't enough room for them all to get to us at once, you could maybe have fitted 8 or 9 in and that's it. We were on the pavement in between the wall and the railings, on the edge of the road, that was the only thing saving us from them swarming us and probably killing us. So we started cracking them and pushing them back, I was more just pushing them and protecting my face, rather than hitting them. But then I saw him at the side of me this big cunt with a tash, it was only Super Mario again, only minus his belt. Not a clue how he had lost his belt, he must have broke it hitting us that hard with it, either that or his jeans were coming down. I thought right Mario you're fucking getting it you are, he seemed somehow oblivious to how close he was stood at the side of me. Bang, fuck off Super Mario, caught him with the perfect punch, couldn't have hit him any cleaner or harder, if I tried 100 times more. Was he knocked out? Did he stumble right back? No this cunt just stood there, he didn't even move, Super Mario was like a fucking bull. Well that was slightly disheartening, now they all started to surround us. I thought we were going to not only get the shit kicked out of us, but stabbed a good few times too and there's no doubt we would have, if GMP hadn't turn up when they did. As soon as GMP turned up I'm not even going to lie, I thought thank fuck for that, it's about time. Not that we were ever going to let them know, that they had just saved us. Police were now all over and these Italians looked even more pissed off than before, they should have by rights fucking battered us but they didn't. Although my back, arms and chest were bruised and sore from all the belts for a good few days after. The police told us they had seen a lot of what had gone on and that us 3 are mad. Nice to know they were watching it from a safe distance! That was pretty much it for the Napoli fixture. I know the away leg in Naples left a few City fans stabbed, a thing that was more just shirters rather than lads though, horrible cunts.

Rochdale – Now people reading this will be thinking, when the fuck did Man City play Rochdale away? Well you're right we didn't but Bury did. Bolton and other firms may have you believe that there's some huge thing between City and Bury, which really isn't the case. They make out we are like one big firm, going to each other's games together, week in week out, which is just utter crap. The vast majority of the City lads and the Bury lads have never even met. But there are a couple of their lads that have been to games with us once or twice and we have done the same once or twice. Bury have a handful of the gamest lads around but if am being honest their fair share of tagalongs and shitbags too. Bury and Rochdale fucking hate each other, the towns are fairly close to one another, on the outskirts of Manchester. With it being a derby game we expected Bury to have enough lads out and to be fair they did, a good 80 of them I would say, we took 6 youth down, met up with the Bury youth and had a few beers with them. Police came and escorted all the Bury lads to the game on foot. We didn't have tickets, neither did around 5 or so of the Bury lot, so we just stayed around there, going from pub to pub. We found ourselves in a part of Rochdale called Norden; it's like a countryside area on the outskirts of Rochdale. It's a far cry from their town centre, with them big dirty tower blocks everywhere.

After the game the Bury lads were supposed to be returning to where we were before the game, only GMP had other ideas. The majority of the Bury lads were rounded up and sent back to Bury, only around 20 managed to avoid the police and make it back. The 20 or so who managed to slip away soon met up with us lot in Norden. Rochdale knew the pub we were in and said they were on their way down to it. Now a good 45 minutes had gone by and still no sign of them, we thought they were a no-show. Another 15 minutes went by and nothing apart from some kids throwing a couple of stones at us and running off into some woods. Not a fucking clue what that was all about, we were all laughing saying it was their youth. A Bury lad came inside the pub and said "I think Rochdale are here now". So we all went outside to have a look and some big fat fucking weird thing, like some hairy gorilla, went "Rochdale are already here" and punched one of our lads Worthy. The cheeky cunt must have been sat near us in the pub, for all that time, and nobody had noticed. Although there's no way anybody would think he was a lad with his long black greasy hair, he looked like a biker, minus the bike. Everyone just paused for a second after he hit Worthy, not sure if they were thinking, where did he come from, or what the fuck is that, he really did look that weird, it seems impossible that nobody noticed him in the pub. After the pause came the scramble to smack this cunt, he was like a big ape, about 4 lads were on him and he was just swinging them about.

Our attention soon moved from the weird looking hairy bloke to the advancing bunch of lads numbering around 30. Rochdale had finally showed up, around 30 of them, mostly if not all older lads from what I could make out. As is the case a lot of the time there was a standoff for a few seconds. People shouting stuff and bouncing up and down full of adrenaline and then we just ran into Rochdale. We smacked a few of them, they all started running back, and we chased them off. Well that was easy enough I thought, Rochdale are a bit crap aren't they? We all turned to walk back to the pub, job done we thought, but within seconds they were back again. Rochdale were back running towards us again, hang on a minute, was only seconds earlier they were running away from us, this is fucking weird. We could see little taxi mini-buses pulling up with more of their lads in, so that's why they had now grown some balls and were running back for more. This time it was more of a proper fight, with lads going at it on both sides on this main road, just outside this pub. It was a nice tranquil setting, semi-rural area with green everywhere, now it had around 60 lads scrapping in the middle of the main road there. No cars were getting through with us on it, some pulled over to watch, others either in shock or in a rush, reversed and turned round and got off the way they came.

After a good half a minute's fighting, we had got the better of Rochdale once more, had backed them off, and now had them on the run again once more. "YOOF! YOOF! YOOF!" went up from our lads, with some of the Bury lads joining in. Our chants soon turned into laughter, as we saw Rochdale running off into the distance, well that was that job done right? Wrong!

In the distance I could see yet more taxis pulling up, with lads jumping out of them. I'm not entirely convinced that these were in fact Rochdale's firm; I think many could have been just blokes from the town of Rochdale who heard there was a fight going on and came along. This was now becoming a bit of a pattern, they run down, get a slap and run off, more lads appear in taxis and they come back and have another pop. Only this time they now had 50-60 lads, they ran into us, only this time the extra numbers took their toll and they backed us right back from the start. We were still giving as good as we got though, just the sheer numbers of them more than anything were giving us trouble. I was having a little fight with some old man with grey/white hair, well I say old man he was only about 40, just made him look older because of his white hair. I caught him with a couple of clean shots, his legs went and he staggered back like a piss head and fell into his own lads behind him. On the whole they were getting the better of us and we were now being pushed right back towards the pub. Some of the Bury lads were starting to get off, it's just like the domino effect, as soon as a few go, loads more follow suit. Police sirens were heard in the distance as well, which never helps does it. I got dragged in by a few of the Rochdale lads; they were smashing my head off this wall. You know them stone walls you only get in the countryside aren't flat like normal brick, so it fucking hurts. I was grabbed and pulled back by one of the Bury younger lads, Gizmo. Gizmo at the time was only dead young and dead small, but he is just fucking mad, as game as they come. It's worth mentioning that while most of the Bury lads had got off, there was still around 8 or so that weren't budging, well were being backed off but refusing to run. The police finally arrived and we all ran off, but this is like the middle of nowhere, and there wasn't really anywhere to run off to. A few of the City lads ran across some field to get away, me and my mate Button ran into the pub beer garden at the back and were soon apprehended. To our amazement we weren't even arrested, in fact as far as I know, no arrests were made at all. I had a nice little black eye and a fat lip, from being smashed against that wall. To make matters worse it was now raining hard, proper pissing it down, and there's nothing worse than soaking wet jeans sticking to your legs. In truth the police turning up when they did probably saved us from a good kicking.

A year or so on from this and Bury had Rochdale once more in the league; this time was a home fixture. I went along once more with a car full of City lads, to see what's what. This time Bury's numbers mustn't have been far off 100 lads. We were all just outside Bury town centre, going from pub to pub, and a couple of these pubs we went in were the worst pubs I've ever been to in my entire life, in fact worse than anything I had seen on telly. They were just fucking disgusting, the seats inside were just park benches which the owners had robbed and used as seats. There was some old bloke with a beard sat in the corner smoking a pipe with only 1 shoe on. It was one fucked up place that's for sure; anyway we soon moved on from there and headed towards the ground to meet Rochdale's lads. All Bury's older lot seemed to want to do was sing songs and drink, so all the younger lot set off to Bury bus station, where it was rumoured Rochdale were supposed to be. There were around 50 of us marching down, and sure as anything there were about 30 Rochdale in Bury interchange, with TAU around them. We tried our hardest to get to them but there was a couple of police dogs there and we didn't fancy getting bitten by them. We were pushed back and given a loose escort to the ground. Now the policing and stewarding in the top flight is pretty decent, on the whole they keep the rival fans apart and stop fans invading the pitch. However as I found out in the lower leagues, it isn't exactly policed to the same standard inside the ground. There were a couple of gimpy looking stewards, an old man and a fat bird, at the bottom of our stand by the corner flag, in-between the home fans and the away fans. Now the Rochdale fans were in a separate stand, they were behind the goal, but it just seemed easy enough to get to them, so we thought we would give it a go. We ran down the steps, onto the pitch and began to get into the Rochdale end, around 15 of us made it down onto the pitch, and right at their end. They did nothing but stand there and wait for the police and stewards to run down. This would be one of the last football matches I would attend, before I would be banned from all football grounds in the country.

Lech Poznan – Poznan from Poland, now these kids and the Poles in general, were starting to get a big reputation for football violence. I couldn't wait for them to come to Manchester, so I could see first hand what all the fuss was about. We had heard one or two things about Lech Poznan, they were apparently one of the Polish firms that didn't use weapons and were just into fist fighting. Another thing we had heard was to expect fucking hundreds and hundreds of them coming over. With them being Polish you just knew as well they were all going to be massive cunts too. We were well up for it anyway, it would be an interesting evening.

Me and Bez went to town to meet all the others, a good hour before kickoff. Walking up the top end of Market Street towards Spoons, and you could just see them all over, wherever you looked there were Poles. Straight away we thought why are they all stood outside Spoons? Thinking they must have been kicked out. As we approached Wetherspoons it became clear they weren't all outside Spoons, they filled the place too. There were masses of them, Spoons was rammed with them and they spilled out onto the street. Hard to say exactly how many there were but we're talking maybe 500, something daft like that anyway. We walked through the middle of them all, pushing our way past as we go. We did this partly to just get a better look of them because we're nosey cunts and partly because we're not going out of our way to walk round people, not in our own town anyway. Was hard to tell what the ratio would have been between shirters and actual lads. Near enough all of them were like giants though, eat more spinach than Popeye this lot. The atmosphere had like a dark undertone, there was tension in the air. It wasn't long before some of the Polish lads started arguing and fighting among each other, with GMP not really wanting to get involved. Me and Bez certainly didn't want to get involved, we were just asking to get battered stood right by them, just staring at them, so we decided to make our move. After all, these lot didn't have any qualms about kicking fuck out of one another, so think what they would have done to us two.

Time was getting on, all the lads were either at the ground, or making their way down to it, so we thought we would do the same. All the Polish lot were now being put in an escort and taken down to the ground anyway, although it was probably more like they decided they were going and GMP thought they best follow. Don't get me wrong, there was a fair amount of police around them but I'm not convinced there was anywhere near enough to control them, if anything went off. Me and Bez decided to pretty much shadow their escort down to the ground. We rang the rest of the lads and told them we're with the Polish kids now, so get ready to come out of the estate when we say. Well we weren't exactly with them, but we were around 150 metres away, on the other side of the road. We carried on down until we got to Toys R Us in Ancoats, we waited there for the escort to catch us up, just in case the police tried to take them a daft way. The escort caught us up and only now could we truly appreciate the numbers they had. Was well over 500 anyway, didn't appear to be any women or children in this escort, although it would still be hard to say how many were their "hooligan" element, and how many just normal supporters. Obviously there were a lot of Manchester based Poles, along with the ones who had travelled over, which would explain why their numbers were so vast. The size of these lot as well, I can't stress how big they were, not just some of them, literally all of them were massive. If you seen this escort with all them lot in it in a film, you would just laugh and say it's unrealistic, I've certainly never seen anything like it before or since. I mean if you see a group of just 50 lads walking down that is loads. The biggest I have ever been in would be getting on for 200, I've been in a couple escorts with like 150 of us too, all against United but for us to have numbers like that wouldn't be a regular thing. We later on heard GMP say there were 700 in the escort before the match. The escort had what must have been not far off 100 police on foot with them and a few horses, not to forget our friend in the sky the helicopter.

Now that we had let the escort catch us up, they weren't too far away from us at all, they were walking down the middle of the road, with us on the grass verge opposite them.

Bez starts hurling abuse at them "Polish pricks, fuck Poland" I was like fuckinell Bez your going to get us killed, half of them will speak English you know. A few of them shouted back "fuck English stickmen" I wasn't amused by that one bit, cheeky cunts. I maybe only 5 foot 8 but I was 15 stone at the time, I spent all my time lifting weights, so I was anything but a stickman. But that was just testament to the sheer size of all of them, to many of them, I was a stickman. We started to walk closer to their escort, goading them, why we were doing this I have no idea, it was a fucking daft thing to do. A couple of our FIOs shouted fuck off to us, "seriously just move away before you get hurt". We felt like naughty children being told off by our parents or something. There was genuine concern in their voice, not like they were arsed about us, just if these Poles decided to kick off and break out of this escort, there was little or no chance of the police controlling them. We decided it was probably best all round if we jogged ahead, and made our way down to the ground.

We headed for one of the pubs on the estate, The Townley. There was probably around 20 youth there, and around 40 older lads, with a few more round the corner in The Manchester. Didn't fancy our chances against that lot much but what are you going to do, hide in your own town, bollocks to that we're Man City. It's a weird feeling knowing that if it goes off, their numbers are so vast that we didn't stand a chance. That was pretty much the feeling we all had but we all made a laugh and a joke about it. So off we went down the side of The Townley, through the ginnels and various back streets on the estate and made our way to the main road. We popped out onto the main road and the police's face just dropped, they shit it. If we tried attacking their escort, the police knew there was no way they could hold the 700 Polish back. The police would also get a beating along with us lot, if they tried to get in the middle of it. I really can't get across how many of them there were and the size of them, it was an intimidating sight if am being honest about it. Now there is being brave, and there is being stupid, you could say there's a fine line between the two but if we ran into that escort that wouldn't be brave, that would be plain stupid. The police had every single copper in Manchester now in between us and the Poles, or at least that's what it felt like at the time. Now I'm not going to lie and say we tried our hardest to push the police back to get to them, because we didn't. I mean seriously what would be the point, there was just too many of them. But we let them know we were there, we didn't hide away we stood as close as we possibly could to them, with the police stopping us going closer. Anyway we knew in the back of our minds, that it would be after the game now, where it would happen. A couple of the lads had managed to get in contact with English based Polish lads, who were at the game. So a meet was arranged for after the game.

The game ended and we set off on our way to the pub we had said we'd be in. The pub was called the Spanking Roger, what a fucking name. While this pub wasn't a million miles from our ground, it was in the complete opposite direction to where 90 percent of the fans would be heading, so it was a completely dead area, nice and quiet. Around 20 of us younger lads were walking down to this Spanking Roger. As we got there we could see around 15–20 older lads already inside. We waited for these Polish lads, half expecting 100 of them to come rushing round the corner at any second. For whatever reason they just never showed, there were other people who turned up though... GMP. Cliff Lea, our main FIO at the time was up to his old tricks again. He was trying to get Tom to become a police informant for money. He gave him his old pitch "it's not grassing on your friends, it's giving us information, which would actually keep them out of trouble, and there's money to be earned, lots of it" We were all given Section 27s and fucked off from the area; I made my way down Queens Road back to Cheetham Hill, and then got the bus back home. A week or two later the police told us that a number of the Poznan lads had been stopped and searched; they were being searched for weapons basically. They didn't find any weapons on them, just many of them had brought gum shields with them, and wraps for their hands, like boxers wear. Them Polish kids are my kind of people. There was the odd little scrap near the ground that day so I was told after the game but nothing big, don't think I'll ever see an escort like that one at City any time soon.

There was an away leg which some of the lads travelled over to. I didn't go; in fact the weird thing is I never had a passport, until I had been banned from football. If I could go back I would have certainly scraped the money together, and gone to a few of these massive European away days. Poznan, the City itself, was modern as fuck, I think many of the lads were surprised by this. But although it may have been modern, it was still dodgy as fuck. For example in the subway leading to their ground, there was blood splattered all over the place. The Polish police would often take money off people and just keep it for themselves. The night before the game it went off a couple of times but with City getting the better of the exchanges every time. They would come and attack the bar that City were in, City would run out, have it with them and eventually chase them off. They didn't seem to have the huge numbers they did in Manchester. So maybe a lot more of them were English based Poles or there were a lot more were shirters in the escort than I first thought, although it really didn't look that way at all. On the day of the game there was a little bit of trouble as well. 40 odd City were in the ground booting down the fences to get in the other end and get to Poznan. Was supposed to have been freezing cold as well but what do you expect it is Poland.

Ajax – We had Ajax in Europe, and despite all the bans we took a decent mob over there. Would be a good away trip for the lads, with all the fun Amsterdam has to offer, not to mention Ajax are supposed to be a fairly decent firm. In recent times they have came over to Manchester in huge numbers and took the piss, not at our place, but at United. Like I said they proper took the piss, after the game battering United's firm all over, which is what I like to hear. There was around 60 City lads in a boozer by the canal, was a fair few other pubs close by, filled with City shirters. A group of lads turned up not too far away, just on the other side of the canal, it was Ajax's boys. There was a good 40 of them. Soon bottles and stuff were being thrown and both sets of lads met on the canal bridge, and steamed into each other. Many of the Ajax lads were using their belts as weapons against the City lads. However it wasn't too long before Ajax found themselves on the back foot and were taking a bit of a kicking. They eventually backed back off the canal bridge and ran, with City in pursuit behind them. City chased loads of them into a nearby bar, and used scaffolding poles to try and smash their way in. Dutch police were soon on the scene and many arrests were made. One of my mates "The German" was nicked that day and received a 500 euro fine for his troubles, bit fucking steep that isn't it. In the Dutch police cells you have your own telly and you get to control the temperature of your cell. I wouldn't mind a bit of that, it sounds alright. A far cry from the freezing cells in England, with them shitty blue mats, and smack heads in nearby cells banging all through the night.

Barnsley – We had Barnsley away in a pre-season friendly in 2009. We didn't see it as a huge game, we didn't have anything arranged either, just a few of us went down for a beer and that. Well I say a few of us, the majority of people had already set off on a previous train an hour before, while we were still fucking about in town. There was just 10 of us younger lot going down there, no tickets for the game, just for the day out and to see what's what. By the time we made it off the train, I was starving. I found a Greggs and went in, was after couple of meat and potato pies or pasties. After going in several bakeries (the only food places open in their town centre) I found out they don't sell anything meat and potato. Well this put me in a right fucking mood all day. We stayed in their town centre, moving around in different bars and clubs, seeing if we bumped into any of their lads. There was a fairly big pub just slightly up the hill. There appeared to be what looked like a couple of their older lads, stood outside having a cig. A couple of the lads decided to have a wander up, just casually walk past and have a glance in, get an idea of roughly how many they had. they came back shortly after and said there seemed to be at least 40, maybe 50. Well fuck that for a laugh, there was only 10 of us, we would have been leathered.

Anyway not long after a couple of their younger lads came outside the pub we were in. They said they knew we were here but it's far too on top in their town centre to have it, every street is camered up apparently. So numbers were exchanged and they said in 10 minutes time we would receive a call telling us exactly where to go. Shortly after they rang and told us to go to some car park which was only 5 minutes walk away and told us how to get there. So we made our way there, not knowing if there would be loads of them or what. We need not worry, because on arriving there it was clear there wasn't masses of them, in fact there wasn't anybody there at all. We rang them and they said "oh sorry. we're by our train station now". So we we're now starting to get a little pissed off with them, messing us around. We made our way towards the train station, down the side streets around there. Sure as anything they actually were where they said, this time at least anyway. Numbering around 25, just literally outside the main entrance to the train station. We rang them and said "we are down this back street now, can't you see us? Come down here and let's have it". They wouldn't move from the front entrance of the station and made enough noise from chanting that the police were soon all over them. Complete and utter mongs, I wasn't impressed one bit. Loads of police now turned up and put us in this pub with loads more City fans, right by the train station. These pregnant birds only around 16, 17 turned up, I'm guessing the birds of some of these Barnsley kids. Then a lot of Barnsley were either moved on by the police or some got off on mopeds. It was all a little bit strange to be honest. So after all that it would be fair to say that I didn't exactly hold them in high regard.

Four years later and we had Barnsley in the F.A Cup quarter-finals at our place. I've got to be honest, my initial reaction was oh god, not these muppets again. But after talking to a couple of my mates in other firms, they all seemed to rate Barnsley quite highly. So I thought well maybe that day it wasn't their proper lads, just dickheads and wannabees, every club has them, I know we certainly do. So I started talking to their youth, trying to arrange something for when they came down. At first, a meet was arranged for Stockport, then they said there were just going straight to Manchester. This pissed me off because of my ban. This really was a massive game for these lot, it was like their cup final, so they would be coming down in vast numbers. To be fair to them, straight from the start they said it's a massive game for them, so there will be loads of them. Although they did say they would be happy to break off as a youth and just have it with us lot. Dry Bar on Oldham Street would be where we all arranged to meet up in the morning, all our younger lot that is. As turns out to be the case on so many occassions, many of our lads were out drinking the night before and late turning up. Barnsley told me there was around 80-90 of them, just pulling into Piccadilly on the train now and said there's roughly the same number again on the next train. Fuckinell we're all in for a fun day aren't we, at that point there were only 15 of us in Dry Bar. There were supposed to be a few older lot in the Millstone and meeting in the Printworks but not the mad numbers Basrnsley were bringing down, in fact nowhere close to even half that. Barnsley were saying they were in the Waldorf, so while waiting for the rest to arrive, me and Rodgers decided to have a walk round and see if there really was that many of them.

Now it's always a little bit dodgy meeting other firms for a "chat" you know everything will be alright, but it only takes a couple of their lads to be dicks and it would kick off. But they seemed proper kids, so we were sure nothing like that would happen but you never know. The Waldorf is only a short distance away from where we were, so it didn't take us long to get there. On reaching the pub we belled them up, said we're here now just the two of us, now they could have been dicks and come out with all the pub but they didn't. Only around 6 or 7 came out and straight away came over to us shaking our hands and we had a quick chat, trying to sort something out. I told them "look there's not enough of us at the moment, give us 45 minutes to get it together and then we will meet youse" they seemed happy enough with that. Just before leaving, we went to the window and had a look inside to see how many there was. It was rammed literally wall to wall with Barnsley lads, must have been not far off 100 of them and as we were leaving, another 20 more arrived from around the corner. That was a decent mob, not to mention the fact there was still a train load of them coming, which hadn't even arrived yet. We returned back to Dry, told the lads how many of them there was and said we will wait a little longer for more lads to arrive. We all agreed that regardless of numbers, in half an hour we are meeting them, because we're not having anybody take the piss in our town. We managed to scrape 20-25 youth together and said "do youse wannit youth on youth?" they said "yeah that's bang on". They were in Bar Rouge on Portland Street, so we made out way there across Piccadilly Gardens. As soon as we got onto Portland Street itself we could see them, all coming out of the bar. But we were still on opposite side of the road and it is a fairly busy road in the middle of town, with numerous lanes of traffic separating us and them. We made our way down the road to where the traffic was thinning out, so that we could get to each other. Someone tapped me on my shoulder "Carl look!" as I've turned round I have seen a couple of police vans turning round, to come back in our direction. Just as we were crossing the road to get to each other, the police vans pulled over just ahead of us. I nodded my head in the direction of the vans, so that Barnsley had seen them. I told the lads to stay on that side of the road, nothing could happen with the police on the same road watching. I went to the middle of the road half way, where there is like a crossing. A couple of their lads came to the middle and met me. I told them now because of the time, me and Rodgers had to leave town because of our bans, it was just too risky being there. But said we will ring you in the next 20 minutes or so, and sort something out. Wasn't such a bad thing looking back, it not going off on that street. The riots that had taken place the year previous year had taken place on Portland Street, so it was camered up to fuck now.

We made our way to the outskirts of town, down Oxford Road past the Mancunian Way and out of the area we're banned from. So we got into a place just off Oxford Road, Zoo Bar or something daft like that it's called. A couple more lads turned up and even a couple of Dutch kids from Den Bosch, who were friends with a few of the lads, had made the trip over. All bar me and Rodgers made their way back to town, to the Northern Quarter to meet a few more of the lads. By this time there was a loads of Barnsley lads in town but with large numbers comes large police presence. The City lads made their way to The Millstone, where there was said to be already a good 50 plus City inside. Now it all kicked off funnily enough in Dry Bar, the place where we had met up several hours ago. A handful of City came into Dry Bar, where a handful of Barnsley kids already were. Words was exchanged between the groups and then it all kicked off there. Digs were flying all over, glasses smashing, chairs being used, lads being bottled, the lot. The fighting went on, with neither side wanting to back off. But at the same time knowing they will be camered up and that GMP would be on their way. With that in mind the fighting stopped, and there was a standoff, with really neither side doing the other one. The City lads who were nearest to the door left Dry Bar, and walked up the street, narrowly missing the police who turned up soon after. Many City were picked up over the coming days and charged and bailed over the incident in Dry that day. Many lads were being charged with violent disorder and were looking at the possiblity of a good few months inside. As we all know court cases have the tendency to drag out, it took over a year after the fight in Dry Bar, for the court cases to be over. With nobody ending up serving a custodial sentence. In all truth it should have been thrown out of court, because the CCTV isn't exactly good quality. It's a shame it didn't go off on a bigger scale, like both firms wanted that day. But fair play to Barnsley, they brought a mob and a half down to our place that day. Certainly one of the biggest firms numbers wise that I have ever seen come to our place anyway. They're good lads, I've got allot of time for them, YOU REDS!

It was pretty much the start of summer 2014. The season was coming to an end and the World Cup in Brazil was due to start shortly. My 25th birthday was coming up, and I wanted to do something for it. Filming had not long come to an end for the first Football Fight Club. I had recently been involved in the Bohs/Shamrock thing in Ireland weeks earlier and around 6 months back, the epic Zulu battle. But there had been a few missed opportunities, planned things not coming off, so it was time to set that right. So with the season over and no banning restrictions, a nice little meet with someone out of the way, would go down nicely for my birthday. Now the job of finding someone to meet us, that would meet us, and aren't a million fucking miles away. I was thinking where we could go and by chance a Barnsley mate of mine happened to text. Perfect, Barnsley away it was then. It's around an hour away in a mini bus, if that, so distance wise it was bang on. He seemed up for it as well so it was happy days. They were some lads away at Her Majesty's pleasure in Strangeways and a few working. Always a few that get steaming the night before and don't end up making it but that's always the way. It was always going to be a small meet numbers wise anyway. We said from the start 10-15 lads, or something along them lines. So when 12 of us made it to town that morning, that was pretty much what I had expected. Instead of getting the train down, we got a 14 seater minibus. Made things easier for getting down there, and more importantly, for getting away. So we had our 12 and set off on our way to South Yorkshire.

It was the same sort of thing as the Zulu one week before, I said to them "tell us where you want us to go, and we will". So a postcode was given to us, for an area called Hoyle Mill. This was only a few hundred metres from their ground Oakwell. As we went over the Snake Pass we all jumped out for a piss and a picture. When we set off again I decided to sit up front with the driver. I did this partly so when we got there, if we saw them I could jump out quicker. But I think the main reason I did it is because I was being a little queer and was getting travel sick. The older I get, the more travel sick I get, fuck knows why. We were soon passing signs saying 5 miles to Barnsley, so gave them a bell, said we're 10 minutes away. We had little or no interest in hanging around in Yorkshire. Find them, smash them, fuck off back to Manchester and get pissed. We arrived at this Hoyle Mill place anyway. It was like a big park, not with swings and slides and shit, more like where you would walk your dog. It seemed like a good spot for a row anyway, so I couldn't complain.

We had parked the bus on some pub car park and we're now walking through this park. Was no sign of them at all though, so I gave them a quick bell. "come on we're fucking here now, where are youse?". He assured me they was on their way and wouldn't be long. I've always found it a strange feeling, that few minutes before a fight. Never really quite know what to do with myself. I make no bones about the fact I get dead nervous before a fight, always been like that, not that I show it though. The lads were now getting restless, so I rang yet again, he said 2 minutes away. Another 10 minutes went by, they were starting to take the piss now. These 2 young lads went passed on bikes and I just knew Barnsley had sent them, to scout as out. It was getting daft now, we had come all this fucking way and the longer it went on, the less likely it seemed they would turn up. I was pissed off, not impressed at all. We decided to have a little walk about for them. The path bent round this wooded area, so we followed it round. After a couple of minutes walking bingo, they're in the distance. Looked about 15 or so of them, mainly kids too. We just fucking ran at them. No word of a lie as we got near them, they all just turned and ran. If I hadn't wasted time and effort arranging it, it would have been funny as fuck. We ran after them, up this path up this steep hill. I was getting close to a couple of them, until they dived head first into some bushes and fucked off, little cunts. It was a weird mixture of feelings among us all. Some lads like me were fuming that they all just ran off, others was pissing themselves laughing at them. If I knew they would just do that, I wouldn't have wasted my time going. They had just messed us about and made themselves look like muppets. That being said, I don't think what happened that day is a fair reflection on Barnsley, because I do think they're alright. That day was just a bag of wank but shit happens, what are you going to do? I'm sure one day we will bump into each other properly and I look forward to it.

LIVERPOOL

IN THE LAST FEW SEASONS, for one reason or another, we just have not had the same sort of rivialry with Liverpool, as we have with their rivals Everton. It would be easy for me to sit hear and say, "oh Liverpool ain't up to much, they never come to our place" because they could flip that around and say the same about us. As we have had far more rows with Everton, they have funnily enough had far more with our rivals United. It would be safe to say that on the whole there is great mutual respect between City and Everton, I don't think the same could be said for United and Liverpool though somehow. A fair few years ago now I heard that Liverpool's youth have been given around 20 or so bans, now that is more than enough to crush any youth firm. This alone may go someway to explain the lack of history youth wise, between the two of us. As a general rule, from what I have seen, there don't seem to be a great deal of Under 5 mobs in the Premier League. Under 5s meaning 14-18 year olds I would say, whereas that age group thrives in the lower leagues. That being said Liverpool seem to be one of the exceptions to that. In the last couple of seasons they seem to have emerged from nowhere, loads of young kids following Liverpool. There's shit loads of them, a good 50 or so easily, all around 17. If they can keep those kind of numbers together, coinciding with many of their lads coming off banning orders, then just through sheer numbers alone they must be one to watch out for.

I've only ever been to Liverpool away one time and that was not really so much going as a firm there, as most people didn't bother. Sunday 4th May 2008, near the end of the season. So I thought fuck it I might as well go down. Went down by the train which just pisses me off, how it can take a relatively short trip from Manchester to Liverpool and drag it out to over an hour, it's a joke. But anyway, we arrived there to the usual police reception, not City FIOs, just Liverpool's, and oh yeah they fucking hated us. Proper nasty scousers they were, just looking for any excuse to give you a whack, or nick you, you know the sort. The train was completely rammed with normal City fans. There were a few older lads on, a lot of whom I know now but didn't really 7 years ago. There were about 30–35 lads from what I could make out anyway. We all left the station together and went in this Spoons near Lime Street station. There were a few more City in there, some of my pals and more of the older lot as well. There was a lot of talk of Liverpool knowing where we are and they were going to come down. So I didn't even bother drinking, I just got a glass of water and a packet of salt and vinegar crisps, McCoys the crinkly ones you always seem to get in boozers. Wouldn't go as far to say I was on edge or owt daft like that but I couldn't fully relax, thinking any minute Liverpool are going to show up. But as time went by it seemed less and less likely to happen.

As a few of us were leaving that pub to head on to another, I saw a group of 8–10 or so lads across the road with their backs to us. One of us shouted 'calm down, calm down' in a scouse accent, was a decent scouse accent to be fair. The lads stopped and looked around sort of a bit confused. We said "youse Liverpool lads, yeah" and started to bounce over the road at the same time. I'm not sure of the street that we were on but it was like in the middle of their town centre, shops and bars on either side of this busy main road. Also I must add that while they were about 8-10 of them, they were probably getting on for 14-15 of us. Some of their lads sort of stood there and froze and you could tell they just really didn't wanna be there. It's surprising how much you can tell about a person and what they're thinking, without actually speaking, just looking in their eyes. Some of their lads shouted something back and bounced over in our direction sort of thing. It was a busy City centre road and surely camered up to fuck as well, so a really silly place for a row but sometimes these things just happen. My head was so set on these scouse kids that we were seconds away from having it. I forgot what I was doing, and I nearly got myself run over by a transit van, my mate pulled my shoulder back just in time. The scouse kids gestured over, as if to say "come on then" as they deffo wanted it and who were we to let them down! So we darted across the main road to them, narrowly getting in front of this bus. Some didn't wanna get run over by the buses and didn't wanna risk it, and had to run down and round the traffic, which consisted of mainly taxis and buses. Would have been a bit embarrassing getting ran over by a bus, people would be like, how the fuck did you not see that, however I can't say owt because when I was 16 I was hit by a fucking fire engine, say no more.

So we were now pretty split into 2 groups. One of the Liverpool lads chucks a bottle which somehow passed directly between my head and my mate's who's stood next to me. Was a cracking shot I'll give him that, couple of inches left or right and would have been bang on. We weren't too impressed at the time, I thought right you cheeky scouse cunt, youse are deffo fucking getting it now! As we got in front of them I thought the momentum of us running would make us just steam right into them but there was what I can best describe as an awkward hesitation from both sides. A bit of bouncing up and down was going on. Whether it was just weighing each other up, or hesitation because it seemed a daft place for a fight I'm not sure. Then thankfully the awkward hesitancy, of jumping up and down like a set of fucking kangaroos, was brought to and end when one of their lads cracked one of our older lot and nearly took his fucking head off. That was when we all just got straight in there. It was weird because it seemed if anything they had more lads than us not the other way round, which baffled my head at the time. I chinned one of their kids, caught him right and proper on the button, and put him on his arse, then started fighting with another two, one with ginger hair, the other one with curly hair. To be fair to Liverpool they gave as good as they got at first. Then all you could hear was "City! City! City!" and about 6 or 7 more lads come running into them. With that Liverpool backed off and a few of them started running off away. Their lads started saying 'the bizzies will be here in a sec lad'. I guess the police would deffo be on there way. So we got off the way we had come from and they got off a separate way, with my heart racing like mad, jogging away from the area to get away from the 'bizzies' as the scouse kid so elegantly put it.

A few of us jumped in taxis and fucked off near the ground, where police sort of shoved us in a pub with other City fans, probably to get us all together, so they could keep an eye on us. After the little thing with a few of them in their town centre, we expected it to go off big time down near the ground but it just never happened, I think I'm right in saying nothing else happened that day probably due to police being all over it, rather than them not wanting to have a go. The match itself ended 1-0 to them, with that little queer for them Torres scoring. Piss take cos we were all over them, Elano hitting the bar and everything, well bar or post, was one of them. So that was my only away trip to Anfield anyway.

But a few months after they would come to our place with a fair few lads. My recollection of the day is at parts a little hazy. I was so pissed out of my head for the best part of the day, really not like me at the match to be honest, but oh well I live and learn.

Apart from recently I hadn't seen a Liverpool mob at our place but this day they turned up off the train with about 40 or 50 of them. It was a nice mix of youth and older lads, it was a nice unexpected surprise for most of us anyway, who I doubt were even expecting anthing to happen at all that day, then word got around, that more or their lads were on their way down. We were on Oldham Street as usual, in the City Arms I think it was. There were too many police around them near where they were apparently. So we made our way towards the ground. We got back onto the estate in Ancoats. At this point there were around 25 of us mainly Blazing Squad lads, with some older lot. We bumped into a mob of City at the bottom near The Bank of England pub. They were just coming out and reckoned that Liverpool's escort had been seen not too far away. There were a few fair in The Bank and loads started piling out of the pub when they heard that. So there were now about 60 maybe 70 of us. Most were lads but to be honest the tagalongs numbered about 10 or so at least. They certainly were not proper lads, just more like pissheads up for twatting scousers. Either way it was a good 60–70 lads. Everyone was saying "Aww we got well over 100 lads here easy" but people do tend to exaggerate, especially when it comes to numbers at football.

I had been drinking the night before, had been asleep for a couple of hours, woke up not hungover but still pretty much pissed, so had gone out and got right back on it at the football that day. I was dying for a piss, so went across from the shops behind the flats, leant against a big tree and had a piss.

At the same time all the lads running down to the bottom shouting "they're here, they're here". Oh fuckinell the last thing I wanna do is miss all the fun because I was having a piss but at the same time I didn't want to risk running down and weeing all over myself. Wouldn't have been a good look for me I don't think! So what seemed to be the longest piss of my life was over, I grabbed my beer in one hand and tried pulling my belt together and fastening it with the other. A tricky task with one hand while pissed, never mind running as well. Ran downhill the 50 or so metre distance and could see everyone at the bottom by the Mitchell Arms, which is on the corner of the main road which goes to our ground. I ran down to see just a wash of people, there was the 70 or so City lads and around 50 Liverpool and about 25 police in between the 2, with more police coming from the other side of the road. I threw my can, which was pretty heavy cos it was nearly full, at Liverpool. As far as I know it didn't hit anyone, but I wasn't watching, we were doing our best at attacking their escort to get to Liverpool. It soon ended up as if it was us against GMP and Liverpool because GMP had fully concentrated all their man power on pushing City back. There were a few punches thrown to be honest a lot of it had already happened before I got there. Now it was more just getting pushed back by police. The police eventually got enough bodies down to hold us back and safely escort Liverpool to the ground. I always say the police are deffo there for the away firm's protection when they come to Manchester, without a shadow of a doubt. I think we caught Liverpool by surprise one minute there were none of us, the next minute 70 lads steamed into their escort. So the police were grabbing people to Section 60, Section 27 and possibly nick, so many of us got off, some didn't, we had moved away from the ground and Liverpool and back to a place we knew they wouldn't look for us...Canal Street, the Gay Village.

There were only about 12 or 13 of us in there, stayed in a bar for a bit and then a place called View on Canal Street itself. Then 25 minutes before the game was due to end, we set off walking back towards the ground. We got in The Bank pub and it really started to fill up. I say around 90 lads, maybe even getting on for 100 – it was rammed with lads, mainly older lads with about 20 youth. Out of the 100, there was the odd tag a long but most were good lads. We set off from the pub when we knew that Liverpool's escort was on its way down from Eastlands. However it would seem the police weren't going to fall for the same trick twice in one day. They brought out the big guns; helicopter, TAU, dogs and of course the dreaded horses, that police just use to trample on you. Before we could get near enough to attack their escort, there were so many police round us we couldn't move. It was proper over the top. There were supposed to have been a few scuffles down near the ground but nothing to write home about. Apparently a few of the older lads got wind that Liverpool were coming down that's why there were loads of them about. It was news to me anyway. We wouldn't have owt with them for around 5 years until the emergence of these new lads, they had coming through.

Early Febuary 2013 would see Liverpool travel to our place. Now in all honesty this was not a fixture that we were looking out for. Around 1–2 weeks before the fixture I got a text off one of the younger lads saying Liverpool were coming down and wanted it. Funnily enough literally the same day I was hearing stories of them doing United and also having it with Oldham at Oldham in a cup tie. So I get the lad's number who my mate had been talking to from Liverpool and took it from there. Now these scouse kids are only young lads, more like say that they were more Under 5's than youth. I said to their lad straight away look I'm 23 and a lot of the lads are my age, some older, but as a fair few are teenagers so maybe youse are a bit too young to be meeting us. He very quickly replied no they couldn't care less about age, they're fighting lads a lot older and bigger, so I thought fair play it's all good then, Then I thought back to us lot at that age and we didn't give a fuck about fighting older lads. I myself had been knocking out men when I was 11 years old, so I certainly didn't want to dismiss them, just on their age. Although I did make it clear a few of us were a lot older and said to him if you want to bring older lads, do that as well. They said they would be coming in by train to Victoria and asked me if I knew the snooker hall near it at the top of Cheetham Hill Road, he said they would probably all go in there as it's out of the way. So I thought this sounded good to me and then thought around that area near Strangeways and the Fort shopping centre, all the side streets round there are used by prostitutes at night but in the day they are fairly quiet warehouses and cash and carrys and the like. With our game falling on a Sunday I thought the place would be spot on for a meet. It's north Manchester as well, my side a town, which was a lot better for me with my banning order, so I wouldn't run this risk of having to go through town and risk being seen breaching my ban.

So on the Saturday, the day before, I had a little drive about and found the perfect place. Perfect not only just to have it with Liverpool but also to attack them from two different sides and sandwich them in the middle. The plan was mint. However football and plans the majority of the time end up fucking up and this was to be no exception. Now with the game being on a Sunday I knew only too well this would leave countless faces either being late or not turning out at all. Why? Well simply because they would be hungover and dying in bed from the night before. I spread the word about to all our lot, get to Dry on Oldham Street at such and such a time on Sunday. I must have text that to around 40 lads, give or take. Think the time I told everyone to arrive was 12, as it was a 4 o'clock kick off that day. Knowing for various reasons there's always a fair few lads that don't turn up, I was expecting around 25 to show. If 25 lads showed I would be happy enough. Both ourselves and Liverpool agreed from the get go, it was far better to get the meet done and dusted as soon as, no messing about. Obviously the longer you leave it, the more chance there is of police rumbling it, before it's even begun.

Like a dickhead, I had spent the Saturday night at some bird's house, drinking all sorts until about 6am. Not the smartest thing to do the night before. I had done the one thing I had told the rest of the lads not to do, go out that night and get fucking wasted. No matter how sick I was, or how hungover I felt, there was never any danger of me not showing. No matter how horrible I felt, you can't be organising meets and then telling your pals, "I'm not coming I feel ill" bollocks to that. How gay would that have made me look? So I begrudgingly forced myself up, got a shower and got dressed. Left my flat and staggered up to Besses Met, feeling very sorry for myself indeed. I remember giving the scouse kids a quick bell, checking we were still good to go. Part of me was half hoping that they weren't coming or that police had them all, just so I could go back to bed. But everything was good from their end they said. I went for some food, hoping that would sort me out. My mate text us saying he is giving it a miss, just what I needed, one of the main lads not playing out. To be fair to him though he had only just been let out, he had been held on remand and had court cases pending, so it was the smart thing to do. Still rather selfishly I hoped he would think fuck it and turn up in the end. Started to then do a quick ring round to some of the lads. Not too many lads were picking up, which certainly wasn't a good sign, this day was going from bad to worse. All the time I knew in the back of my head there was going to be a right mob of this lot, fucking shit loads of them. Ah well, what was done was done. It had all been arranged and there was no way in the world I was backing out, couldn't care if there was only 5 of us. Although I knew it wouldn't come to that, well I hoped anyway.

The plan originally was for me to go by car, and get the other banned lads from town in the car with me. We were going to sit in Cheetham Hill, so they didn't have to walk around town, breaching their bans. And the rest of the lads would meet in Dry. But this was now all fucked up and it looked like I was going to be the only banned lad out. I decided I was going to come into town to sort all the lads out and to see how many had actually turned up for the meet. I would say going down Oldham Steet when City are home, there's probably more chance that I would get seen and arrested, than wouldn't. But at that point I was too pissed off and hungover to care. Besides, if I did get nicked I could just sleep all day in the cell. Easier said than done when there's normally tramps and smackheads booting the cell doors but there you go. So I got into town and made my way to Oldham Street. Certainly not with the attitude of wanting to get nicked but the attitude of, well if it happens it happens, do you know what I mean? With these banning orders they call them radius bans, it basically means you're not only just banned from all football grounds but also from around the ground and the town centre and surrounding areas on match days. Not to mention banned from any town or City that City play in, plus if City or England play abroad the police have to have your passport, and you've gotta sign on, breaching a ban may not even mean fighting, just being where you shouldn't, it can be 6 months inside and a £5,000 fine, I've been held a couple of days on remand for it but not 6 months inside, yet. So my passport pretty much lives at Bury police station. Another thing they do that really winds me up, they don't let you just sign on at your local police station, some lads have to travel 8-9 miles to theirs, mine's around 4-5 miles and have to pretty much pass another police station in Whitefield on the way. They just make you do it to be awkward, so you breach and they can have you for it. Also not so long ago, the media got wind that the police forces were being paid money for every football banning order that was issued. Food for thought that is, I'll leave you to make your minds up on that one.

Back to the Liverpool thing and my hangover was getting worse, I felt fuckin' awful. Truth be told I just wanted to go home and curl up in bed and that is what I intended to do after we smashed these scousers all over the place. Got to Dry which really is a smart as fuck bar, and in many ways just doesn't fit in with the other pubs on Oldham Street, Dry Bar is like the posh, smart places you would find like down Deansgate locks or summat. I near enough always use it as a meeting place. It was pretty much bang in the middle of Oldham Street, which is a two minute walk from Piccadilly Gardens and Market Street. It's also pretty much situated half way between Piccadilly and Victoria stations as well. A handy spot with a seating area at the front, you could see right up and down the street for GMP or rival firms. As much as I didn't want a beer I knew a pint would probably sort me out, hair of the dog and all that. There were around 8 or 9 of us there so far, which was nothing short of embarrassing. Liverpool had not long been on their train, so I knew we had a good half hour, if not longer. One by one lads started turning up. Yet we were still a million miles away from the turn out and show of strength that I had hoped for. All the time knowing these lot were going to turn up with good numbers.

Now it was said that it would be just fists, meaning no tools, but scousers do love a blade, so I've been told. Leading up to this day, several lads weren't happy with the lack of stuff happening, as regards to fights and what not. I agreed it had been rather quiet for some time now, so this was good opportunity to sort that out. So I arrange this do with the scouse kids and what happens, hardly anybody turns up, typical that. We now had around 15 lads, a few my age group, but mostly younger, 16-20 that sort of age. Liverpool had arrived in Manchester and were eager to have it right now. In fact it struck me as a bit mad, how keen they really were. I tried to buy a little more time and stall, 'just give us 10 more minutes to get it together' I said to the kid on the phone. With them being so up for it and wanting it right now, led me to agree with my original assumption, that there were loads of them. For all we knew could have been 60, even 70 of them, although they said they had 20, which I knew was bollocks. The really annoying thing was that in an hour I could have pulled together 30 lads, in just half an hour we could have got 20 odd. My idea of sandwiching them down near Strangeways was off, not with these numbers anyway but no way were we backing out of the meet, I can honestly say we have never done that.

Liverpool were now ringing pretty much every minute, passing the phone to various different lads. 'come on City, you boys want it or not? stop fucking us about'. Now they had a point, if this was the other way round I wouldn't be impressed one bit. I told them five more minutes and we are on our way. Told all our lads, finish your drinks, go for a piss, then we're on our way, no matter how many we have. Wasn't half fucking annoying, knowing another 6 or 7 lads were actually on their way to town, with more about to set off. It was their own fault though for being well over an hour late. I couldn't fob the scousers off any longer, the time had come, we were on our way. As long as there weren't millions of the cunts we would be alright, person for person I knew we would be far better. Although I bet if you ask any firm that, they will say exactly the same thing...

I rang them and said right, 15 of us now walking to meet youse, where are you now? Their responce was they couldn't get served in some pub, so they were outside Tesco. Couldn't get served in a pub? Fuck me how young are these lot, we were all wondering and also and maybe more to the point, why were they standing outside a Tesco's, what's all that about. Robbing the place blind no doubt! Tesco was only just round the corner from where we were as well. So our walk turned into a purposeful march. Now as cringey and gay as I know this sounds, older and more experienced lads turn to younger lads and reassure them. "Dont worry these are wank compared to us, we will smash these, all stick together, don't give them an inch. We're Man City, and nobody comes to Manchester and takes the piss. Let's use these scouse kids to send a message to all youth firms, this is what you get if you turn up in our town." Sounds like stuff some daft American action film but at the time, with your heart racing, adrenaline pumping and when you're seconds away from a mass brawl, it all makes perfect sense. At that moment nothing else in your life matters, nothing has any importance but the fight which is moments away.

As we got nearer to Tesco our walking got faster and faster, and was bordering on jogging. In fact in the end I think a few of us did end up jogging down. But as we got near to Tesco one thing soon came apparent, there was no mob, not a single lad to be seen. Where the fuck were they? I rang back – no answer, belled them back again and still nobody picked up. Well this wasn't looking good. Then the lad rang us back and said they are now by Primark. It then occurred to me that they were next to a different Tesco, than the one we were at. They meant the Tesco on Market Street, Market Street being the main shopping street, in the centre of town. Market Street wasn't really the sort of place where you would be wanting a big meet, it's a very packed area full of shoppers. So we made our way down another 100 or so metres to where they said they were. We sort of went the long way round, doing a half circle shape, coming back on ourselves. We did this so we wouldn't be directly on Market Street, we were on a street just set off from it. We made our way round the corner, which directly led to the side of Primark. We all started to spread out to cover the street. There they were at the bottom of the street, pretty much where they claimed to have been. From Pizza Hut to Primark, they filled the street, there was a fair few of them that's for sure. Not a clue where this kid learnt to count, if he thought they had 20! Not that it mattered now, plus it wasn't like it was unexpected anyway. Both sides now started shouting stuff to one another, bouncing and gesturing towards each other. 'CITY! CITY! YOOF! YOOF! YOOF!' chants went up from us lot.

A couple of our lot had glasses and bottles that they had acquired from Dry. They were launched at Liverpool, proper lobbed in the air. They seemed to be in the air forever, seemed to go a lot higher in height, than further in distance anyway. While they were in the air, we charged at them, making as much noise as possible. The noise and aggression maybe going someway to overcompensate for our lack of numbers. However being outnumbered was defo nothing new to us, in fact it would be fair to say we thrived off it. It made the victory that little bit sweeter. Some of our lot reckon there was a good 50 of them, I'm not sure about that but I would say anything between 30 and 40. So if you bear in mind we only had 15, their extra numbers should have made quite a difference. Loads of their lads ran forward, proper game for it, whereas many of the others half-heartedly followed. This straight away filled us with even more confidence. We already had the advantage of seeing what their lads at the front could not see. Which was half their lads didn't seem to wanna know, and were bouncing forward together with them. Whereas I didn't have to look to know that we were all together, as one. What did strike me was it appeared the young kids were the ones at the front for them and the lads in the early to mid 20s, seemed to be more the ones at the back. You would automatically assume that it would be the other way round, if anything.

Straight away after minimal punches were traded, Liverpool were on the back foot. So we stayed on them, gave them no room to think or do anything and sure enough their front line crumbled and retreated. Once they realised they weren't going to win they sprinted away up Market Street. 'Stand, stand Liverpool!'' went up but it was too little, too late by that time. We weren't content with that, we wanted to proper teach them a lesson. So we legged it after them, up Market Street, which was rammed with shoppers, locals and tourists. Not a clue what most of them thought was going on. I do remember vividly two women shouting 'go on City, smash the scousers' and laughing, well words to that affect anyway, oh how it's nice to occasionally be appreciated. A couple of lads arrived at this point, who were late for the meet, they quickly saw us chasing them and joined in the pursuit. One almost tripping up a couple of them as they sprinted past, they must have thought even the locals were out to get them. We were now sprinting down the met lines, towards Piccadilly Gardens after them, the chase was in vain as unless they turned round and wanted it, we weren't going to catch them. Police sirens now rang clear in the air, so GMP had been alerted to what had gone on and must have been fairly near by.

We made our way towards Oldham Street once more, to a pub just off it, the Crown and Anchor I believe it was. I was sick a couple of times on the floor, from the drink a few hours previous I am guessing. Although it wasn't exactly fight of the century, we were still on a buzz from it. Went outside and had a picture taken, went back in the pub and a fair few more lads come. Fair few older lads turned up too, was 40 or so of us in this pub now. I knew I was pushing it being in town, what with my ban, so gave it another half hour, then fucked off on the Met back to Whitefield. As I was leaving Liverpool rang again, saying they wanted it again, I laughed and said "not a chance, see you next year kid" and put the phone down. Straight away he belled us back, saying they aren't going to run this time, where are we? As tempted as I was to stay, I knew it was for the best that I got off. It was home time for me, the way I saw it my work was done, it was back home to die in bed and wait for the game to come on telly. I passed their numbers over to a couple of my mates, and left it to them to sort it out with the scousers. Now it was 10 minutes on the Met from town and another 10 or so walk back to mine but before I had made that journey my phone was going off again. It was going off all over near the ground. It was supposed to be madness down there. City chasing Liverpool, the police chasing City, went off all up and down the main road by our ground. After the game a mob of City converged outside The Mitchell but GMP were all over it and that was pretty much that.

Like I said though if Liverpool can keep all them lads together, plus all their lads coming back off bans, in a couple of years they more than likely will be one to watch out for.

ZULUS

BIRMINGHAM'S FIRM GOT THEIR NAME the Zulus from Man City many years ago now. Well it was away to City at Maine Road, in the 80s anyway. Obviously well before my time, I wasn't even born till '89. The Zulu warriors or Zulus have long been regarded as one of the best firms in the country. With their firm being one of the biggest numbers wise but unlike one or two other firms that spring to mind, they didn't just rely on numbers. Now with a name like Zulus you would expect them all to be black lads but that's not entirely the case. While they do have a lot of black lads in their firm, it's more the older lads. I suppose that's maybe just one of the reasons why there is so many of them, if your blues your blues, regardless of your background. Now for whatever reason whenever I've tried to arrange a scrap with them, something fucks up and it doesn't end up happening. I'm sure you can imagine that gets pretty annoying, especially if you've just spent the last couple of weeks arranging it with them. But I wasn't going to be deterred and at something like the fourth time of trying it finally came off and everything went like clockwork. With both sides agreeing afterwards that it was the best do at football they had ever been involved with.

Football violence is weird at times, it's like you can have no fights for months, then bang, you could have three in a month. It's just the way it goes, well that's always the way it seems to be with us lot anyway. I had taken my eye of the ball, as regards to sorting out meets and what not. I had been busy writing this book and being filmed by the BBC for a hooligan documentary. It had been a few months since the majority of us had had it proper at the match, also bans didn't help but even so I had been too wrapped up in other stuff, I had let things slide. Lads were getting a little frustrated that not a lot seemed to be happening and rightly so – something had to be done. So I sat and had a long hard think about it all, and decided an away day was needed. Not just any old away day, our away days with Blazing Squad differ slightly from others. Most firms get tickets to the game, go down there, get pissed go the match, if they see the opposing firm they kick off, if they don't they don't and then they go home. Fair enough if that's what you into, for me and the lads that's all a bit too boring, maybe not so much boring, just ordinary. Who wants to be like everybody else?

What I proposed was a little bit different from that sort of away day. The plan was to go to south Birmingham, right out of the way, and have it with the Zulu youth. According to the Zulu youth lads nobody has ever dared come right into south Birmingham to meet them, let alone has anybody ever done them there. So it would seem the odds were stacked against us, good job I like a challenge. It would have been easy to just pick a mediocre firm and just go and smash them but where's the fun in that? We want to be known as one of the best and to do that we need to beat the best, or at least give it a good go. So that was it, it was all arranged we were to travel to south Brum and have it with their youth. I even picked a game where Birmingham was at home, so there could be no excuses that they had loads of lads at the away match. Everybody thought we were mad doing what we were doing, other City lads and mates in other firms alike. "Carl you're fucking mad going down there when they're at home, your gunna get set up, there's going to be like 100 of them". Now if we went down there and did the business, it would be some fucking achievement and would make us look mint. However if we went down there and got smashed, which is what the majority of people seemed to think would happen, it would make me look a right cunt. People would think I didn't have a clue what I'm doing and I've just taken lads down there to get battered. The last thing I wanted to do was get my mates hurt, just due to me being too proud to turn down the chance to go there and fight them. All along I was quietly confident, well what am I on about quietly confident, I was going round telling everyone we were going to go down there and destroy them, whether I fully believed that or not, is another thing.

The morning of the fight was a little different to what I was used to, before a big away day with the lads. I was up at half 7 out with the BBC filming and would be filming all that day, right up until we got on the coach and made our way to the West Midlands. To say I was nervous about the day would have been an understatement but I wasn't going to let the rest of the lads know that. People only see what you allow them to see, if you portray nothing but confidence, then that's what they see. The last thing I wanted was some of the younger lads there seeing me nervous about it all. I just kept telling everyone "look I know a few of their lads, have done for years, they're game lads and that, but we're better, trust me". I was doing similar thing all week to Zulus on the phone, telling them I know they're a top firm, which is why I wanted to meet there, but I just can't see us losing to them at all. Wanted to try and make them doubt themselves, or at least think, City must really be that good, look how confident Carl is. When really a part of me was fucking bricking it. We were having trouble booking a bus or coach leading up to the date. It was stressing me out to fuck; I started worrying it wasn't going to even happen, like so many times before.

But with the help of a couple of other lads, it was sorted out. After the first 3 companies had let us down, after agreeing initially to take us, we found one that was willing to take us. Good job really because I would have never lived it down after all the mouthing off I had done, if we then didn't even go. The coach was a 32 seater. We didn't have 33 lads though, you know what we didn't even have 23. 20 lads we had that turned up and paid their money. I was hoping for a good 25, but 20 it was, I can't really moan at that because out of the 20, there were some proper top lads. Any lad will tell you a top 20 lads, will destroy an average 40 lads all day long. Not to say these Zulu kids were average though, far from it.

Now it had been almost 5 years since we last travelled to Birmingham and that day the majority of the lads got nicked after we did Stoke. So ever since that day I've always had to take a bit of stick for not proper turning up in Brum, but I mean it wasn't my fault the police were waiting for us near Walsall. Today was the day we were setting the record straight, we wanted to send a message out to every firm in the country. We didn't have to worry about seeing any of our FIOs in town; we had Southampton away, so by the time we were setting off, they would have been long gone. So we set off in our bus on our way to South Birmingham. Suppose one good thing about a few lads not turning out is there were enough seats for us all to chill out and not be squashed together. In the past we have had like 18 of us in 16 seaters all the way to London and it's fucking horrible being all squashed together for that length of time. Out of the 20, there were a couple of lads who had been going even longer than me and a few young lads who it would be their first ever time. One of which was my 16 year-old little brother Matt, talk about throwing people straight in at the deep end.

Now for me, an away day isn't an away day without the

music blasting on the bus, as sad as it sounds I look forward to that as much as anything else. So I was fucking distraught to find we must have had the only coach in the world which doesn't have a CD player, well a working one anyway. This was no good, it was fucking depressing me, I had a few big bottles of Micky Finns, which I was happily necking back, but no fucking music. Well this was no good at all, somewhere just outside of Stoke we pulled into the services. While all the other lads was on the rob, I had more pressing matters to take care of, the music. Found some little speakers that went into phones, so I bought one of them, £30 fucking piss take, thought it would only be a tenner max. Anyway we took a couple of pictures and then dived back on the bus, only around 30-40 miles away from Birmingham now. The world seemed a far better place with the music on the bus, until Blood got hold of it and started playing god knows what. It was soon confiscated back off him and normal music was put back on, Oasis and Arctic Monkeys etc.

We were now past Walsall and nearing the centre of Birmingham, we had gone past Villa Park on the motorway also, so we needed a postcode. I got the postcode gave it to the driver and we were on our way into South Brum. We were still a good few miles away though, purely because we were on like a ring road and it was taking us all around the City in a big loop. Zulu lads knew that we weren't too far away, they said they were all in a pub just down the road from the postcode that we had been given. The weird thing is, the closer we got to Brum the more I fancied our chances, and the more confident I felt about it all. If anything I suppose you think it should be the other way round, the closer it got the fight the more nervous I got but just wasn't the case at all. I suppose there was a sense of us having nothing to lose, but everything to gain. Meaning if we go down there and get done, is it really the end of the world? Because it seemed that's what an awful lot of people expected to happen, with it being on their turf and us only bringing 20 lads. So here we were now, pulled off the motorway and we're on normal roads only a couple of miles from the postcode they have given us. I had no doubts in my mind over whether they would turn up, I knew for a fact they would. So now it wasn't if it's going to go off today but when and we were now surely a handful of minutes away from the biggest fight of our lives.

We found a spot about a quarter of a mile past the postcode they had given us and jumped off the coach there. We were now making our way up this hill on foot. I later found out the big hill we was walking up was called "Cock Hill", would have made us laugh if we all knew that at the time. We wasn't so much walking up the hill, more marching up it, half expecting them to rush towards us at any second. We passed a pub on our right hand side called The Cock, a couple of lads ran over to look through the windows, but there didn't appear to be anybody inside. We continued to walk on until the road started to level out. We were now on the edge of some estate, just off from the main road we had just walked up. There were several tower blocks around us and we thought right they will certainly be coming out us from off this estate. So I rang them again and gave them the street name which we was on, they said they're only two minutes away now. The majority of the lads stayed back from the main road, behind some big bushes, with a couple of lads stayed across the road by the pub to see if they were coming from that way. I was stood on my own just bang in the middle of the pub and the rest of the lads on the estate.

Now this area we were in wasn't exactly posh, Frankley it's called, in proper deep South Birmingham, this was proper Zulu country. Nobody had ever come to this area before to have it with the Zulu younger lot and standing there by the road side I started to question my decision to do so. I started to doubt myself and think maybe I had been a little naïve thinking we could just come down here and take the piss. This really wasn't the time or the place to start doubting myself. A car slowly drove passed me, you could see he was having a good look at me, and the lads set back from the road, who were making a poor effort to hide behind this bush. Them lot would have been fucking awful at hide and seek that's for sure. The bloke in the passenger seat of the car, wound his window down and said "you're Man City aren't ya" to which I replied "yeah were City", to that he just nodded his head, smiled and the car drove off. I presumed he must be one of their older lads who had been made aware about the meet today. Rumours had been going round that in fact a few of their older lads were going to be there alongside their youth today, although that could have been just people chatting shit, as so often turns out to be the case. I now needed to clear any doubt from my mind whatsoever, this wasn't a time to start shitting it. I also didn't want any of the other lads to see how nervous I was, not so much from a pride point of view, more because it would make them more nervous. I took a few deep breaths and took my gloves out my back pocket and slowly put them on. The couple of lads that were by the side of the pub shouted, "They're here, Zulus are fucking here" and with that we all made for the other side of the road and down the ginnel at the side. All the doubts or nerves that I had moments earlier, had now evaporated as quickly as they appeared.

We were now all together 20 handed at the top of the hill, with the Zulu lot around 100 metres away down the hill. The higher ground I suppose would be a slight advantage, well certainly it isn't a disadvantage anyway. I was screaming at one of our lads who ran ahead, to get back with the rest of us. The last thing I wanted was somebody running too far forward towards them on their own. We needed to all be together, all as one. The chants went up from both sides, but from them first I think it was. "ZULU! ZULU! ZULU!" from them lot and "YOOF! YOOF!" and "CITY!" being chanting from us lot, as we were running down towards them. The alley way we were running down wasn't so different to that Banana Walk in Radcliffe, where we had had that fight with Bolton all those years ago. "Come on you fucking Zulu cunts" and various other things were shouted, as we drew nearer to them. Like I said before, any doubts that I had earlier, had completely gone away. It really was make or break for us now, I knew that whatever happened in these first few exchanges, would set the precedent for the rest of the fight.

Us lot running downhill gave us a slight advantage, gave us the momentum as we were coming down. We didn't exactly full on smash into them; I would say we slowed beforehand. Think that had more to do with not being able to punch when you're running, more than anything else. I wasn't the first one in, was probably more like the 5th or 6th, something like that anyway. Whether that's a true reflection of me being the 5th or 6th gamest lad, or me just being a fat fuck, and not as fast as I used to be, in truth it's probably a bit of both. With me being only a couple of metres at most behind the front lads, it gave me a chance to just watch and see what was going on. So for around only 2 or 3 seconds I stood and I watched, before I ran in. Now I know that will sound weird as fuck, you're probably thinking what the fuck are doing standing and watching you queer, steam in and just fight. Not really sure why I do it, it's not something I purposely do, just something I have always done without thinking about it. I stand and take everything in around me, just for a couple of seconds and then I start fighting. I think in situations like this you just go on autopilot, I know I do anyway. I don't really think well I'll do this, and I'll do that, I've been there and done it so many times before that I just do whatever I do, without really thinking. I guess it's the same sort of thing for many other lads as well.

Now this was a proper fucking war, there was no standing off from each other or bouncing about throwing the odd punch. The best way I can describe it would be close quarter fighting; both frontlines of lads were pretty much pressed against each other. We were both like on top of each other, like when in the ring when a boxer comes dead tight to his opponent and he smothers his work. A bottle just missed my head by centimetres, I later found out it was my close pal from Zulus that had thrown it and had purposely aimed it for my head. Well with friends like that who needs enemies? We were both going at it proper, suppose that's pride for you. Punches were flying in all over the show, with lads on both sides going down on the deck. The level of respect shown between us and them was admirable. I mean here we were kicking the fucking shit out of each other but when someone went down, they were left to it. Don't get me wrong they were hit a couple of times on the way down and maybe the odd kick as they were down but that was it, then they weren't touched, no being booted in on the floor or owt like that. One of our lads was on the floor right beside me, didn't see how he went down, I am guessing from a punch or punches. I've gripped him on his shoulders and arm from behind and pulled him up. So as I've first pulled him up his body and face were facing them, I've turned him round and turned myself round at the same time, so now we were both facing away from the Brum lads. So the back of me was now facing them, and loads of them were just a couple of feet away from me.

Not a single one of them smacked me, or my mate that I was helping up. At the same time one of their lads, now I'm sure it was the same one, kept running into us and kept ending up on his arse. When he went down, he was getting a couple of digs and the odd kick and then was dragged up to his feet, on two occasions by me. I pulled him up and pushed him back into his own lads. He was a game little cunt though; he just kept coming back for more and more, fair play to him.

So the fighting went on. My nose was dripping with blood, although I don't actually remember being hit that hard for it to bleed like that, even though looking back I must have been hit a fair few times because I was right there in the thick of it. There were certain ones of their lads that were just bang at the front all the way through and just refused to budge. One of them had this black bally on, I remember fighting with him for a while and I'm guessing it was him who did my nose in. I just remember looking and seeing his head in the perfect position for a right hook, so I proper stepped into it and caught him sweet. The punch landed bang on, it made him like take a little step back but he didn't go down, he carried on fighting, little bastard. The fighting was just relentless, if there was a crowd I'm sure they would be up on their feet applauding, well maybe not, but you get what I mean. Both sides still going toe to toe battling, it could only carry on at this pace for so long. It now ended up being a standoff, a chance for a breather, because we were all fucked, but at the time you don't really notice, your adrenaline carries you through.

Now for a few brief seconds began the war of words, verbal insults exchanged and stuff shouted to each other. It all went quiet for a second and one of them started laughing and shouted "COME ON THEN, CARL" it's always nice to be thought of I suppose. The fighting then carried on, but only for a handful of seconds before there was yet another brief standoff. All the way through the fighting, which had now been going on for well over a minute, it had been even stevens I would say. However since the first breather, it seemed to be us who were maybe just slightly getting the upper hand, and getting the better of things. This gave us a huge boost in confidence and I'm sure had the reverse effect on them.

Now leading up to this fight, and in fact for a few years previous, there's been some friendly banter between me and one of their lads. It wasn't the fact we didn't like each other, it's just the fact we both wanted to kick the fuck out of each other, if that makes sense. So it had been building between me and him for years. He has a reputation for being a hard cunt and a mad bastard and we both said we would go for each other in this meet. Now I had seen him out of the corner of my eye at the front all the way through the fight, but I wasn't really able to get across to him, not until now anyway. We were now just a few feet away from each other, now was our chance to go at it. He had been in the thick of it all the way through; his mouth was pissing with blood. I later found out he had been smacked there by one of our lads with a cosh and he was still there bang at the front battling away. Now a lot was made of us "using weapons" yeah I'll admit two of our lads had coshes but that's it. One of theirs, some black kid in a bally, had a knuckle duster on, and right at the start I was almost smashed in the face with a bottle. So I don't think anybody can really moan about 2 lads having coshes. Anyway we were now practically facing each other and I know he had now noticed me too, because our eyes were locked on one another, not in a gay way, but you catch my drift.

"Come on B...." I shouted his name "Fucking Come on" he put his arms out gesturing come on then, and we both went for each other. My mate later told me that when

I shouted that everybody seemed to stop for a couple of seconds, as if to watch what would happen. He threw the first dig but I anticipated it and moved and rolled with the punch, which took much of the sting out of it. I stepped forward and smacked him, with what I can only describe as a cross between a jab and a left hook. It caught him flush, and he stumbled back a couple of steps into what I think was one of them green electrical boxes. With that all the rest of City rushed forward, ploughing into the Zulu lads and pushing them right back. One of their lads got smashed in the thigh with a cosh, and he let out a big "ahhhhh". He was hobbling and couldn't walk proper, so I grabbed him and helped him a few feet to his mates. While this was going on there was still more fighting going on to the other side from me. The lad I had just cracked, had been hit by a couple of lads straight after I whacked him. He put his arm up to protect his face and ended up getting a broken wrist I think. A handful of their lads who were at the front throughout, carried on defiantly fighting with us, as a fair few of their lads now began to run off. We carried on fighting with them and they backed off as well and in the end they jogged off. A couple of the lads ran after them, I shouted them back, and said leave it, "the job's done, we have done them, we have done the Zulus!".

The scrap was that good I just felt compelled to run over and shake hands with some of their lads, just out of respect. There was no animosity or tension between us at all, we had just had a massive fight and kicked the shit out of each other, but there was no anger or hatred between us, just respect. We made our way running back up the hill towards our bus, and we were all fucked from the fight. The hill was so much harder going up than it was coming down, which I know obviously you would expect but all our legs were just dead going back up this hill. Now just a few metres from the top of the ginnel, which leads us back onto the main road, on to the oddly named "Cock Hill". No sooner had we almost reached the top we had to come back down, there were police cars flying about everywhere. Wasn't just 1 or 2 cars, was a good 4 or 5, so they were definitely on to us. We were running down the hill the way we had come and dived down this alleyway, leading onto this new housing estate. We followed the road round which lead us back to the main road at the top. We were now running slightly downhill, we could see the Cock Inn in front of us, with what looked like our bus parked up on the car park. We frantically made for the bus, with sirens gaining on us in the back ground. It was now a race to see if we could all get on the car park and hide behind the bus, before the police drove past and spotted us. We made it just, and I mean just, another couple of seconds and we would have been too slow, the police would have seen us. We all broke out into laughter, fuckinell that was a close one, too close. We jumped straight back onto the bus, I did a quick head count, we had 20, we were good to go. Told the driver to set off and get us back to Manchester.

For me that felt bitter sweet, that fight with them lot had been on the cards for 5 years now and finally it had actually happened. We had pulled off what no other youth firm had done, gone to Zulu's turf and had it with them. We didn't only just have it with them; we did them and ran them. I felt on top of the world, that was without a shadow of a doubt, the biggest thing I have ever done in the eight years of going to the football. Everybody thought we were mad going down there with 20 lads and meeting them, on their estate, when they had a home match the same day. Enough people doubted us, at times I even started doubting us but we pulled it off and we were now on our way back to Manchester in jubilant mood. Everybody was buzzing their tits off as you would expect. Everyone was talking about the fight and telling their part in the battle and what they did. One of our lad's heads was split open and bleeding, I think it looked a little worse than it actually was though, which is often the case with blood from the head. I knew from bitter experience the best thing was to get some sugar in him. So at the services I got him a couple of chocolate bars and a big bottle of water as well, told him that should make him feel miles better. I asked the driver of our bus how long we were actually in Brum for, he said he from getting off the bus, to us jumping back on it was less than 20 minutes. We had come all that way for 20 minutes, but it was worth it. Another thing that didn't take long was for word to get around. Within half an hour it seemed half the firms in the country were aware about our fight with Zulus. Before we had even made it back to Manchester I must have had a good 7 or 8 firms ring or text me, congratulating us and asking about the scrap. One of our older lads on Facebook gave us the nickname the "magnificent 20" after the fight. By the time we had made it back to Manchester, we were all drained and tired. Not sure if it was the beer and that wearing off, or the adrenaline had now gone or what. What a mad scrap for the several young teenagers we had with us that day, for what was their first proper scrap for City.

So the day had gone well, actually it had gone perfect, couldn't have gone any better if I wanted it to. If Carlsberg did away days…. I have nothing but respect for the Zulu lot, can't find a bad word to say about them whatsoever. I've spoke to them numerous times since then, and we have all agreed that it was the best fight any of us had ever been involved in at the match. Them lot are without a shadow of a doubt are the best firm I've had it with anyway and I know they say exactly the same thing about us too. They say good things come to those who wait and since we had it with Stoke on the way to Brum, and it messed that day up, it had been almost 5 years. They could have taken the piss and turned up with 60 lads that day and turned us over, but they didn't, they came with same numbers. That made the fight that much better, nobody set anybody up, it was a 20 on 20 and they were true to their word. So not only are they game lads, they're honest too. There aren't too many firms knocking about that can claim to be either of the two, never mind both. Sometime in the future Zulus said they're going to repay the favour, and turn up at our place. Now win lose or draw, that's going to be yet another fight to remember.

THERE IS A LIGHT AND IT NEVER GOES OUT

WHEN I FIRST SET OUT to write this book, I said the most important thing is to be honest, I hope that came across. The same could be said with the BBC3 hooligan documentary (Football Fight Club) that I was being filmed for; throughout the period I was writing this book. It would have been so easy for me to miss out fights we have lost, or even change the outcome of them, to make out we won. As sad as that sounds, many people have done that in books in the past. If a story is going to be told, then it may as well be told fucking properly. The last thing people want to read is yet another hooligan book with fake tales of never being done, with delusions of grandeur, and being the best firm around. That shit bores me to death it really does, as I'm sure it does you as well. I now find myself at a sort of strange age (25) where I'm certainly no longer a kid but maybe not quite old enough to be a proper grown up adult, if that makes any sense. Same as regards to City as well, I mean how many more years can I run around claiming to be youth? 1 year maybe 2, if in fact any more years at all? 5 or 6 years ago I would have pissed myself at a 25 year old "yoof" lad. I suppose sooner or later there comes a point where you think enough is enough, I've had more than my fair share of fun, maybe it's time to think about calling it a day.

Throughout this book and indeed on camera for the BBC, I struggled to find the words to get across how top it is being a football lad. The highs you have with you mates, it's sometimes a rollercoaster of emotions, because believe me, there are as many lows as there are highs. The constant paranoia that maybe someone in the firm isn't all they seem and could in fact be giving GMP info for cash. Those thoughts can seriously fuck your head up and drive you mad. I think the police defo add fuel to the fire in those situations, it's the perfect way for them to get inside people's heads and create doubt among friends and in some extremes watch the firm tear each other apart over it. I've always tried to be level-headed when it comes to things like this, never one for jumping on the bandwagon in calling somebody a grass. In certain cases in the past I've stood up for people, when many were turning against them. My decision to do so was just, when it turned out the lad had done fuck all wrong anyway. Also there is always the hassle and in some cases borderline harassment off the police themselves. When the police are coming round to your house several times a week because there's a warrant out for your arrest or whatever, it's enough to piss anybody off. But every time I think right enough is enough, I'm done with it now, the urge to go back grips hold of me once more, it really is like a drug. If it's a huge game, or just a meet, the last thing you want is your mates belling you up, telling you they've just had some mint fight and just smashed a firm to pieces.

Quite recently I took a little step back from things, to concentrate on turning professional at boxing. Lost over 3 stone, was set to turn pro and have my first fight, a few weeks after and I got injured, quite badly as well. The cartilage had gone in one of my knees, all worn away, leaving the bones to rub and scrape together, fucking piss take after all that hard work too. I have tried to take a tiny step back I suppose, and be a better dad to my 4 year-old Katie. However that being said I'm still fairly confident of being one of, if not the, most active banned lads in the country. My version of taking a step back and taking it easy is still being far more active than the majority of lads that aren't even banned anyway.

The future at City is looking good, with some decent lads that have come through the ranks in the last year or so. So I think Blazing Squad is looking good for the coming few seasons, although how many of the original members will still be there, is another thing entirely. Since we came together to form in 2007, I must have seen a good 50, 60 lads come and go, some good and some not really up to much. It used to proper do my nut in, every year we seemed to gain 5-10 lads, but at the same time lose 5-10 lads, for one reason or another. Just one of them things I suppose, I'm sure we're not the only ones it happens to. I've more than done my bit at trying to get new lads at City, as have some of the other lads as well. Always trying to make them feel welcome (as gay as that sounds) and introducing them to the rest of the lads. Would still be nice to have a few more numbers but I suppose we wouldn't be who we were, it just wouldn't be City if we weren't going into pretty much every scrap being outnumbered. That made it even sweeter when we won and the majority of times we did win, trust me. Stuff like going into fights knowing you're outnumbered and coming out on top makes you closer as a firm.

That's what I think nobody seems to get, there's not just one reason for why people fight at football, there's loads. Every person will have a slightly different view on this I'm sure, so I can only speak for me personally. Some lads may like the idea of fighting for their own town or city, or indeed football club. Others may like being in a big firm, you know like the "pack" mentality and the unity that goes with it. Some lads maybe want to initially be in a hooligan firm because of the reputation that goes with it, may have watched all the films and think it's the "cool" thing to do. Maybe they're attracted to the rush of adrenaline that goes through your body moments before you go into battle. Or just crave that almost indescribable sensation after the big fight, like you're on top of the world. Then you have got the nasty violent bastards, who literally just want to fight, don't care who they fight, or why they fight, they just love to fight. I'm sure everybody knows somebody like that. I think for me it's a mixture of most of them things. I love the friendship side of being in a firm, knowing your mates are there for you no matter what, is very humbling. But I also just love to fight; it's what I'm good at. How close you get standing side by side with someone week after week, it's a unique bond. After all you're only as strong as the people around you. I suppose I feel sorry for anybody reading this that has never experienced that kind of friendship and can't relate to what I am saying. The memories I have over the past 9 years are truly priceless and I wouldn't swap them for all the money in City's owner's bank account.

Violence and football will always go hand in hand, if you ask me. The so called "hey day" of the 1980s, has well and truly gone, I don't think anybody is denying that. Will it ever reach those heights again? I really can't see it and I very much doubt it, more's the pity. However, that being said, I think if football violence was ever going to go away, then by now, I'm sure it would have done. But it's true that the dynamic of fighting at football has well and truly changed over recent years. From fighting literally on the terraces, to now outside the grounds, or even pre-arranged meets several miles away, the forest fighting which seems to be taking off all over Europe, I just can't see ever taking off here, although I can understand why they do it and fair play to those that do it. Over the last few years lads have had to be far more clued up over what they do and where they do it. I'm referring to 2 things here, CCTV cameras and the police. Over recent years CCTV cameras have popped up everywhere, you'll be pushed to find many streets in town centres without several cameras on them, never mind just one on them. That's why they call us 'The Stars of CCTV'. The police are also far more clued up on the scene than they were decades ago; millions have been spent to combat football violence. Things like Facebook and even mobile phones are just perfect for police to gather evidence. Another thing that I've noticed is the life expectancy, if you will, of a football lad seems to be getting shorter. Lads seem to do it for a couple of seasons, rather than a couple of decades, I guess police have a huge thing to do with that. The average age of the young lads coming through seems to have changed; I've noticed that in the time I've been doing it. Especially in the lower leagues, where it's fairly common place to firms all made up of 14, 15, 16 year olds. City, as well as many other firms, are finding it hard and struggling with the amount of bans they have. It will be interesting around the 2016 season, when an awful lot of people come off their bans. There's already lads getting excited about France 2016, so I know myself personally I cannot fucking wait for that. With various new youths and under 5s popping up all over the country, it seems fighting at football has an interesting next few years to come. I honestly can't see anything more that the police can do to combat it. I mean they're already giving lads harsh custodial sentences, and dishing out banning orders like they're going out of fashion. So whether people like it or not, it would very much appear that football violence is here to stay.

In the words of Stephen Patrick Morrissey – there is a light and it never goes out!